Borders, Territories, and Ethics

Shofar Supplements in Jewish Studies

Zev Garber, Editor
Los Angeles Valley College

Borders, Territories, and Ethics

Hebrew Literature in the Shadow of the Intifada

Adia Mendelson-Maoz

Purdue University Press
West Lafayette, Indiana

Printed in the United States of America.

Cataloging-in-Publication data is on file with the Library of Congress.

Paper ISBN: 978-1-557-53820-8
ePDF ISBN: 978-1-612-49535-4
ePUB ISBN: 978-1-612-49536-1

Front cover painting, *Mt. Canaan #2*, 1992, courtesy of artist David Reeb

Contents

Acknowledgments

This book was written at the Open University of Israel, my academic home, and at Harvard University between 2015 and 2016, where I spent a one-year sabbatical. I am grateful to the Open University Research Authority for providing initial funding for this project (grant number 37056), and to my colleagues at the NELC Department at Harvard University.

This book was written with the assistance of several people. I would like to express my gratitude to Tom Kellner, who worked with me closely, throughout this project, with great diligence and intelligence that came across so clearly in her reading and editing, thoughts and ideas. I would like to thank Tamar Gerstenhaber for translating the literary excerpts from Hebrew to English while preserving the complexity of the Hebrew source, and to the book's English editor, Esther Singer, for her practical attitude and thoughtful comments. I would like to thank the reviewers for their helpfull comments and suggestions.

I thank my colleagues and friends at the Department of Literature, Language and Arts at the Open University of Israel for their support and friendship, and in particular Tammy Amiel-Houser and Mei-Tal Nadler for fruitful discussions during the last few years, and Tzahi Weiss and Galia Benziman for their advice. Finally, my heartfelt gratitude goes to my family, my parents and brothers, my partner and my children, for their encouragement, inspiration, and love.

Early versions of chapters 4, 6, and 7 appeared in the following publications: "The Bereaved Father and His Dead Son in the Works of A. B.

Yehoshua," *Social Jewish Studies* 17.1 (Fall 2010): 116–40; "The Face of the Dead Other—A Levinasian Reading of Contemporary Israeli Novels by A. B. Yehoshua and Shifra Horn," *JNT: Journal of Narrative Theory* 46.3 (2016): 395–423; "Borders, Territory, and Sovereignty in the Works of Contemporary Israeli Women Writers," *Women's Studies* 63.6 (2014): 788–822. I thank all the publishers for their permission to reprint.

Introduction

> *The citizens of Israel have no clear concept of a border. Living this way means living in a home where all the walls are constantly moving and open to invasion. A person whose home has no solid walls finds it very difficult to know where the next home "begins."*
>
> —David Grossman[1]

> *I came from a place of Zionism, from a place of the realization of dreams, which is supposed to be full of meaning. A place with no emptiness. A place filled with myths, vocations, missions. But there is something utterly paradoxical here. Fifty years have passed, and this state still does not have any borders. They weren't marked. People don't know where the line is, where it is dangerous, and then we wonder why people walk in strange directions.*
>
> —Orly Castel-Bloom[2]

David Grossman, an iconic Israeli writer, outspoken peace activist, and bereaved father, describes the Israeli situation through the concepts of home and borders, while depicting the abnormality of both the Israeli state and the Israeli identity. Israel was founded as a home for the Jewish people; however, in the aftermath of several wars since the establishment of the state and its complex military and security circumstances, this home lacks stable borders. This lack of borders creates an intense and continuous sense of insecurity and fear on both sides of the presumed line. Borders are the subject of Orly Castel-Bloom's passage as well. In her sarcastic style, Castel-Bloom, one of the leading female authors in Israel, admits that she was raised on the love of country and its ideology, but finds it difficult to pursue these ideals in a state where the borders are not defined.

Both Grossman and Castel-Bloom refer to borders to make more general observations on the "Israeli condition." In their view, borders are not only geographic locations or points, but also a major factor in Israel's cultural and political identity, and a source of malaise. In their works, as in others, the geographic abnormality of a state without stable borders is both a reality and a metaphor for confusion, contradiction, fear, and aggression. This state of affairs also deviates considerably from the humanist ideals that were the cornerstones for the establishment of Israel in 1948, in the wake of the Holocaust.

Space and borders are the main topics of this book, which focuses on contemporary Hebrew prose written in the shadow of the Occupation and the Intifadas from 1987 to 2007. It explores the relationship between ethics and space, and illustrates the symbolic role of borders, or the lack thereof, as a key leitmotif. Israeli literary representations of the Occupation and the two Intifadas raise immensely important moral questions that include, but are not limited to, militarism, humanism, national identity, the citizen-soldier duality, Zionist education, the acknowledgment of the Other, the nature of the State of Israel as a democracy, and the sovereignty of the subject. In these literary-ethical inquiries, space is a major player in its own right. The political situation immediately following the 1967 war, which resulted in redefinitions of Israel's borders and made the Occupied Territories a liminal zone under martial law, was accompanied by a sense of great strength and pride. Today, however, this situation constitutes the core of what is perceived by many as the tragedy of contemporary Israeli society. My main argument is that in Israeli literature, this ambiguity in the concept of Israeli borders articulates the pathology of the Occupation, substantially as well as metaphorically, while creating a twilight zone that captures the inherent tension between the Zionist humanistic legacy and the heavy price of ruling over the Palestinian population. This introduction provides a background to what I consider to be the prime sources of Israeli abnormality and presents an overview of the main theoretical perspectives of space and ethics discussed in each chapter.

Space, Borders, and Ethics

National borders and identity are the foundations of the modern nation-state. Borders are generally considered part of the territorial building blocks of the state, while constituting a national identity is viewed as a facet of nation-building. Adriana Kemp suggests differentiating between borders and identity in terms of hardware (border) and software (identity), and underscores the cultural and ideological importance of a border that exceeds its formal role of land.[3]

In the Israeli context, the land is both a state and a home.[4] In the aftermath of the 1948 War of Independence, Israel applied the principle of territorial sovereignty to its land; it employed rhetorical and institutional mechanisms that generated commitment to guarding the borders and strengthening traditional bonds with biblical Israel after millennia of diaspora.[5] Shaping a space as a national territory is clearly not solely a Zionist idea. National movements use sets of mechanisms to create commitment and belonging to specific areas, and to instill love and loyalty to a land. However, the case of Israel is different, since most of its citizens were not born there, but came from various countries, and they made Palestine-Israel their homeland while shaping the new territory in the spirit of their national inspirations.

The Six-Day War in 1967 introduced the new concept of the Green Line that divided the State of Israel from the Occupied Territories in the West Bank.[6] This was the turning point that destabilized the equation between nation and territory. Prior to 1967 there seems to have been a consensus that Israeli space has already been defined and charted.[7] Numerous researchers concur that there was no public debate on a change in the borders at that time.[8] Michael Feige notes that in 1967, only a few weeks before the war broke out, the right-wing Israeli politician and journalist Geula Cohen asked David Ben-Gurion, one of the founders of the state and the first prime minister of Israel, and at that time a member of the Knesset (parliament), what he would say to his grandchild if he asked him to define the borders of his homeland. Ben-Gurion did not hesitate: "I would say to my grandchild today: the borders of your homeland are the borders of the State of Israel as they are today."[9] Feige claims that Ben-Gurion's answer was not at all rare at the time.

However, the concept of national territory altered dramatically after the 1967 war. The new territories encompassed major sites linked to the Jewish past and associated with strong biblical references such as Hebron, Nablus, Mt. Sinai, and the Western Wall of Herod's temple in Jerusalem. These sites, which were now accessible to Israelis, elicited a messianic drive to forge a Jewish nation within these wider borders corresponding to Jewish heritage. At the same time, because these territories were densely populated with Palestinians who were not part of the Zionist enterprise and demographically threatened the Jewish majority in greater Israel, it was impossible to Hebraize or Judaize the territory (as was done for the 1948 borders).[10] This new situation led to tensions between appropriation and estrangement; in other words, between the promise of the new land and the fact that it was impossible to turn it into an integral part of the state.[11] The outcome created an ambiguity in the concept of the Israeli borders and the entire space of the Territories.

Eyal Weizman suggests seeing the Territories as a frontier zone:

> Against the geography of stable, static places, and the balance across linear and fixed sovereign borders, frontiers are deep, shifting, fragmented and elastic territories. Temporary lines of engagement, marked by makeshift boundaries, are not limited to the edge of political space but exist throughout its depth. Distinctions between the "inside" and the "outside" cannot be clearly marked. In fact, the straighter, more geometric and more abstract official colonial borders across the "New Worlds" tended to be, the more the territories of effective control were fragmented and dynamic and thus unchartable by any conventional mapping technique.[12]

A border presumably demarcates the "here" from the "there," and "my country" from a "foreign country," which can be hostile. However, Weizman maintains that the normative role of borders to concretize the state and differentiate between states has taken on a different role in the Israeli context, as can be seen by the different terms that illustrate its ambiguity such as boundaries, frontiers,[13] checkpoints, separation walls, no-man's-land, closures, fences, and barriers.[14]

Writers have noted that within the Occupied Territories, barriers and checkpoints were designed to create a division of the land, mainly to cut off the Palestinians from their land and to pose the Israeli soldiers as the "owners" of the space. This separation also refers to the binary oppositions of purity and impurity, similarity and difference, but, as Karen Grumberg maintains, "since 'outside' and 'inside' are easily shifted, the contours of the no-man's-land between them become increasingly blurred, defying delineation."[15]

In a book published in 2008, Adi Ophir and Ariella Azoulay emphasize the symbolic nature of borders and their psychological implications.

The Occupied Territories, they claim, are not "external" like some remote continent that can easily be ignored. They are "external" in the sense of a looming shadow: in order to feel normal, to resemble a free democratic society, the "external" must be repressed, and people must make immense efforts to prevent it from rising to consciousness. Parenthesized, forgotten, and denied, the Territories are nevertheless part of the Israeli identity.[16]

While the original 1948 borders were considered to justify the national struggle and elicited solidarity, the liminal region of the Occupied Territories, which has not been fully appended to Israel, violates the clear connection between the nation and the territory, hence complicating the national-Jewish identity and eliciting ethical debates. The juxtaposed spaces on the two sides of the Green Line create an apparent split between the declared national morality, which is based on the broad consensus of Israel as a democracy with Western and liberal values, and the oppression that Israel enforces in the Occupied Territories on the Palestinian people.[17] While on the declarative level Israel has sought to establish an "enlightened occupation" (*kibush naor*), an oxymoronic phrase intended to preserve the moral facade of the country, these territories are in fact in a "state of exception," to use the term of Italian philosopher Giorgio Agamben.[18] They operate as a designated space employed by governments in times of emergencies and crises, where constitutional rights are restricted, suspended, and rejected as the result of an exceptional decree.[19] However, although the "state of exception" usually refers to temporary (radical) actions, the rhetoric that repeatedly employs promises of "calmness" and "security," actually defines it as an interim situation that can continue ad infinitum.[20]

The Occupation of the West Bank, which began in 1967, remained remote to most Israelis for the next two decades. The First Intifada thrust this twilight zone into broader Israeli society in a dramatic and tangible way. The popular Palestinian uprising of the Intifada, in particular the fact that Palestinian civilians were involved in the rebellion and that it was the first time that Israelis, who were not soldiers, had heard the voices of the inhabitants of the Territories, all confirmed that the repression engendered by the Occupation was no longer possible. Yaron Peleg points out that "when the Intifada broke out, it acted like a sudden shock that revealed the large gap between words and actions, between the self-righteousness of Zionism, the magnitude of its hyperbole, and its ugly policies toward the Palestinians."[21]

The outbreak of the Second Intifada (the al Aqsa Intifada) in 2000, after the failure of the negotiations led by Ehud Barak and Yasser Arafat, sparked a second crisis. Terrorism and guerrilla warfare became commonplace, and terror attacks were carried out within the State of Israel. The Second Intifada constituted a different phase of the conflict, but it also brought to the surface the collective memory of the First Intifada. Though the Occupation itself created an abnormality, it was the two Intifadas that created the shock and highlighted the ambiguity of the concept of borders and its professed temporariness. This situation pinpointed the problematic nature of the border, both geographically and morally, as its lack of a fixed hierarchy or a linear order undermines normality and violates all equilibria.

This book offers a spatial reading of contemporary Israeli literature written in the shadow of the Intifada. Although it is part of what can be termed the "spatial turn" in the research on Israeli literature, my reading takes a distinctive philosophical perspective. As shown in the works of Karen Grumberg, Lital Levy, Hannan Hever, Shimrit Peled, Yigal Schwartz, Barbara Mann, and Nili Gold, reading Hebrew prose in the context of space and place has proven to be very fruitful. A few of these works explore certain questions and texts that constitute the focus of this book. Grumberg's *Place and Ideology in Contemporary Hebrew Literature* (2011) adopts the spatial vernacular to raise questions about ideology and identity. She investigates the works of Amos Oz, Orly Castel-Bloom, Sayed Kashua, Yoel Hoffman, and Ronit Matalon and illustrates different concepts of space in Israeli literature and culture. Grumberg suggests that Zionist ideology shaped an idea of place, and explores the manner in which different manifestations of space can challenge its ideological power. Her perspective on the hierarchy of space, the concept of border and roadblock, and her illustration of the spatial themes in the context of Israelis, Palestinians, and Arabs are linked to this study. Levy offers a spatial reading of the landscapes of Arab villages in the works of Anton Shammas, Emile Habiby, and Elias Khoury.[22] By reading canonic writers, as well as Mizrahi and Palestinian writers, from Yitzhak Shami to Emile Habibi and Ronit Matalon, Hever argues that the uses of place and space in Israeli works challenge hegemonial stances.[23] Both Levy and Hever reveal specific strategies of identity and literary resistance, issues that are explored here as well. In her book, *Ha-ribon ha-israeli- ha-sia'h ve-ha-roman 1967–1973* (The Israeli Sovereign: Discourse and Novel 1967–1973), Peled explores the Israeli discourse on space and sovereignty between 1967–1973, and its literary complex constellation. Yochai Oppenheimer's book *Me'ever la-gader: itsug ha-aravim ba-siporet ha-ivrit ve-ha-israelit 1906–2005* (Barriers: The Representation of the Arab in Hebrew and Israeli Fiction, 1906–2005) provides a wide-ranging account of the image of the Israeli Arab in Israeli-Hebrew prose. While the book is not primarily an analysis of spatial representations and does not discuss ethical concepts, it contains readings of a wide spectrum of works, some of which are also analyzed here.[24] Yaron Peleg's book *Israeli Culture between the Two Intifadas: A Brief Romance*, published in 2008, unfolds a cultural and literary mapping of the 1990s, a period of escapism, bounded by the symbolic milestones of the two Intifadas. Peleg sheds light on the effects of the Intifadas on Israeli culture and discusses the works of Orly Castel-Bloom, Etgar Keret, Gadi Taub, Uzi Weil, and Gafi Amir, but rarely touches on the military context or the Occupation.[25]

The theoretical framework of this book relates to these works but also differs from them in a number of ways. The core issue explored here is the question of the Occupation and the Intifada. The context of territories and borders is associated mainly with the Israeli-Palestinian conflict and to places of direct and indirect confrontation between soldiers and citizens. The book innovates in its theoretical development of the relationships between spatial concepts and ethics. Space and place in this book do not merely involve an examination of historical and ideological concepts, but also form a theoretical bridge between spatial thought and theories of ethics.

The key point of departure for this new theoretical framework is Gilles Deleuze and Félix Guattari's concept of deterritorialization. Although Hever uses this concept mainly to articulate his postcolonialist reading, I demonstrate the ethical insights that derive from implementing this term as a prism.[26] Deleuze and Guattari describe deterritorialization in a variety of ways and contexts. In this book, it serves as both a descriptive term (the realm of unclear borders) and a normative term (underscoring normative and ethical issues). Primarily, I show that deterritorialization can be used to define the abnormality of a border, by conceptualizing this abnormality as a subversion of the concept of territorial boundaries and a decontextualization of the relations between culture and place.[27]

In his preface to Deleuze and Guattari's *Anti-Oedipus*, Michel Foucault notes that deterritorialization can be perceived as an ethical theory.[28] I extend Foucault's conceptualization and show that in the context of the Occupation, deterritorialization can be perceived as both a risk and an opportunity. Traversing automatic and fixed borders and categories may lead to a downward spiral that negates all ethics and morality, thus rapidly reestablishing reterritorialization by building up new concepts of borders and roles. However, this situation also fractures time and space, providing the possibility for an uneasy contemplation that can lead to new paradigms. Deleuze and Guattari differentiate between "relative deterritorialization" and "absolute deterritorialization." The former is "stratic or interstratic" and does not impact the order of things, whereas the latter marks an "absolute drift"—the impossibility of being territorialized again.[29] They claim that the two forms of deterritorialization can be positive and negative. Relative deterritorialization is negative when it is immediately subjected to forms of reterritorialization that block any line of flight. It is positive when the line of flight dominates secondary reterritorializations. Absolute deterritorialization is positive when it leads to the creation of something new, but is negative when it leads to total chaos and madness.[30]

Marcelo Svirsky employs deterritorialization as his basic concept in his studies of Arab-Jewish activism in Israel-Palestine. He views deterritorialization as a revolutionary element that is interlaced with movements of reterritorialization, and produces rearrangements of the surroundings.[31] In literature, however, deterritorialization does not only refer to a political situation but also to poetic strategies, and specifically to the effect of defamiliarization, alienation, changes of viewpoints, as well as figurative and metaphoric writings, all of which are basic aesthetic concepts that can bridge artistic experience and ethical contemplation. By implementing the concept of deterritorialization, this book shows that the literary texts presented here, though differing from one another, depict worlds, spaces, and narratives that shatter authoritative concepts of meaning, either by changing the setting from a known environment to alien places, or by adopting a nonlinear or nonrealist style. The main argument is that there is an ethical basis within the concept of deterritorialization; namely, that lack of compliance is a vital condition for any form of moral inquiry.

In this book, the political and social structures constitute the settings for an analysis of specific narratives, images, formats, and structures in Israeli literature that express the rich and diverse representation of this spatial crisis and its ethical implications. Its basic assumption adheres to the "turn toward the ethical" in contemporary literary criticism, which, as novelist and philosopher Iris Murdoch states, provides a "new vocabulary of attention"[32] in its interchanging relations between the raw material of particular reality and the abstraction of philosophical theories.[33] Literature and reality have multifaceted relations and a multidirectional influence. Nevertheless, this book aims to show the power of literary texts to reveal problematic situations and encourage a new ethical gaze. Thus, it combines the concept of deterritorialization with other key concepts and notions in the field of moral philosophy, such as the ethics of military conduct, the controversial concept of *moral luck*, the ethics of bereavement, as well as the Levinasian notion of ethics, not only to reveal the importance of territory and borders in ethical controversies, but also to show how a literary work can be a source of ethical insights.

Hever claims that "in the teleological narrative of national identity construction we encounter the confluence of literary text with space [. . .] in many ways, this particular narrative of identity construction intersects the issue of territory and the quest to achieve sovereign rule over it."[34] From this perspective, this book examines what happened to this national narrative as a result of the Occupation, specifically in the Intifada era, when the issues are no longer related to achieving sovereignty over the land and defining national identity, but rather to coping with the multifaceted relationships between borders, territory, and identity.

The literary community in Israel has always been an important part of the cultural arena, whether by supporting hegemonic stances or criticizing them in direct or indirect ways. During the 1940s, Hebrew literature was influenced by social realism and depicted protagonists considered to be contemporary prototypes who settled the Land of Israel and fought for its sovereignty. Writers were considered obligated to shape the new national identity while promoting humanism and moral norms. In the 1950s, the author Haim Hazaz wrote that the role of literature is to bravely and responsibly illustrate the circumstances in Israel, reflect the voice of conscience, capture the greatness, and reveal the corruption.[35] This position was part of the cultural consensus that encouraged constant inner criticism and subversion in which authors shed light on injustices to foster the ethos of the new state and its people.[36] However, as exemplified in S. Yizhar's stories from the late 1940s, authors who challenged the Zionist ideology still identified with its general ideas. Glenda Abramson notes that:

> Generally, the political dialectic in Israeli literature was, therefore, not simply a matter of protesting against unpopular government, since it spanned the entire history of the State of Israel from 1948 [. . .].

> The liberal intellectuals, who constituted the mainstream group of Israeli writers from the start, exhibited subversive tendencies even when nominally supporting and traditionally identified with Labor.[37]

In fact, generations of Israeli authors from the 1940s up to the 1970s identified with the ruling political parties. This did not silence criticism, but may have moderated it. This may also explain the delay and the hesitation in the literary response to the Occupation after 1967. The Occupation forced Israeli society to examine its basic Zionist narrative and face the contradictions inherent to Zionism as a movement that believes and supports universal humanistic liberal ideas, while simultaneously enacting a national ideology that allows military control over the Palestinian population. This responsibility was not simple to shoulder.

Correlatively, since the Occupation was not the center of attention in the first two decades following the Six-Day War (1967–1987), it is not surprising that canonic Hebrew prose of the time rarely engaged with this issue. During the 1970s and the beginning of the 1980s a few playwrights (e.g., Joseph Mondi, Hanoch Levin, and Yehoshua Sobol) and poets (e.g., Meir Wieseltier) related to the Occupation, but Hebrew prose was slower to respond to the political situation and tended to focus on the Israeli-Arab conflict and the 1956, 1967, and 1973 wars (see, for example, Amos Oz's and A. B. Yehoshua's writings from the 1960s to the 1980s). While several of these texts were highly critical of Zionist ideology, they still did not address the Occupation and the new ethical and spatial issues it raised.[38]

According to Dan Urian, the first Lebanon war provided the initial spark for the debates on the Arab/Palestinian question and the Occupation, although the Israeli consensus had started to crack as early as in the 1973 war but primarily in the 1977 election, which ended thirty years of Mapai Party rule and led to a vast shift in Israeli politics. The Lebanon war disrupted national solidarity and created an oppositional movement,[39] which prompted civil disobedience for the first time. This became more extreme during the 1987 Intifada and led to a radical change in literary discourse. Along with the moral and intellectual involvement of literature in political discourse, many literary texts began describing the Occupation and the Intifada, and its extreme violence and guilt, as a reflection of a national pathology.

Literary prose on the Occupation and the two Intifadas has dealt with the political and cultural debate and posed interesting spatial ideas. Although not all these texts raise the question of spaces and borders directly, or in the same manner, the range of spatial issues they present illustrate this abnormality and constitute it as the kernel of corruption. Analyzing these complex representations of the Occupation and the Intifadas often reveals the internal conflict between the humanist tendency of Israeli literature, which is usually perceived as aligned with the political Left, and an acceptance of the reality of the Occupation. This analysis holds a mirror to Israeli society, its writers, and its intellectuals, which points toward a kind of dual morality.

Overview

The corpus of works written between 1987 and 2007 reveals a variety of themes, narratives, and poetic strategies. This twenty-year time frame serves to examine Israeli writing from the beginning of the First Intifada up to the aftermath of the Second Intifada. It paints a variegated portrait of the Israeli soldier, depicts the settings of the Occupied Territories, but also describes life in cities such as Tel Aviv and Jerusalem. It examines realistic writing as well as fantastic-grotesque images from both the soldiers' and the Palestinians' points of view, and discusses texts that use both first-person and third-person narration. While the issues discussed are not limited to this time frame, these two decades can be considered a historical and literary period in their own right in which these works, despite their variety, manifest the overriding theme of an intensive articulation of the sickness of a society in a state of confusion. One of the key purposes of this book is to show that this illness can best be understood through readings of the concepts of space, borders, and ethics.

This volume is made of two parts. The first part, "In the Heart of Darkness," is centered on the Israeli soldier and the Occupied Territories from the First Intifada in the 1990s to the Second Intifada. The second part, "Does Literature Matter?" discusses literary works set in civilian spaces of Israel and explores the ways in which everyday life in Israel has been affected by the conflict.

The first section is composed of three chapters that analyze the transformation of the Israeli soldier from an admired hero to an agent of evil. The first two chapters trace the ways in which literature has mirrored an evolution in the perception of soldiers from initially viewing them as subjects of a greater power, through envisioning them as the victims of the national war machine, and finally leading to critical stances toward the military ethos and its ethical shortcomings. The third chapter examines literature depicting the lives of the Palestinians in the Occupied Territories.

The first chapter, "On a Hot Tin Roof," examines the relationships between space and ethics, as manifested through a recurring scene in many literary texts where soldiers requisition a Palestinian home or take control of its roof so that they can monitor the Palestinian street and track down wanted individuals. Gilad Evron's story "Ha-baz" (The Falcon) from *Mar'eh makom* (Reference, 2003), Asher Kravitz's *Ani Mustafa Rabinovitch* (I, Mustafa Rabinovitch, 2004), Shai Lahav's *Lekh le-aza* (Go to Gaza, 2005), A. B. Yehoshua's *Esh yedidutit* (Friendly Fire, 2007), Yaniv Iczkovits's *Dofek* (Pulse, 2007), and Eshkol Nevo's *Mish'ala ahat yemina* (World Cup Wishes, 2007) describe this type of scene where the soldiers have a spatial and topographical advantage that may lead to a kind of superiority, which, in turn, they eventually lose along with their humanity, their friends, and/or their lives. This investigation is initiated by Dave Grossman's book *On Killing* (1995) and the issues of space and distance. Grossman, a scholar who has explored the psychological and social aspects of soldiers in battle, analyzes the effect of physical distance between soldiers and their victims. The spatial concept of topography moves in this chapter from a bird's-eye view, in which the soldier cannot see his victims clearly, to a face-to-face encounter with the Palestinians. As the distance begins to close, and a more intimate encounter takes place, the feeling of deterritorialization sharpens and the horror is increased, as does the soldiers' "emotional burden." The reading also draws on Orly Lubin's analysis (2006) of Dina Zvi-Riklis's film *Nekudat tatspit* (Lookout, 1991) to explore the impact of this recurring scene and the changes in distance, and discuss the manner in which these literary texts make use of spatial superiority through a variety of poetic twists.

The conflict of the soldier and his position is articulated in the second chapter, "No Luck." This chapter introduces an ethical architecture designed to better understand what motivates authors to write rooftop scenes and describe the soldiers' feelings of distress and guilt in such detail. The leitmotif of the Israeli soldier in these texts often revolves around issues of personal responsibility and free choice, and concretizes the soldiers' continuous feeling of guilt in terms of the catchphrase *Yorim u'bokhim* (shooting and crying). This phrase, which expresses a kind of "Catch 22" in which soldiers are trapped in a designated space with a different reality and deviated norms, refers to the dual notion of the soldier as both the perpetrator (causing Palestinian suffering) and the victim (of the military and political situation). Hebrew literature and culture, from the 1948 war to this day, has presented fictional and nonfictional writings of war testimonies along this line. To formulate this dualism, I present the philosophical concept of *moral luck.* Thomas Nagel, an American philosopher who wrote several books in the field of moral philosophy and ethics, developed the notion of moral luck, which refers to a state where a moral agent is assigned moral blame or praise for an action, even though a significant part of what she or he does depends on factors beyond his or her control. The connection between deterritorialization and the dualistic nature of moral luck is evident: the soldiers' spatial disorientation is a fundamental component of the process of losing control over their actions, which eventually leads them to military conduct they would be unlikely to perform under any other circumstances. Reading prose from the Intifada through these concepts of deterritorialization and moral luck engenders a philosophical account of the phenomenon of Israeli war testimonies and the concept of *Yorim u'bokhim.* In this chapter, I read Yitzhak Ben-Ner's *Ta'atuon* (Delusion, 1989), Roy Polity's *Arnavonei gagot* (Roof Rabbits, 2001), and Liran Ron Furer's *Tismonet ha-mahsom* (Checkpoint Syndrome, 2003), as well as the texts presented in the first chapter.

The third chapter, "The Third Eye," focuses on works that describe the Palestinian perspective through Palestinian narrators. Moral philosophy has often explored the notion of "point of view" by questioning its claim of objectivity and underscoring its problematization. Thomas Nagel, for instance, chose the title *The View from Nowhere* for his 1986 book, in which he articulates the theoretical assumption that ethical questions should be addressed from a neutral point of view. Although it is clear that this type of position is impractical in real life, fiction provides a unique opportunity to switch perspectives and adopt different points of view. In this chapter, I read works by Israeli Jewish authors who ostensibly give voice to Palestinian elders, women, and children, and depict their suffering under the Occupation. I discuss the cultural and ethical issues surrounding the appropriation of the voice of the subaltern by the conqueror, and analyze the authors' esthetic choices, such as the use of the grotesque and unrealistic spaces.

The power of deterritorialization appears in this inquiry in two different contexts. The first is the writers' decision to alienate themselves from their innate position as Jewish Israelis and engage with a different perspective. The second is their choice to abandon a causal linear narrative for nonrealistic writing. This chapter analyzes three texts: David Grossman's *Hiyukh ha-gdi* (The Smile of the Lamb, 1983), Dror Green's *Agadot ha-intifada* (The Intifada Tales, 1989), and Itamar Levy's *Otiyot ha-shemesh, otiyot ha-yare'ah* (Letters of the Sun, Letters of the Moon, 1991).

The second section of this book is composed of four chapters, each chapter discusses two literary texts that deal with the ways in which everyday life in Israel has been affected by the conflict. Most of these texts were written after Prime Minister Yitzhak Rabin's assassination in 1995 and during the Second Intifada, when the optimism regarding the possibility of peace agreement faded rapidly. During this period, a sense of uncertainty filled the hearts of mainstream Israelis. Since these works do not center on the friction points between Israelis and Palestinians, and their setting is not the Occupied Territories, they often tend not to ask direct questions about the Occupation and do not aim to describe military conduct. Instead, they depict the lives of individuals under daily terrorism, controversial forms of army service, and bereavement, all of which cast a different light on the theme of spaces and borders. Because the chapters analyze literary works by canonical writers, they also discuss these authors' political personas and the tension between the acceptance of the central Zionist ideology and its subversion.

The fourth and fifth chapters revolve around different works by a single author, which depict changes in Israeli society from the 1970s and 1990s up to the first decades of the twenty-first century, or a time period from the First to the Second Intifada. The fourth chapter, "A. B. Yehoshua and the Moderation on the Left at the Turn of the Millennium," discusses Yehoshua's depiction of the character of the bereaved father. This character appears in many of his works from the short stories he published in the 1960s to the novel *Friendly Fire* that was published in 2007. While the Israeli *akeda* myth and the issue of national bereavement have been discussed in relation to Yehoshua's work, here I stress the evolution of this myth, its specific connotation in relation to the Occupation and the Intifada, and its ethical burden. In a sense, the concept of the *akeda* (the binding of Issac), which depicts the soldier as a son who is sent to sacrifice himself on the altar of the state, is but another variation on the notion of moral luck, since the soldiers are doomed to be part of a social mechanism that negates their free will, and hence defines a political perspective that perceives the soldiers as innocent. In recent years, Yehoshua has been taken to task for tempering his highly acerbic criticism of Israeli politics and moving closer to the political center. This change in attitude toward the military-national consensus not only illustrates the political-ideological crisis that the Israeli Left has experienced in the past twenty years, but also stems from Yehoshua's status as a major author in the Israeli canon, which implicitly demands a certain national role. The analysis shows that in his early works, such as *Be-t'hilat kayits—1970* (Early in the Summer of 1970, published in the early 1970s), he was very critical of the idealistic concept of national bereavement in particular and militarism in general, while in his later work, when depicting a soldier in a Palestinian village, Yehoshua moderates his position to reflect and internalize an acceptance of the national concept and the myth of national bereavement.

The fifth chapter, "Orly Castel-Bloom between the Two Intifadas," discusses two novels by Castel-Bloom—*Dolly City* (1992) and *Halakim enoshiyim* (Human Parts, 2002). In this chapter, I explore Castel-Bloom's use of literary techniques such as supernatural, grotesque, and plastic images of the human body as a metaphor for the political, which in turn come to reflect a unique take on the concepts of borders, the Occupation, militarism, and terrorism. As many literary critics have already stated, Castel-Bloom's style obliterates the basic structures of space to create an alienated world that appropriates parts of Israeli reality, while at the same time infuses them with postmodern images. The chapter analyzes the differences in Castel-Bloom's deterritorialization of the Zionist space in the two novels. In *Dolly City*, Castel-Bloom voices uncompromising criticism of the Occupation and the questions of borders, and takes a blunt, provocative, and active approach. In *Human Parts,* she presents a more passive description of the sensation of oppressiveness, in which Israelis are shunted from moral decay to great fear, prefer to perceive the world through the all-encompassing eye of the media, and let their fears turn them into puppets on the historical and political stage.

The readings of the works of Yehoshua and Castel-Bloom suggest there was a paradigmatic shift in literary representations after the Second Intifada. The sixth and seventh chapters present an alternative ethical and spatial view. In the sixth chapter, "Terrorism and the Face of the Dead Other," I offer a reading of Shifra Horn's *Himnon la-simha* (Ode to Joy) and A. B. Yehoshua's *Shlihuto shel ha-memune al mash'abei enosh* (A Woman in Jerusalem), both published in 2004 and both dealing with terror attacks in the heart of Jerusalem. The daily lives of the protagonists in the two novels are disrupted by a deadly terror bombing when they encounter one of the anonymous victims, a casualty who is a total stranger. This chapter proposes an ethical reading of these two novels through Emmanuel Levinas's ethics, by exploring the protagonists' surprise and shock at their encounter with the Other. I discuss the way in which the journeys in both novels reveal the face of the Other, and examine how these novels deal with the issue of one's responsibility for the dead Other, beyond his demise.

The final chapter, "Dismantling Borders: A Female Perspective," examines ethical alternatives to the question of borders in Ronit Matalon's *Sarah, Sarah* (Bliss, 2000) and Michal Govrin's *Hevzekim* (Snapshots, 2002). These two works, through their context and style, systematically dismantle borders—not only those of the liminal space of the Occupied Territories, but also the entire national space and sovereignty—and create deterritorialization. The analysis draws on Deleuze and Guattari's concept of space along with Rosi Braidotti's more recent ethical-feminist perspective, to underscore the new position reflected in these novels toward territorial sovereignty and its significance. This final chapter explores the aesthetic and ethical approaches in the two novels and the possibility of their realization.

The book ends with a short epilogue that discusses the nature of contemporary literary criticism and examines this era from today's perspective.

Overall, this book attempts to shed new light on the multifaceted relationships between space and ethics in contemporary Israeli prose written during the Occupation and the two Intifadas. From realistic to nonrealistic fiction, from the soldier's point of view to that of the noncombatant, from male protagonists to women and children, this book presents a collage of voices, which illustrate the role of Israeli literature in today's Israeli cultural and political arena.

PART 1

In the Heart of Darkness

Meyer, the soldier narrator of Etgar Keret's story "Darukh ve-natsur" (Cocked and Locked), finds himself in a narrow passageway in a Palestinian village. A Hamas activist, who likes to curse and intimidate soldiers, is standing in front of him calling him a "cocksucker" and "homo." He asks him if "Your cross-eyed sergeant bush [push][1] it up your ass too hard yesterday?" and makes crude sexual remarks about Meyer's sister or mother.[2] Later he points at his heart and urges Meyer to shoot him, knowing that Meyer will not do a thing.

Keret's story, published in Hebrew in 1994, illustrates the asymmetric power relations between Israelis and Palestinians and raises crucial questions about military conduct. It does so by depicting a single point of friction between a Hamas activist and Meyer, the narrator, a soldier who is positioned facing him, but is duty-bound not to respond in kind.

Meyer, whose friend Abutbul was severely injured and will probably remain in a coma, is frustrated by the situation and feels completely powerless during his everyday encounters with Palestinians. When he points his rifle at the Hamas activist just to scare him, the sergeant approaches and shouts at him: "what the hell do you think you're doing, standing there like a damn cowboy with your weapon smeared over your cheek? What do you think this is? The fucking Wild West or something?"[3] The sergeant admits that he is also upset about Abutbul and has fantasies of revenge; however, the role of a soldier is to refrain from these actions, which are those of terrorists—"if I did that, I'd be just like them. Don't you get it?"[4] Unlike the Palestinians who use any means at their disposal to hurt and kill (as they did with Abutbul), Israeli soldiers must act differently, be better than them, and not shoot.

The next day, the Hamas activist continues, as usual, to call Meyer names, inquire about Abutbul's condition, and send the Hamas' regards. But this time, Meyer cannot stand this situation in which his power to act and his masculinity are continuously attacked and finds an original solution. Meyer makes an unexpected gesture: he tears the wrapping off his field dressing and ties it across his face like a kaffiyeh. He takes his rifle, cocks it, and makes sure the safety is on. He swings the rifle over his head a few times and then, suddenly, lets it go. It lands about midway between him and his Palestinian counterpart.

> "That's for you, ya majnun" I scream to him. [. . .] He's faster than me. He'll get to it before me. But I'll win, because now I am just like him, and with the rifle in his hands he'll be just like me.[5]

Meyer feels he can only win and vindicate his manhood by relinquishing his weapon. He decides to throw down his rifle and confront his antagonist with his bare hands. He approaches him, knocks him down, kicks him hard, grabs his face, and bangs it into a telephone pole, letting his anger fuel his actions. The ending is clearly a nod to cowboy movies, when a rifle flies into the sky and spirals slowly downward in slow motion as the protagonist shows his manly power.

This story is about space and ethics: cowboys could shoot whenever they wanted, whereas the Israeli soldier in the Occupied Territories must refrain, to preserve his moral superiority over his enemies. Meyer is depicted as a gentle soldier who cares about his friends and family, but the nature of the situation prompts him to commit an act of brutal violence. Eventually, the solution has much to do with this Wild West image. Meyer tries to internalize the rules of engagement as formulated by the sergeant, and thus abandons his rifle so he will be on an equal footing with his counterpart and will be able to smash his head, just like what happened to his friend Abutbul. Throughout the story, the Palestinian points at his heart, as though he is ready to be killed. He feels free to expose his genitals and say whatever he likes. This "freedom" reflects the cynical behavior of a person who has lost all notion of the value of life. Meyer, on the other hand, has a lot to lose, including his morality. At the end of the story, after he "takes care" of the Palestinian, he symbolically recovers his masculinity and power, but has incurred a great loss.

Keret's unique style in "Cocked and Locked" employs radicalism and sarcasm to capture the ethical challenges posed by warfare in the Occupied Territories. These challenges stem from the unclear nature of military intervention in the Territories and the asymmetric power relations between Israelis and Palestinians, as Uri Ben-Eliezer states in his book *Old Conflict, New War*:

> These wars are not waged between professional, conscript, or mass armies, even if such armies take part alongside other military groups. In fact, these wars involve a welter of forces: private armies, militias, autonomous military units, paramilitary groups, regional armies, segments of national armies, tribal armies, national movements, underground organizations, mercenaries, terrorist gangs, and even criminal organizations.[6]

Ben-Eliezer, a sociologist who writes on militarism in the context of Israeli society, discusses how these new wars differ from conventional ones between states. New wars are often asymmetric, in particular if they are conducted between a state and a non-state. The stronger side can have greater technical capabilities, but the weaker side can surprise the stronger side with unpredictable tactics, such as guerrilla warfare and terrorism. Many such wars do not have differentiated battlefields, and the dichotomies between the front and the rear, soldiers and civilians are often conflated. Thus, "the violence often shifts from the battlefields to the big cities, refugee camps, and villages—in short, to civilian habitats."[7] In many cases these wars are not declared; they have clear objectives, such as to conquer enemy territory or appropriate material resources. Thus, it is unclear when the war is over or who the winner is. Another aspect of new wars is the involvement of media, both traditional and local and also new and global. Thus, stories and images are quickly redistributed and become part of the conflict.[8]

With no such clarity of objectives and successes, and with the big eye of the media, perfect military conduct is impossible, as illustrated in Yuval Shimony's text "Omanut ha-milhama" (The Art of War, 1990). This short allegorical text unfolds the story of a commander who decides to train for combat in a built-up area by constructing a perfect life-size model of a residential combat zone. In a Kafkaesque manner, the model becomes the essence of the operation, as the whole group works on every detail, trying to model the people and even the birds. They never carry out the operation, because they cannot make the model perfect.

Unlike Shimony's model, in Keret's story the protagonist is plunged into an actual residential combat zone, in which he cannot engage in rule-book military conduct. The contrast between Shimony's ideal model and the forlorn appearance of Keret's protagonist underscores not only the problematic circumstances of soldiers in the Territories, but the literary power of the authors, who articulate these situations through images, myths, and concepts.

CHAPTER 1

On a Hot Tin Roof

> We climbed the slope of a hill, which had never even in its dreams seen anything driving over it with such dizzying boldness [. . .] and there we sought out a place and surveyed the entire land below us.
>
> A first glance and the great land stretched out before you, emphasizing all its sharp-hewn outlines, hunched and hollowed with drenched lushness, in a light that was growing whiter, and with a bit of a breeze that had started in the meantime and blew upon us a breath of beauty [. . .] suddenly here was the checkerboard of fields, plowed and verdant, and the patches of shade-dappled orchards, and the hedges that dissected the area into peaceful forms stretching into the distance.[1]

These lines are taken from "Hirbet Hiz'a," a story written in 1949 by S. Yizhar. It takes place during the 1948 war, as a group of Israeli soldiers is ordered to demolish an Arab village and expel its inhabitants. The story documents their cruelty toward the helpless villagers. Apart from the narrator, a soldier himself, whose feelings about the incident are mixed, the other soldiers act with insensitivity and are completely unaware of the heinous nature of their deeds.

This passage highlights the spatial setting of the story by placing the soldiers on a hill overlooking the surrounding countryside. The village, located beneath them, blends into the carefully nurtured fields. Here, while the "village lay spread out before us,"[2] the soldiers "took position, set up machine guns, and were ready to start." However, since "there was still a wait until zero hour,"[3] they sit together relaxing and eating their tinned rations, playing games and enjoying themselves, as if they were on a school outing. Soon, however, their spatial topographic position, combined with their boredom and the acknowledgment that "this whole Khirbet Khizeh presented no problem"[4] (that is, no military challenge), inspires them to start a kind of hunting game in which the soldiers target people (or animals) and try to score points by shooting.

"Hirbet Hiz'a" was one of the first stories to criticize the events of the 1948 War of Independence. Soon after its publication and to this day, this story is considered one of the most important and controversial literary texts on the 1948 war.[5] Yizhar was brave enough to paint unflattering images of Israeli soldiers, and to demonstrate a mechanism that can lead to unethical and unlawful military conduct, which earned him both praise and condemnation. The commentary on this story is extensive. This chapter does not dwell on the richness of the text, but rather examines elements that have not been widely discussed elsewhere that are critical to the context of space and ethics and evidenced in contemporary prose on the Intifada: the power of the topographic settings and the portrayal of physical and mental distance.

This chapter focuses on scenes found in almost every literary text that describes a friction point between soldiers and Palestinian civilians and families, when soldiers requisition apartments and roofs for military purposes. They are suggestive of what Karen Grumberg calls "the hierarchy of space in Israeli society,"[6] since they create a realm where the Palestinian home is always penetrated, and the Israeli soldier is the master of the landscape. On the other hand, the spatial presentation emphasizes that the soldiers are doomed to play a certain role they did not anticipate. They are ordered to leave their natural environment and are plunged into a completely foreign territory with different rules. This creates a state of deterritorialization—a state of movement or process, in which something escapes or departs from a given territory, which may be a marked space, or any other system, whether conceptual, linguistic, or social.[7] This deterritorialization blurs individuals' familiar system of thoughts and affects later traumatic recollections of these events. Though these literary works are often influenced by concrete events, they do not so much copy reality as endow a space and topography with a tangible, figurative, and symbolic role. This, in turn, reveals a range of ethical issues and the responses to them.

On Distancing

Former chief of staff Dan Halutz, who served as a military pilot, was asked how he felt when bombing from the air. The context of the question was a debate on the role of pilots in the Second Intifada, after the IDF adopted a policy of "targeted elimination," which consisted of aerial bombing of wanted Palestinians that often caused the death of family members and other innocent people and children. Halutz only responded to the physiological notion of sensation. He said that when the bomb was dropped he felt a jerk in the aircraft that only lasted a second.[8]

The psychological mechanism of distancing is widely recognized as one of the key reasons why ordinary individuals can be made to kill. It involves a process of dehumanization the Other, and thus enables people to deny the fact that they are killing human beings.[9] Physical distance ranges from impersonal and long range as in the case of artillery, to short and even intimate in the case of hand-to-hand fighting.[10]

When engaged in artillery fire, soldiers cannot see their individual victims without using mechanical devices such as radar, binoculars, or a periscope.[11] Dan Halutz's response is indicative of the effect of topographic distance on pilots, whose exposure to the sights and sounds of war is muffled, and for whom the outcomes of bombings are not tangible.

Another type of long-range warfare involves situations where soldiers can see the enemy but cannot kill him without special weaponry such as sniper guns, tank fire, or antimissile missiles. Unlike when they use artillery, the soldiers have an idea of what is taking place on the battlefield, but use mechanical distancing devices to observe the target through their weapons; by contrast, at mid-range, soldiers can see their counterparts but cannot see their facial expressions. The soldier can only see his opponent at close range, when "looking at a man's face, seeing his eyes and his fear"[12] eliminates denial. At this range the interpersonal nature of killing shifts: "instead of shooting at a uniform and killing a generalized enemy, the killer must shoot at a person and kill a specific individual."[13] There is even greater intimacy in close combat, which has been related to sexual abuse or even rape.[14] Clearly, while military action at long range blurs the attributes of the scene and makes the strike more sterile and thus more probable, getting closer to the enemy emphasizes individuality and makes the act of killing more difficult and traumatic for the soldier.

Distance can be mental as well as physical. Mental distance is created by military education (formal and informal) and the process of becoming accustomed to violence. Research has shown that violent acts such as causing severe injuries and mutilation, torturing bound prisoners, and humiliating people can escalate as a function of soldiers' exposure to this behavior and their perception of it as part of military service. This type of conduct can take place in almost every army, as was seen in the Abu Ghraib incidents in the U.S. military.[15] From their first days in the military, recruits are subjected to a set of rituals, such as donning a uniform, receiving the regulation crew cut, taking an oath, and undergoing basic training, which create bonds between soldiers.[16] These rituals nurture group spirit and group loyalty, and whet their appetite for battle.[17]

Military service in Israel is perceived as essential to an adolescent's right to belong to the inner circle of adult males.[18] Especially in elite units, this underscores a dichotomous notion of gender, in which masculinity is contrasted with femininity and homosexuality, and consists of the adoption of "manly" values such as "power, coarseness, bluntness and emotional distance."[19] The homosocial masculine group often absorbs sexual content such that becoming a soldier seems to enhance a man's sexuality. Hence, it is not surprising that a similar sense of anticipation that precedes a man's first sexual experience may precede his first battle.[20] UNESCO's expert group meeting report *Male Roles, Masculinities and Violence: A Culture of Peace Perspective* (2000) argues that "boys' peer group life, military training, and mass media often promote a direct link between being a 'real man' and the practice of dominance and violence."[21] Thus, accountability to one's friends, and anonymity that reduces one's sense of personal responsibility,[22] along with common notions of manhood, are among the attributes that promote soldiers' psychological distance and often create a fertile breeding ground for illegal acts of violence.

Topography and distancing take on realistic and symbolic meaning in many literary texts. Yizhar's text is a good example. The physical distance in Yizhar's story varies from long range to mid-range: the soldiers can see the villagers, but from a distance they cannot identify whether they are young or old, male or female, and they cannot kill them without special weaponry. Since the villagers look smaller from a distance, it is easier for the soldiers to dehumanize them. As masters of the land, their physical distance prevents them from seeing the faces and expressions of the villagers, so the soldiers perceive them as uncivilized, like animals "running around desperately"[23] like ants. They are not perceived as human: "forget these Ayrabs—they're not even human,"[24] "They don't even have blood in their veins, these Ayrabs."[25]

The soldiers in Yizhar's text illustrate not only physical but mental distancing. They continue to dehumanize their victims even when the physical distance is reduced. When the soldiers encounter one of the last men who did not flee or was killed, they give him two alternatives: "Your life or the camel,"[26] as though the two could be equated. They later kill old women as if they were wounded animals: "I would do them a favor and finish them off with a bullet to the head."[27] These attributes of animalism are consistent with another mechanism of mental distancing, as the soldiers start considering the situation to be a hunting party. The soldiers measure lengths and positions and refer to the villagers in terms of "pieces" ("How many pieces do you have?"[28]), and to the act of killing with the verb "screw" (*li'dfok* in Hebrew), which was translated in the English version as "blast."[29]

Using the word "screw" instead of kill exemplifies the "overlap between the language of sex and that of battle," and stresses the relationship between fighting and masculinity.[30] In Yizhar's story the soldiers behave in an extremely chauvinistic way toward "girls." For example, they chat at lunchtime about Rebecca and Arieh, saying "Just watch out [. . .] that you don't end up the same way with her as you did with the horse"[31] in reference to a beautiful colt that ran away as soon as they untied it. Thus, Arabs and women in general are perceived as animals that need to be tamed.

Yizhar's story was written decades before the Intifada broke out, but his description of soldiers' physical and mental distancing remains pertinent. The concept of physical distancing, the hunting game, the dehumanization of the Palestinians, the animalism, and the overlap of sexual and violent terminologies continue to be leitmotifs in literature about soldiers in the Intifada.

On the Roof

> I'll take an example any soldier who served in the Territories will know: manning a lookout post above a civilian house. [. . .] I vividly remember the first lookout post I manned in the town of Halhul near Hebron.
>
> First, the house's entire external walls were stained black from leftover coffee, which the soldiers would spill from the roof. The yard

> was filled with excrement and toilet paper, since it was used as the soldiers' outhouse. The roof had piles of garbage and cans.
>
> The M462 that would come at every shift, would crush the pavement and the entrance to the house. Whenever a shift would change at two in the morning the entire household would wake up, and because they also had a baby in the house, he would start howling. I remember the look on the faces of the household members whenever I would run into one of them in the staircase, a look of humiliation.[32]

Dina Zvi-Riklis's short movie *Nekudat tatspit* (Lookout, 1990) chronicles the moves of an Israeli soldier located on the roof of a building in a refugee camp in the Occupied Territories. While positioned on the roof he can observe the everyday life of the Palestinian family next door: the father, a child of around five, and his sister. His deterritorialization enables him to witness the sister's arranged marriage against her will, her morning sickness, the dovecote on the roof, and the little boy who plays with the doves and sets them free. He sees soldiers take a ball away from children and knock vegetables out of a Palestinian woman's bag. He views soldiers checking the identity card of the sister's husband and arresting her father. The plot reaches its peak when the husband asks his wife's younger brother to take a box to a friend. The boy goes out and is excited to see his father returning home after being arrested. He sees a few soldiers on the corner and gets confused. His sister's husband, who is standing on the roof, encourages him to give the box to the friend, but he panics and throws it. The box blows up and the child dies. The soldier on the roof shoots the husband. In the next scene there is a different soldier on the roof, while in the next building the woman (the sister), dressed in black, is rocking a baby.

In *Isha koret isha* (A Woman Reads Woman) Orly Lubin argues that the soldier on the roof in this film wields the enormous power of a weapon and the power of gaze. By being in an elevated position and often using binoculars, he sees everything below him, while he is protected. The camera in this film never pans from bottom to top, but from a parallel point of view or from the soldier's higher location downward. Thus, the soldier and his point of view constitute the dominant orientation.[33]

Asher Kravitz's novel *Ani Mustafa Rabinovitch* (I, Mustafa Rabinovitch, 2004; second edition, 2008) depicts an Israeli sniper on the roof of Palestinian houses, in which he was placed by the army. Yair Rabinovitch, the protagonist and narrator, serves in the Duvdevan elite unit of *Mista'arvim*, where soldiers often disguise themselves as Palestinians. *Mista'arvim* are specific units made up of soldiers trained to assimilate into the local Arab population. They learn the language and the dialects, dress like locals, and disguise their identity to collect intelligence and perform undercover military activities. Yair's Arab name in the field is Mustafa, and his role is to shoot and kill specific targeted individuals from a distance. These are the opening lines of the novel:

> I lie on a whitewashed roof. My feet are covered in wood chips. Carpentry waste. [. . .] Only the barrel of the 24M sticks out a bit. Three exes are marked on the butt. A silencer is placed at the end of the barrel. [. . .] A tiny microphone rests two centimeters from my mouth. And I am also wearing headphones.[34]

Kravitz's protagonist is lying on the roof of a building. As in Zvi-Riklis's film, he looks at women and children during their intimate moments, sees the soldiers on the street, and observes the moves of the wanted Palestinians. In Zvi-Riklis's film, the soundtrack is based on music played by radio stations and on walkie-talkie conversations, thus making it impossible for the soldier to hear what he sees below. Yair is also unable to hear, so when he watches the street, he feels he is seeing a pantomime. He cannot clearly distinguish men from women: they can be men, women, or men disguised as women.[35]

In both the text and the film, it is clear that a topographically distanced position is a position of power. This topography of power is reminiscent of Bentham's eighteenth-century panopticon,[36] a circular prison with a watchtower in its center. The prisoners are visible to each other and to the guards in the watchtower, but they do not know whether they are being watched. The panopticon was also built to increase security in other institutions, where close surveillance is necessary. Foucault used this concept in *Discipline and Punish* as a metaphor for anonymous disciplinary mechanisms.[37] Avi Valentain's *Shahid* suggests a parallel description when depicting a Palestinian refugee camp and the topography of the IDF soldiers:

> Five paths embark from the same point—from the central square, a place that was once filled with houses in the same horrible and impossible density as the other parts of the town until a tractor came and

> in half a day cleared, with its steel spoon, a pristine surface. Then the construction crews came and raised a magnificent building in the center of the square, reinforced it with concrete, armed it with glass and closed it with bars. Five stories to the sky and three stories in the ground. We live in a tower.[38]

Valentain's description is suggestive of a panopticon, but a panopticon is not necessarily physical and can operate metaphorically. The crowded Palestinian village is usually not constructed or reconstructed in this manner; however, the adjacent windows and roofs of the buildings form an architecture where all the apartments are visible and no secrets can be kept hidden from the soldiers watching from above. In "Children of Palestine," Graham Usher provides a striking illustration of this claustrophobic existence. The daily traumatic experiences of a child under the Occupation are projected in images of incarceration and burial: "[A]t school, we feel the soldiers are on top of us. On breaks, we feel they are on top of us. When we go home, we feel they are on top of us."[39] The soldiers on the roof have the power to silently spy on suspects, to learn their routines, and, in fact, make them feel trapped in their own homes.

Although the spatial superiority of Israeli soldiers is not surprising, the movie and Kravitz's text suggest not only a military supremacy but also a seemingly moral superiority. These texts turn the position of superiority (and the panopticon settings) into a variant on the enlightened Western perspective, as though the Palestinians were savages examined by anthropologists, natives under a colonial regime, or even caged animals.

Lookout ends with the shooting and the killing of the young husband. Kravitz's book also ends with a scene of shooting and killing. It is logical to expect that narratives of snipers will eventually describe what they were sent to do. However, these scenes do not present brutality on the part of the soldiers, but rather their humanistic dilemmas. Zvi-Riklis's movie depicts the tragic death of a young boy who was unwittingly sent on a mission, which risked his life. Throughout the narrative, the father is depicted as wanting to live in peace, whereas the daughter's husband is more politically active. Thus, when the child dies, it is clear that the husband is to blame because of his anti-Israeli activity, but even more so because of what he did to the little boy. Although there is no trial, the soldier's shooting and killing of the husband after he exploited the child emerges as a kind of justice rendered by the soldier.

Kravitz's text can be viewed along these lines as well. Yair is not a violent soldier but rather the stereotype of a well-educated Ashkenazi with a religious background and a yearning to be a good citizen and therefore a good soldier. Because he is fluent in Arabic and highly motivated, he is selected for the Duvdevan elite unit. He is a perfect sniper with a mathematical ability to calculate distances and hit his targets. However, his religious and humanist education prompts him to make a vow that is almost impossible to keep:

> I decided to spend my life on this wretched planet without killing. I don't want the responsibility of cutting down the soul of a human being weighing on my conscience which, according to the best of sources, was created in God's image [. . .] most people would find it very easy to adhere to such a vow. Not me. That's the way it is when you're a fighter in Duvdevan.[40]

Throughout most of the narrative, Yair does not compromise his values. He informs his superiors about the extremely aggressive attitude of his commander, First Lieutenant Nimrod, toward the Palestinians, which leads to Nimrod's removal from the unit. He deliberately shoots a wanted Palestinian in the leg and does not kill him, and he gives water to arrested Palestinians, while putting himself in danger. Yair stands against animal cruelty, and this is also part of his moral attitude. The only episode in which he wants to shoot Palestinians is when he sees three children aggressively strike and kick a donkey they are riding to school.[41] The narrator, who is sitting on the roof, sees them through his telescopic lens and is tempted to pull the trigger.[42] On another occasion, he decides not to shoot wanted Palestinians, who are in the process of transporting weapons, because a dog is lying on the ground next to the car nursing four pups. He knows that if he hits the landmine carrier, they will all blow up and no one will be left alive, so he decides to "to keep the dog and her pups outside the circle of violence."[43]

Thus, while the Palestinians in the story abuse animals, Yair defines himself as their protector. In contrast to the soldiers' abusive attitude toward animals in Yizhar's "Hirbet Hiz'a," in *I, Mustafa Rabinovitch* the attitude toward the well-being of animals seems to rule out an abusive attitude toward the Palestinians. However, this humanistic vision can also be interpreted as suggesting that Yair cares more about animals than the Palestinians.

Yair manages to keep his oath until the final pages of the novel, when he notices a woman emerging from behind a large bush near his officers. The other soldiers do not see her, but Yair knows that she will blow them up. He has no choice but to save his friends from the terrorist; if he shoots her, even without killing her, she will detonate her explosive belt and be killed, and since he does not have the time to aim at her legs, he shoots at the center of her body. When the bullet hits her explosive belt, a massive explosion is heard and her head is splattered everywhere. Yair knows he prevented a horrific disaster, but he has broken his vow: "Two souls occupied my body. One was a savior, the other a murderer."[44] After this incident, the soldiers search for the woman's three young children and contact the Red Cross, which promptly arrives and takes them into care.

In her article on the representation of children in the context of Third World emergencies, Erica Burman analyses the symbolic power of the image of children, suggesting that they "speak for the ways childhood has come to carry signification of truth, nature, spontaneity, innocence and dependence."[45] The Western world tends to sentimentalize childhood, and images of suffering children in a state of poverty or misery are considered disturbing. This makes it impossible to maintain a psychological distance from the scenes, and often sharpens the criticism. The exploitation of children in the Palestinian struggle has prompted strong criticism from Israel and other countries. This may be why in both Zvi-Riklis's film and in Kravitz's text, children attracted a great deal of literary attention, as their deaths may be seen as justification for the soldiers' actions.

As shown in *Lookout*, Yair's actions increase the reader's empathy for him, and his torment reinforces this sympathy, since he betrays his vow but saves the lives of his friends. *Lookout* and *I, Mustafa Rabinovitch* appear to justify the killing of Palestinians, while ignoring many other injustices deriving from the Occupation. Thus, they follow the well-established Israeli concept of "enlightened occupation," which suggests that soldiers shoot to kill only in extreme situations, in response to Palestinian actions, which are much more brutal.[46] This enlightened vision of the Israeli army appears in other texts that deal with related scenes, including novels published after the Second Intifada, such as A. B. Yehoshua's *Esh yedidutit* (Friendly Fire, 2007) and Yaniv Iczkovits's *Dofek* (Pulse, 2007).

In *Friendly Fire*, Yirmi's son Eyal is killed in an accident while serving in the West Bank. Members of his unit are waiting on the rooftops for the arrival of a wanted man they are instructed to gun down. Several minutes before his shift ends, Eyal climbs down from the observation point on the roof to empty a chamber pot and rinse it out. His friends, seeing someone slipping away from the house onto the street, shoot the figure, thinking that he is the wanted man. Amotz Yaari, Eyal's uncle and Yirmi's brother-in-law, uses the term *esh yedidutit* (friendly fire) to describe what happened. Yirmi demands to see the place where his son was killed and asks to climb up to the roof and talk to the family that lived in the house. For Yirmi, as well as for his family members, Eyal was a good person, whose sensitivity and good manners prompted him to clean the bucket and not leave bodily waste on the roof. His father describes his gesture as follows: "he goes down with it, not to dispose of it in some corner, but to rinse it thoroughly, to rinse it, you hear? So he can return it to the family as clean as he got it."[47] However, when Yirmi meets the Palestinian family, he is surprised to discover that Eyal's gesture did not move them. Rather, they choose to describe his death as a *teunat avoda* (work accident), which in military jargon usually refers to the premature explosion of a bomb during its assembly process by Palestinian terrorists. It is considered a tragic event that is related to combat, and thus may apply to the death of Eyal. However, the term "work accident" is used in Israel solely in the context of terrorists' deaths and is hence inappropriate for Eyal, who is perceived by his family members and the readers as a good person, who served his country without losing his humanity.

Udi, the missing son in Iczkovits's *Pulse,* has been living in northern India for two years. Coping with the mental breakdown and finally the suicide of his comrade Naduv, who served with him in the army, he does not plan to return to Israel. Naduv's mental state deteriorated after he developed a deep feeling for a Palestinian family and their little boy:

> His division took hold of some Palestinian house in Jenin for a look out spot, and he was responsible for providing the family with food and taking care of their other needs. And slowly he began spending more and more time with them. But he mainly liked to play with the youngest son of the family. Some four-year-old kid. The soldiers began to talk about him. Until it eventually reached the commanders and they called a mental health officer to evaluate him.[48]

Udi finds a poverty-stricken substitute family in India that reminds him of the Palestinians in their simplicity and poverty. He thus takes it upon himself to be deterritorialized and dedicate his life to this family to fulfill the same type of mission as Naduv. When Udi's mother starts searching for him after he goes missing in India, she meets Omar from Jenin, who knows the Palestinian family where Naduv and Udi were stationed. As in Yehoshua's novel, Udi's mother tries to obtain some form of acknowledgment of her son's humanity but fails. Omar tells her: "How did you know he was 'all-righty'? Look. I can't help you. I don't know your son. But I can tell you, as a father of two sons: he was not all-righty. Do you understand what I'm telling you? He was not all-righty."[49]

All these examples highlight the effects of vantage points that alter the way events are perceived by the narrator and the reader. In Zvi-Riklis's film and Kravitz's novel, both the soldier and the reader/viewer are placed as judges who can see the whole picture and do the right thing from a distance. The presence of the soldiers is perceived as pristine, as though they were untouched, uninvolved, and clean. In Yehoshua's and Iczkovits's texts, the distance between soldiers and civilians is not physical, rather, it is part of the unfolding of the narrative in a distant country, and later in the parents' reconstruction of the events. Distance can help foster a primary empathetic attitude toward the soldier. However, a more in-depth analysis suggests that the texts and the film show that although rooted in the humanist legacy of Zionism and the concept of the enlightened occupation, the combination of military superiority and moral superiority is a misnomer, and the spatial distancing (as well as the spatial reconstruction of the event) is in fact fictitious.

Intimacy—Down from the Roof

Kravitz's sniper, Yair, is used to seeing his targets from above, from the rooftop, and through his binoculars or the telescopic lens of his rifle. When he gets physically closer, he not only understands that seeing from a distance is misleading (and he can be mistaken about the identity of the people he sees), but also that killing is not as quiet and clean as it appears from a distance.

> We identified a car that was speeding towards us down the mountain. We moved closer to the road and signaled it to stop. The driver increased his speed. [. . .] Avishai opened the door next to the driver's seat. The driver's dangling head splattered on the wheel leaving a

> trail of red smear. [. . .] The driver's body spilled into the road, and his organs dangled out of the car. [. . .] This was the first time I saw the horror from touching distance, without the barrier of the lenses. Broken pieces of glass from the shattered window pane were wedged into his cheeks. One of his eyes was pierced with a bullet.[50]

The dead driver is Sami Sheetrit from Be'er Sheva. He is married with an infant. He is a vegetable smuggler who did not stop when ordered to do so. He was not a wanted target, but he lost his life nonetheless.

Moving closer may prompt soldiers to challenge the validity of the Occupation and experience the effects of deterritorialization directly. As long as distance is preserved, an Arab can be perceived as a legitimate victim, and "becomes an unknown character or a collection of shadows moving on the horizon," as Yochai Oppenheimer phrased it. However, collapsing the distance, "through a [. . .] lingering glance at the victim's broken body, his abandoned home" exposes the crime.[51]

Eshkol Nevo's *Mish'ala ahat yemina* (World Cup Wishes, 2007) illustrates this movement clearly. The episode begins with the same familiar scene of soldiers on the roof. The narrator is with a group of soldiers who are supposed to spend three days on a rooftop in Nablus but end up spending three weeks there. They are short on food and tired. The narrator begins to calculate which one of the soldiers would be the tastiest, all the while knowing that he is the weakest and probably would be chosen by his friends to satisfy their hunger.[52]

The description of the narrator and his friends reveals that the soldiers perceive the rooftop as an ex-territory. It is so remote that they practically ignore what is taking place in the Palestinian street below them. However, things change when they see a television in one of the apartments. The World Cup is on, and the soldiers, who all enjoy soccer, miss all the fun of the World Cup series. When they see the television, one member of the group hints that they may have an "opportunity to catch England-Cameroon," and Commander Harel gives his blessing. With no further discussion, the soldiers start to prepare their weapons and put on their combat gear. They move in two lines toward the house, invading an apartment where a family of parents, children, and grandparents are watching a quiz show.[53]

To justify their presence, one of the soldiers intimates that a young family member is a suspect, and from this point "the wrath of god began and ended with all the stuff in the living room, with the exception of the television—vases, pictures, bowls—shattered." The Palestinian boy is cuffed, the old women and other family members are forced to go into a small side room, and the soldiers watch the game, sitting relaxed on the sofas, eating hummus out of the refrigerator, while hearing "the sounds of pain made by the handcuffed boy, and the women's pleas to go to the bathroom."[54]

This scene shows the banality of cruelty, the abuse of power, and the way in which the notion of superiority spirals into immoral conduct. Paradoxically, the soldiers do not shoot or kill like Yair Rabinowitz or the protagonist in *Lookout*, yet they appear in Nevo's novel much worse in their full ugliness and corruption.

After this episode, the narrator is full of regret and guilt, and depicts this episode as a traumatic event that revealed to him that he is no better than the others. However, the narrator then describes a picture taken three weeks later with a friend who was part of the unit that came to replace them on the roof:

> In the picture we look like these "before" and "after" commercials. Only with us, the "after" is me, looking dreadful: unshaven, tired, with a blue ink stain on my shirt, and bloodshot eyes. And the "before" is Amichai, actually looking great: spruced up, clean-cut, gazing boldly into the camera. [. . .] And in the background, without noticing, the camera picks up a Palestinian boy—five or six years old, standing on one of the other rooftops observing the entire scene.[55]

The presence of the young Palestinian boy in the picture is no coincidence. The boy is located on the same level as the soldiers and serves as a witness, serving as a reminder of why they are there. This propels the Occupation into this symbolic picture of "before" and "after"; that is, before losing all values, while still believing that it is possible to behave morally.

A child's gaze also takes on powerful form in Shai Lahav's *Lekh le-aza* (*Go to Gaza*, 2005). When the protagonist drives into Gaza for the first time, people gather around the car and he sees the children "standing and observing us in the middle of the day." He tries to understand what motivates their curiosity: "they walk towards the car and turn their heads towards my window, they push their faces against the glass and look at me. [. . .] It will take me two more days in Gaza to understand. It's hatred. Burning," comments the narrator.[56]

In both Nevo's and Lahav's texts, children are on the same level as the soldiers and can look into their eyes. The symbolism of the image of the children make them the harshest critics. However, in this scene, as well as many others, the author decribes children not only to suggest their innocence but also to point toward the future role they will play as adults.

Nevo's book revolves around male brotherhood constructed through the military service and soccer games, but it is also built upon the ruins of Palestinian masculinity, as depicted in the rude invasion of an apartment that violates the family's privacy and undermines the power of the father and the other men to protect their family.

In Boaz Neumann's *Hayal tov* (Good Soldier, 2001), this tendency is even cruder. In Neumann's narrative, soldiers enter a house and interrupt a family with several children. In one of the rooms there is a woman "covered up to her neck with a thin blanket";[57] it is clear that she is naked. They ask the couple to go into the living room, and she covers herself and goes. While conducting the search, the couple stands with their children in the corner. The husband realizes that his zipper is open, and his wife is not wearing a bra. Her nightgown clings to her body and she tries to adjust it but cannot because she is holding two infants in her arms.[58]

The soldiers are amused by the fact that they have caught the couple "in the middle of a fuck" and refer to the woman as a sexual object and tease her. Their gestures are extremely offensive to her, as well as to her husband, who cannot protect her. Like *Hirbet Hiz'a,* the homosocial masculine group injects sexual content and often uses sexual terminology in the context of war. In Lahav's *Go to Gaza*, the soldiers watch porn films during their free time and phrase their relationships with the Palestinians in sexual terms to express their victory. They even borrow porn videocassettes from the Palestinian grocer and discuss their pros and cons with him, in a scene that emphasizes a lack of distance. However, the shared porn interest does not bring about any type of brotherhood between the soldiers and the Palestinian man, but rather underscores the archetypical conflict between men over controlling women and territories.

Porn films are also the source of offensive behavior in Evron's story "Ha-baz" (The Falcon), where a military unit requisitions an elegant house located on the outskirts of the village. It is inhabited by a man and his male housekeeper who is in charge of the cooking and the cleaning. When the unit arrives, the owner accompanies the commander and shows him the house. The commander "expressed a formal apology on behalf of the

IDF for entering the home of Shaaf Sayed and promised to keep the disturbances to a minimum,"[59] but when he decides that all his soldiers will move there, the noise and the mess are terrible. They track mud with their boots all over the house, they shout on the stairs and between rooms, they cook in the backyard and take the food inside, and clog the drains. When they find the home owner's porn video collection, they make fun of him:

> At first it was the soldier's scornful fits of laughter as they stick the tape into the video slot, then teasing, catcalling, and then fake female moans flooded the staircase. [. . .] Orgasms screamed their way into the study and Shaaf Sayed screamed in a shocked voice [. . .] What are you doing? [. . .] Why don't you just rip me apart, strip my clothes off, spit me to the hill?[60]

The soldiers manhandle the owner's personal belongings, which constitutes a disastrous humiliation for this respected, affluent man. Although he is not physically hurt, his dignity and masculinity are insulted in a way that represents the loss of Palestinian masculinity in general. Amal Amireh points out that in Palestinian symbolism, as well as in other national movements (including Israeli nationalism), the land is often symbolized as a woman, whereas "the Palestinian is a male lover, a groom, and a defender."[61] The loss of Palestinian land is often perceived as rape that leads to Palestinian male impotence:

> This metaphor of the loss of Palestine as rape [. . .] signifies the loss of Palestine as loss of female virginity but also of male virility, since the virile actor now is the rapist/enemy. This male loss of virility is inscribed as Palestinian defeat.[62]

Sexual struggles between Palestinians and Israelis are interpreted obliquely as a metaphor for the conflict in the well-known Israeli rock opera *Mammy* written by Hillel Mittelpunkt in 1986. In this opera, a Jewish woman is raped by seven Palestinian men who promise to redeem Palestine with "a hard on and sperm":

> Baby yo baby / Open your legs / to the seven depressed / Seven Palestinians / Twenty years of occupation / We wait no longer / With a hard on and sperm we will save Palestine.[63]

This highly provocative critical rock opera suggests a relationship between Israelis and Palestinians in terms of a sexual war, in which the winners are those who have the greatest potency. Interestingly, in *Go to Gaza*, Lahav uses the same line—"with a hard on and sperm we will save Palestine"[64]—with the opposite meaning to show that Israeli soldiers occupy the Palestinians not only through the use of military weapons, but also by imposing their masculinity. This struggle is symbolic, but also reflects a real fear in Israeli Jewish society concerning the power of reproduction, since the Palestinians have more children and thus can pose a "demographic threat." Mahmoud Darwish's famous poem "Bitaqat Huwiyya" (Identity Card, 1964) expresses this fear in verse. When the speaker addresses the Israeli official, who asks for his ID, he emphasizes his connection to the land, mainly through the many generations who have toiled the land and his power of reproduction: "I have eight children / And the ninth will come after a summer / Will you be angry?"[65]

This quarrel over masculinity and reproduction is also illustrated in a scene from Kravitz's *I, Mustafa Rabinovitch*, when he sees a woman showering in a room with no roof and can see a part of her body. In this scene, reminiscent of David and Bat-Sheva, he fantasizes about this woman and her "Palestinian bush, which must be hiding behind the plaster wall, refusing to expose itself to me," yet his thoughts quickly move to imagining "all the potential terrorists, who might emerge from this frizzy bush."[66]

The offensive sexual language and context depicted in these texts exceed the soldiers' jargon. They articulate the concept of a short intimate distance between males fighting over sexual power and reproduction and territory for their offspring. The young Palestinian boys who can watch the soldiers, and those who are waiting to be born in the "Palestinian bush" of the bathing woman, are the ones who have the power to challenge the soldiers. This suggests that the war over masculinity is not over; after their fathers' masculinity is doomed, these boys will represent the next generation's masculine struggle.

Animalism

The shift from long to short distances introduces issues of intimacy and masculinity to the forefront and leads to a condemnation of the soldiers' actions. As the distance is reduced, the effect of deterritorializaion is heightened: a soldier can deny the fact that he is located in a foreign sphere if he stays in a remote place, if he cannot see the details, or if he has a panoramic view of an area. But as he moves closer, he finds himself in the house and even in the bed of his counterpart. The face-to-face confrontation with the Palestinians in the texts here deteriorates the soldiers to a more primitive state of animalism and cuts them off from any moral or enlightened position.

The episode after Nevo's scene on the roof and inside the Palestinians' house tackles the narrator's feelings of shame, which are phrased in animalistic terminology. He tries to explain to himself that this was a one-time lapse, but he knows that it was not and that he has turned into someone else, a member of the horde, a kind of a beast, a rhinoceros.[67] Nevo's protagonist uses the Hebrew word *hitkarnefut*, which literally means turning into a rhinoceros, with enormous power and tough skin, and metaphorically insinuates that he is blindly following the herd. The use of this verb in Hebrew is actually an accurate reference to Eugène Ionesco's play *Rhinoceros* (1959), where the people of a provincial French town turn into rhinoceroses. This play is often interpreted as a criticism of fascist conformity and mass movements. The play was translated into Hebrew and performed in 1962, and soon afterward theater critics coined the word *rhinoceros* to refer to the herd-like behavior of people who become bestial.[68]

The basic assumption behind the use of animal terminology is to challenge people's fundamental assumptions regarding human behavior, and primarily that human beings are better than animals, since people are supposed to have a sense of justice, control their physical desires, and have individual personalities. Animal terminology is used in many texts when dehumanizing Palestinians. However, when Israeli soldiers turn into beasts (as Nevo puts it), when they act according to their impulses or focus solely on their physical needs, when they cannot have a real conversation, and when they attack their counterparts without mercy, it suggests that they are no better than the Palestinians, and are in fact worse.

In *Go to Gaza*, Lahav describes a military unit that serves mainly in Gaza. The narrative depicts the process of becoming a beast as the loss of individual thought and judgment; it shows the power of the group over the individual, and physical forlornness. The text is replete with descriptions of brutality and unlawful military orders such as breaking the arms and legs of Palestinians,[69] torturing the mentally ill,[70] shattering shop windows and calling it *Leil ha-bdolah* (Kristallnacht),[71] along with other acts of revenge and destruction.

Two long scenes in the novel take place on the roof. The first is on Christmas Eve in Bethlehem and the second is on the seventeenth floor of a building in Gaza. In both scenes, the description of the soldiers emphasizes their animalism. In the first scene, the narrator describes how the unit is divided into pairs who go up to the roofs of Bethlehem to secure the area during the Christmas celebrations. The soldiers can see each other with their binoculars, and soon the story focuses on the different pairs on the roof instead of what is happening in the streets. The pairs on the roof have to cope with bad weather, cold, rain, and hunger. They are not allowed to wear their coats since it is not considered appropriate for their mission to secure Christmas Eve. Since they were given the order to man the rooftops at the last moment, there is no food delivery. During the day and a half they spend on the roof, they are described as completely forlorn. One pair starts to fight when they get hungry. They think about going into one of the apartments, but they know that the Palestinians have been under curfew for more than two weeks and assume that even in the apartment there is nothing to eat. When one of them sees a Palestinian peddler in the street, he leaves his observation point and runs to buy some warm pitas, clearly violating military orders. His companion tries to dissuade him, but his empty stomach is stronger than any command. He then refuses to share and they fight like animals over their prey: "Within a few seconds the two are rolling on the cold concrete floor in a wild burst of free wrestling."[72]

The other pairs suffer from fatigue, but instead of dividing the hours between them, they try to get through the shift together. One pair leans on the edge of the roof and falls asleep standing up. Soon they lose control and one of the soldiers falls onto a sloping awning and lands without injury. These scenes emphasize both the homoerotic facets of being in a masculine group and the ease with which people become animals when deprived of their basic needs.

In the second scene, Itay gets mad and throws a pile of newspapers smeared with feces from the roof. A senior Palestinian physician who lives on the ground floor goes up to the roof and tells them in English, politely, that he has an idea what was in the pile.[73] Unlike Eyal in Yehoshua's novel, who insists on cleaning his bucket at the end of his shift and is shot by mistake by one of his friends, Lahav paints a totally different picture. The roof is turned into a psychiatric institution, like Ken Kesey's 1962 novel *One Flew over the Cuckoo's Nest*. Thus, although their role in the village is to be guards while the Palestinians are imprisoned by the curfew, they see themselves as the prisoners and behave like animals in a cage, losing their sanity and injuring each other out of despair.

Conclusion

In subsequent sequences of Gilad Evron's "The Falcon," Shaaf Sayed keeps one thing for himself: the falcon that the family used for hunting, but that now has become the family pet. The falcon is full of pride, strength, and even male potency, and although his owner claims that it does not hunt anymore, it is still fully able to do so. When the soldiers "sensed, with a primal instinct, the tension between a predator and its prey, between an animal running in terror and the shade hovering and growing over it,"[74] and are tempted to play with the bird and abuse it, the falcon reverts to its original state. It becomes more aggressive, hunts a mouse, and swallows it forcefully: "The bird of prey has indeed returned to hunt."[75]

This transformation is a metaphor for the dignity and the male power of its owner and, through him, of the Palestinians as a whole. This is also the reason why the soldiers want to subdue it. Mully, the commander, wants the falcon and feels it suits his personality. He starts to discuss the issue with the owner, who then invites him to dinner to continue the discussion. In a move that mimics "The Falcon" in Boccaccio's *Decameron*, Shaaf Sayed prepares a wonderful meal. He sets the table magnificently with expensive dishes and cutlery and serves wonderful food including stuffed meat, rice with almonds, raisins, and special chives and sauces. While Mully is enjoying it, he imagines his life with the falcon, how he will hunt, likens himself to an aristocrat, a count or a king in the open fields. When he asks Shaaf Sayed where the falcon is and is told he has just eaten it, "The commander of the 'Gihon' removed his Uzi from the back of his seat, opened the pin and shot Shaaf Sayed in the head."[76]

In Lahav's initial description of the unit's arrival in Gaza, the narrator feels trapped, as though the soldiers were "in a scene from an Arab movie directed by Hitchcock. It seemed that giant birds would descend upon us in just a moment."[77] Lahav uses the metaphor of Hitchcockian ravens that swoop around the car in circles to emphasize the unspoken Palestinian power, like the dignity and nobility of the falcon, which cannot be crushed. These birds, along with the doves that were set free from the dovecot in *Lookout,* show that even if the soldiers are located in a distant topographical space, where they can presumably preserve their humanity and feel that by doing so they are superior to their Palestinian counterparts, the birds are flying free above. The birds' topographic advantage symbolizes the Palestinian spirit that cannot be destroyed. Thus, although the parting shot, in each of the texts, emanates from the Israeli weapon, these texts suggest that distancing and superiority is doomed to fail over and over again. The roof does not provide protection or guarantee victory.

CHAPTER 2

No Luck

In "A Soft Focus on War" (2010), Slavoj Žižek discusses Kathryn Bigelow's film *The Hurt Locker* (2008), and criticizes the way it prompts a sympathetic reaction toward U.S. soldiers. Žižek compares this movie to two Israeli films that deal with the 1982 Lebanon war: Ari Folman's *Waltz with Bashir* (2008) and Samuel Maoz's *Lebanon* (2009):

> The re-focus on the perpetrator's traumatic experience enables us to obliterate the entire ethico-political background of the conflict: What was the Israeli army doing deep in Lebanon? Such a "humanization" thus serves to obfuscate the key point: the need for a ruthless analysis of what we are doing in our political-military activity and what is at stake [. . .].
>
> More generally, such a "humanization" of the soldier [. . .] is a key constituent of the ideological (self-) presentation of the Israeli Defense Forces (IDF). The Israeli media loves to dwell on the imperfections and psychic traumas of Israeli soldiers, presenting them neither as perfect military machines nor as super-human heroes, but as ordinary people who, caught into the traumas of history and warfare, commit errors and can get lost as all normal people can.
>
> It is easy to discern the falsity of such a gesture of empathy: The notion that, in spite of political differences, we are all human beings

> with the same loves and worries, neutralizes the impact of what the soldier is effectively doing at that moment.[1]

Žižek states that the Israeli media and filmmakers depict Israeli soldiers (in Lebanon and the Occupied Territories) as innocent young individuals, who find themselves doing horrible things and later suffer from posttraumatic syndromes and endless sorrow and regrets. He argues that this mythic description is driven by ideology designed to reduce public awareness of soldiers' violent conduct. Thus, instead of raising difficult questions about soldiers' military activities and acknowledging the suffering of their victims, the media and the arts continue to depict these young soldiers as humane.

Gil Hochberg, an Israeli scholar in the field of literature and culture, responds to Žižek's claims in her book *Visual Occupations* (2015), and specifically addresses his take on the humanization of the soldier:

> While I have no dispute with Zizek regarding the Israeli media's role in circulating the image of the Israeli soldier as innocent and clueless, I nevertheless question the logic of his objection: Are we to conclude that the soldiers are not ordinary people? Are we to assume they are categorically different from "us" or that their crimes are ones that we "ordinary people" would have not committed under similar circumstances?[2]

Hochberg refuses to strip Israeli soldiers of their humanity and claims that they are, in fact, "ordinary people." To refute the humanity of a soldier means to distance him from ourselves, so there will be no commonality between him and us, the so-called "ordinary people." It is a way to refrain from asking under what conditions an "ordinary man" can become a soldier, or from assuming that this "ordinary man" can have different emotions and a complex personality.

This chapter elaborates on the dispute between Hochberg and Žižek. Drawing on the previous chapter's presentation of distancing and the rooftop setting, it combines the spatial with the ethical, to examine the consequences of deterritorialization in literary texts. It poses the duality of the Israeli soldier as both a perpetrator in terms of his deeds and a victim of the Israeli war machine, examines the symbolic phrase *shooting and crying*, and formulates this ethical complexity through the philosophical concept of *moral luck*.

The realm of the Occupation is rife with dissonance. Soldiers find themselves in a state of deterritorialization that is both spatial and ethical. As seen in the previous chapter, they enter a foreign territory where they are supposed to be the masters, but are in fact violent intruders; and once there, they experience a loss of their familiar systems of values, thoughts, and behavior. Tamar Libes and Shoshana Blum-Kulka show that soldiers often experience a conflict between the orders they must obey during their IDF service and their personal ethical creed to behave in a humane way.[3] Soldiers have a variety of ways to handle this dissonance, ranging from refusing to serve in the army altogether or refusing to take part in designated actions.[4] Alternatively, soldiers may retreat inward and not voice their complaints to their commanders, or modify their personal values to accommodate psychological distance when brutality occurs and perhaps condone it. Many soldiers, who continue to serve in the army and are involved directly with the Palestinian population, become brutal to a certain extent, and the physical/mental price to pay is often high for the individual soldier as well as for Israeli society as a whole. Charles Greenbaum and Yoel Elitzur have argued that while the mechanism of justifying brutal conduct may enable soldiers to get through their military service and for some even to continue with their lives as though nothing has happened, in many cases these mechanisms do not dispel their feelings of shame and guilt, which can turn into a long-term posttraumatic stress disorder.[5] These psychological issues relate not only to deterritorialization in general but to the notion of absolute deterritorialization in particular. Unlike relative deterritorialization that does not break the rules but proceeds to create reterritorialization, absolute deterritorialization may lead to absolute repercussions; namely, a "state of escaping spatiotemporal and even existential coordinates," or even falling into "the black hole of consciousness."[6] Hebrew and Israeli literature and culture have dealt intensively with the character of the soldier and feelings of deterritorialization and dissonance. From its earliest manifestations in the Hebrew canonical literature on the 1948 war, to contemporary prose and poetry, soldiers are depicted as *shooting and crying*; in other words, they are portrayed as individuals who often suffer from a disorientation associated with their perceived dual role as perpetrators and victims.

Shooting and Crying

In 1968, in the immediate aftermath of the 1967 war, during a time of great euphoria in Israel when the Kotel (the Western Wall) in Jerusalem was again accessible to Israelis and many biblical holy places in the West Bank came under Israeli control, a book entitled *Si'ah lohamim* (Fighters' Discourse) was published. This book was based on a series of recorded conversations held after the war with kibbutzim members.[7] It was edited by Avraham Shapira and among the discussants were Muki Tzur, Amos Oz, and Yariv Ben-Aharon. The background was the shock and mourning in the kibbutz movement over the terrible losses in battle, but also the trauma of war and the soldiers' exposure to killing.

Although the text was heavily censored in an attempt to mask what was considered inconsistent with the Israeli ethos of army morality, the book (and the recorded material) still contained testimony referring to atrocities committed by Israeli soldiers.[8] People were shocked to discover how easily they were able to shoot and kill, and when they confronted their memories, they were tormented. Moshe Zartal, a kibbutz member, a journalist, and an editor, wrote about the volume a short time after its publication, and stressed the combination of the love of one's country confronting ideological rifts (specifically the issue of land and territory) and continuous debates on morality.[9] Muky Tzur termed the overall feeling that stems from the volume *sliha she-nitsahnu* (we apologize for our victory),[10] and in the 1970s, writers, journalists, and historians used the phrase *yorim u'bokhim* (shooting and crying), which was associated retrospectively with *Fighters' Discourse*. The phrase was probably coined in Kobi Niv's satirical column in *Ha-olam ha-ze* that told of parents who decide, out of patriotism and morality, to call their first son "shooting" and their second son "crying," so that while the first shoots the second can cry. The column mocks the hypocrisy of the national discourse that encourages the use of harsh military power on the one hand but on the other weeps out of sorrow.[11] A search in databases of Israeli newspapers shows that the phrase was only used a few times from 1967 to 1987, but its use increased dramatically after 1988 when the First Intifada broke out. In March 1988, Israeli singer Si Himan composed a rock song entitled "Shooting and Crying" that described acts committed in the Occupied Territories. Yoav Kutner, a well-known music editor at Galey Tsahal (the IDF radio station), played the song before it was officially distributed and without asking for the necessary approval. Nachman Shai, the commander and chief editor of Galey Tsahal, banned this song and had Kutner expelled from the station. Nonetheless, the song made its way to the public through other radio stations and big concerts.[12]

The phrase *shooting and crying* was designed to ridicule the fact that the country and its soldiers cry after killing, rather than simply refusing to shoot altogether. However, in some political contexts, people perceived the term as demonstrating bravery and moral rectitude, since soldiers were criticizing themselves and their violence. The role of this phrase in Israeli culture, and the debate that raged over *Fighters' Discourse*, both when published and recently when the uncensored recorded materials were released, as well as the impact of this phrase in Israeli culture, illustration the heated discourse over cultural practices and the ritual of war testimony.[13] In these cultural rituals, soldiers describe the disturbing things they either participated in or witnessed, which responds to these soldiers' need to confess so that they can assuage their consciences, or at least help them to heal.

During the first months of the Intifada, when violence made daily headlines, soldiers' feelings of guilt were accompanied by a need to express it. As Yaron Peleg notes, on the first Yom Kippur after the Intifada broke out, Tel Aviv newspaper *Ha-ir* devoted its cover to a confession signed by "Ashamnu" ("we are guilty," the opening of the Yom Kippur liturgy). This confession related to "collective guilt in oppressing the Palestinians," followed by a list of deeds: "we sealed [houses], we beat, we expelled [Palestinians], we oppressed, we transferred." The list goes on: "we shot, we handcuffed, we came down hard, we embittered, we clubbed, we sealed, we pulled out an eye, we blew up, we censured, we buried, we were wicked, we defaced." However, the ending of this "prayer" is somewhat ironic:

> O Lord, we ask for your forgiveness—what do you want from our lives? We were not guilty, we felt no shame, we did not stammer, we shed no tears, we felt no remorse, we could not care less.[14]

At first sight, this ending appears to reject the blame altogether, yet the contradiction between the long list of transgressions and the blame that is denied plays a critical rhetorical role.

In 1990, Roli Rozen and Ilana Hammerman published a collection of soldiers' testimonies from the First Intifada, along with military documents and court rulings on cases of unlawful acts against Palestinians.

Unlike the Tel Aviv newspaper that published a sarcastic confession, the Rozen and Hammerman book had a different tone:

> We shoot and weep, yes—we shoot—we, all of us because we are part of this society, and we live within it and function within it, and eventually we are also a part of the mechanism that sustains that which happens there. So everybody shoots—in that sense—and then we also weep—for instance, write these kinds of books, and even take pride in this, saying "how wonderful it is to be able to write such things, how wonderful we are that we also cry."[15]

Since 1990, numerous testimonies have been made public, including a volume entitled *Ad kan* (Refusenik!), edited by Peretz Kidron in 2004, and through the activity of the organization Shovrim shtika (Breaking the Silence) that was set up to expose "the gap between the reality [the soldiers] encounter in the [Occupied] Territories, and the silence they encounter at home,"[16] since "Israeli society doesn't want to know or doesn't care about"[17] what is happening there.

Breaking the Silence and *Fighters' Discourse* have been criticized in different ways. The activities of *Breaking the Silence* are often blamed for betraying the State of Israel, and their legality has been examined carefully; it is claimed that the organization is financed by foreign sources that orchestrate criticism outside Israel and thus fuel hatred and boycotts of Israel.[18] On the other end of the spectrum they have been criticized for presenting a troubled realm without articulating a way to change it. The positioning of soldiers as witnesses may mark them as victims. Erella Grassiani notes that "witnessing" is a practice associated with victims who are the survivors of terrible atrocities (such as Holocaust survivors or those who survived genocides as in Rwanda and other places in the world). Hence, it is somewhat surprising to see that a group of former combatants would use this method to accuse themselves of being perpetrators.[19]

This anomaly may stem in part from the age-old perception of Jews as victims. It is inherent to the canonic Zionist narrative, in which Jews were persecuted in the Diaspora and then sought refuge in their ancestral homeland, where they then became victims of Arab violence. To present the issue of the Occupation in this manner elicits empathy for the soldiers rather than the Palestinians, while not "dealing with the question of responsibility for the injustices" as Raz Yosef claims.[20]

It is true that in the public discourse, arguments often tend to be one-dimensional. Nevertheless, contemporary Hebrew literature presents a more complex and nuanced picture than Grassiani, Yosef, and Žižek seem to suggest. Although literary works have focused on the misery of the Israeli soldier and the tradition of Jewish victimhood, they have also dealt with military atrocities and often portray soldiers as perpetrators. While typically victims tell their stories to have others recognize their personal pain, in many literary texts the loss is that of morality, and the texts explore the issue of ethical conduct and responsibility. This complex situation and its literary representation can usefully be viewed through the controversial philosophical prism of *moral luck*. This chapter explores Yitzhak Ben-Ner's *Ta'atuon* (Delusion, 1989), Roy Polity's *Arnavonei gagot* (Roof Rabbits, 2001), and Liran Ron Furer's *Tismonet ha-mahsom* (Checkpoint Syndrome, 2003) in this light.

Moral Luck

Thomas Nagel, an American philosopher who wrote several books in the field of moral philosophy and ethics, defined *moral luck* as a situation where "a significant aspect of what someone does depends on factors beyond his control, yet we continue to treat him in that respect as an object of moral judgment."[21] Nagel stresses that "ultimately, nothing or almost nothing about what a person does seems to be under his control,"[22] yet we judge people by these actions, and we are obligated morally to do so. Nagel considers four types of *moral luck*:

> *Constitutive luck*—one's personality, inclinations, capacities and temperament. These depend, at least partially, on factors beyond one's control.
> *Circumstantial luck*—the kind of problems and situations one faces.
> *Causal luck*—the way in which antecedents are determined.
> *Resultant luck*—the outcome of one's actions.[23]

The term *moral luck* refers to a kind of "flaw" in modern morality, in the sense that individuals who do not control a situation cannot be blamed for what they do. Clearly, however, in many situations people are not entirely free, but are indeed responsible for their actions. Despite the debate in the field of ethics, which has prompted some writers to argue that morality is in fact immune to luck, the term has the advantage of injecting the complexity of life into the abstract thinking of philosophy, and can be especially fruitful with regard to the analysis of literary representations, since literature is able to illustrate the unorganized and raw nature of real life.

Literary descriptions of Israeli soldiers often appear to reflect two features of *moral luck* associated with rooftop scenes and other similar episodes. The first is a sense of entrapment in an alien space with different rules stemming from the feeling that the soldiers need to deal with events that are *not fully under their control.* The second is a sense of guilt or personal disorientation (sometimes so great as to engender absolute deterritorialization) stemming from soldiers' sense of *responsibility* and guilt for their actions. These two separate facets coexist and create a paradoxical effect, which is often addressed in literature. This is what makes *moral luck* such a controversial term in philosophy, but what defines the perpetrator-victim pathology of the Israeli soldier extremely well. Whereas the second attribute, which involves guilt or personal disorientation, refers to the image of the perpetrator, the first, the entrapment in a foreign space the soldiers cannot control, refers to a feeling of victimization (being a victim of the situation, the army and its orders, or the political situation).

Circumstantial Moral Luck

Circumstantial *moral luck*, according Nagel, refers to specific circumstances that individuals face over the course of their lives: "the things we are called upon to do, the moral tests we face."[24] Nagel claims that many situations are "importantly determined by factors beyond our control" and shape people's ethical experiences. Thus, while someone who finds himself in a dangerous situation can behave in a cowardly or heroic fashion, another person, who did not have to face this situation, will never be judged for these actions and his moral record will be different. Nagel illustrates circumstantial *moral luck* through the case of Nazi Germany:

> Ordinary citizens of Nazi Germany had an opportunity to behave heroically by opposing the regime. They also had an opportunity to behave badly, and most of them are culpable for having failed this test. But it is a test to which the citizens of other countries were not subjected, with the result that even if they, or some of them, would have behaved as badly as the Germans in like circumstances, they simply

> did not and therefore are not similarly culpable. Here again one is morally at the mercy of fate, and it may seem irrational upon reflection, but our ordinary moral attitudes would be unrecognizable without it.[25]

It may seem harsh to compare Israeli soldiers to Nazi officers. This comparison appeared for the first time in Israel in a statement by Yeshayahu Leibowitz, an Israeli philosopher and scientist known for his outspoken, often controversial opinions on Judaism, ethics, religion, and politics, who accused Israeli soldiers of becoming "Judeo-Nazis." His words prompted a public outcry among Israelis, and even today any reference to Nazis with regard to the Israeli army is perceived as illegitimate. Nevertheless, the comparison has never ceased to impact the collective unconscious of Israeli society, and it is cited extensively in soldiers' testimonies.[26]

Nagel's argument can be used to formulate a general claim to address the Žižek and Hochberg debate on "ordinary people." While Žižek does not consider soldiers to be "ordinary people," Hochberg's reasoning is based on the fact that they are indeed "ordinary people," for this is what "ordinary people" often do in certain circumstances.[27] In "Luck and Moral Responsibility," Michael Zimmerman discusses the problems that can arise from this reasoning, and argues that *moral luck* can easily release people from moral responsibility since "the Nazi collaborator would be no more blameworthy than the non-, but would-be, collaborator."[28] In his inquiry he refers to an unstable mental condition that relieves people of their responsibility for their actions, and warns about overusing this category. However, Nagel's concept does not dismiss responsibility, but rather shows the impact of circumstances on moral actions.

Daniel Statman notes that "if morality is immune to luck, then the option of being moral is open to everybody everywhere and furthermore, it is open to everybody *equally*."[29] *Moral luck* nevertheless pinpoints an inequality that arises in situations that place a person in extreme circumstances and constitutes a moral test. For instance, young men of eighteen who do not live in Israel and are not obliged to enlist are spared such circumstances. For the ones who do live in Israel, the moral test is much more difficult.

This can also be seen in the literary works examined here. Whether they describe moral or immoral protagonists, in all of these texts, the characters are exposed to extreme situations and unfamiliar circumstances. Ben-Ner's *Delusion* describes how Holly Sidon, the protagonist, who was raised and educated by a family that believed in the liberal values of justice and eschewed violence, gradually learns to be violent and cruel and finds satisfaction in torturing Palestinians. The novel poses space and territory as central elements in his decline.

> What motivated Holly to do what he has done and not do what he has not done [. . .] could not have taken place anywhere else. [. . .] This process, which brings together a good boy like your Sidon'chik and such a brutal role, could only have taken place, as they say, in very special circumstances of time and place.[30]

Holly's military experiences, which includes being bullied by his fellow soldiers, lead to his deterioration. He is constantly trying to preserve his sanity: "Just to keep my sanity. Only to keep my sanity. Let everyone go insane, I don't care. I'm staying normal, I have to stay normal."[31] He repeats this phrase obsessively when he is taken to a military jail for unlawful conduct. Later he starts to stink, and since no one can explain or cure the odor emanating from his body, he is sent to a mental institution.

Checkpoint Syndrome by Ron Furer is an experimental work based on the author's experiences during his army service in Gaza in the mid-1990s (a relatively quiet period). His fragmented texts, composed of short, broken lines that do not form a linear narrative, was rejected by major publishers in Israel. Even after its publication with Gvanim Press, Steimatzky, a major Israeli bookstore chain, refused to distribute it.[32] However, the book was adopted by the Palestinian Ministry of Information in 2003 and posted on their site as propaganda.[33] Ron Furer's text, like Ben-Ner's novel, identifies the spatial rift as a precondition for the moral decline that could not have taken place in a different setting. "The army conscripted me at the age of eighteen / and discharged me at age / twenty one."[34] The army is not an integral part of his life but rather a different reality, a kind of a jail that robbed him of three years of his life. This setting encourages young soldiers to engage in a routine of torture, competing among themselves as to who will carry out the most "awesome" actions out of boredom, such as the soldier who "[. . .] stood above / the Arab, took out his cock / and started pissing on / the Arab's head."[35] As discussed in previous chapters, other works also reflect the view that place and time are crucial factors in the moral deterioration of the protagonists. Lahav's *Go to Gaza* or Neumann's *Good Soldier* portray the way in which soldiers in the Occupied Territories enter a new, very extreme world that deviates from the civilian life they knew.

Roy Polity's novel *Roof Rabbits,* also refers to the power of the setting over its protagonists but does so in a different manner. The tragic encounter between Opher, an Israeli Secret Service (Shabak) officer and Samir, a Fatah activist, could not have happened under different circumstances: Opher would not have paid any attention to Samir, a young junior activist in the Fatah, if Samir's father had not had cancer. Opher decides to exploit Samir's distress, brought on by his father's desperate need for cancer treatment in an Israeli hospital, and forces him to cooperate with the Shabak and disclose information about militant groups. Opher admits that this is part of the asymmetric power relations that create this "shameful and unjust" reality.

The crucial effect of the setting is also evident in *I, Mustafa Rabinovitz,* which reveals the contradiction between Yair's vow not to kill and his military profession as a sniper. Thus, while a person can enter the world of the Intifada with the intention of retaining his values and morality, he is inevitably doomed to compromise these values. Entering the realm of the Occupation, standing on the roof of a Palestinian home, and facing these extreme circumstances corresponds to the definition of circumstantial *moral luck.* However, as Nagel puts it, these circumstances in which a person does not have full control over the situation *do not imply* that individuals have no responsibility for their actions.

The protagonists in Ben-Ner's and Ron Furer's as well as in Lahav's and Neumann's books are trapped in activities they perform mechanically, in order to be part of the masculine military group. Their mental deterioration is a result of the repression of their civilian and personal values. They are absorbed into a realm of violence and act like blind automatons, while turning torture and violence into neutral, normal behavior. However, the authors make a straightforward though implicit statement concerning their characters' responsibility. For example, it is clear from Ben-Ner's novel that it is the situation that led to Holly's mental decline and that he may not understand what he is doing. However, the novel uses a powerful allegorical device to stress his guilt and broaden it. Holly is arrested for his sadistic behavior and begins to emit a stench. The smell is clearly a metaphor for the moral turpitude of the army and the state.

The question of responsibility and blame is raised in Polity's *Roof Rabbits* as well. Opher, the protagonist, tends to rationalize his actions: "It's very brutal to become the father of a hostage, but it's also very brutal to allow terror cells to roam around and murder [. . .] you hurt one limb in order to help the rest of the body. That's exactly how I see my work. To help society as a whole, I have to hurt part of it."[36] Opher views his mission a necessary evil. His argument is utilitarian, since it authorizes certain (limited) evil acts to avoid a greater evil.[37] Though Opher tries to convince himself he is doing the right thing, he cannot get rid of his distress. Failing to nurture his relationship with his girlfriend, he moves to a new apartment but is unable to unpack, and instead of going home every evening, he wanders the Palestinian streets and takes unnecessary risks.[38] Opher's spatial disorientation is a clear illustration of deterritorialization: he cannot minimize the gap between the two—the civilian and the military worlds—and finds himself with no home.

The effect of Opher's deterritorialization is combined with a state of burnout. Opher compounds his risks, and "as with all pain relievers, he has to increase the dosage from time to time,"[39] and he becomes overloaded and exhausted. Ayala Malach-Pines defined burnout in the context of the First Intifada as a "sense of emotional, physical and spiritual exhaustion caused by constant and continuing psychological overload."[40] Opher's behavior becomes increasingly obsessive, he ignores his personal life, hardly sleeps, and is totally immersed in his tasks. His obsessive state ultimately leads to his murder.

Opher's death, like the smell in Ben-Ner's novel, enables the narrative to take moral responsibility over its protagonists even when the characters are not capable of doing so. Polity's text follows the lives of both Opher and Samir. This gives the reader the opportunity to see how Opher's actions affect Samir's life. Through the eyes of Samir, the reader sees how much he loves his father and the price he needs to pay to help him. The reader understands the difficulty of betraying his own people by agreeing to help the Shabak, and the realization that he is at constant risk both from his own people, who may discover he is a collaborator, and from the Israeli side, which may find that he is no longer useful. Killing Opher after his father dies becomes a kind of poetic justice: Samir has nothing to lose, and Opher is punished for his actions.

In her article on *moral luck*, Margaret Walker introduces the concepts of *pure agency* and *impure agency*:

> Pure agents are free, on their own, to determine what and how much they may be brought to account for determining the intentional acts

> and commitments they will undertake and recognizing the limits to their control beyond these. [. . .] Impure agents are saddled with weighty responsibilities and the open-ended possibility of acquiring more, due to circumstances beyond their control. Yet agents who recognize their vulnerability to fortune are primed for dependability of humanly invaluable sorts.[41]

Although pure agents can be moral, according to Walker, impure agents are more humane. The former can live without referring to *moral luck*, since they do not feel morally reprehensible for actions governed by issues beyond their control, whereas impure agents take responsibility over themselves.

Literary works represent a type of *impure agency*. The texts show that the soldiers lack full control over the situation in the sense that they have no control over the political moves that led to the situation, and they have no control over the military mission or its underlying reasons, or over the nature of military orders. It is nevertheless clear from these narratives that as perpetrators they are responsible, and they have to cope with the moral cost of their actions: it is they who ultimately experience a permanent sense of guilt or disorientation, and it is they who are punished.

Constitutive Moral Luck

I suggested earlier that the concept of *moral luck*, as it applies to the Israeli soldiers in the texts above, is composed of two features. The first is a sense of responsibility and acknowledgment of moral blame on the part of the authors for the soldiers' deeds, while casting them as the perpetrators; the second is the depiction of a sense of entrapment in a foreign space with different rules where the soldiers have minimal control over the situation they are caught up in and in which they may be viewed as victims. The previous section focused on extreme circumstances and showed that the texts perceive their protagonists as responsible, and therefore guilty. This section further analyzes the situation of entrapment and the protagonists' limited control over the situation.

Liran Ron Furer's *Checkpoint Syndrome* opens with the following monologue, with a special typeface and no punctuation marks:

> Hello to all you human beings the little slaves how are you [. . .] now I'm finally free and far away from all the crap you have there in your

> crappy country fuck I'm never going back now I'm free the crazy energies of Goa have opened up my head and my chakras [. . .] I forgot what I was you stuck me in stinking Gaza and before that you brainwashed me with your guns and the training you turned me into dirt until I couldn't think anymore and the only thing that kept me sane at the end was the drugs [. . .] you used me like a robot [. . .] it all came together and I saw what you tried to do to me I was afraid of smiles you turned me into something else I wasn't me it's somebody else.[42]

In this passage, the narrator depicts himself as a puppet on a string. His monologue refers to the military experience as a trap, as though he was doomed to play a role in a game whose rules he did not set. He therefore takes metaphorical and literal "lines of flight," which, according to Deleuze and Guattari, display the movement of deterritorialization, which negates the system of control: "Lines of flight [. . .] never consist in running away from the world but rather in causing runoffs, as when you drill a hole in a pipe; there is no social system that does not leak from all directions, even if it makes its segments increasingly rigid in order to seal the lines of flight."[43] The narrator finds the leaks in the system when he understands the source of power and its mechanism (brainwashing), which turned him into an automaton who is willing to do things he would never have approved. The only possibility suggested in this introductory text is to run away—not only from Israel, but also from his conscience.

Through his flight, Ron Furer underscores the unnatural situation where soldiers do not exercise their free will when they have to face moral issues. To a certain extent, soldiers do have control over their military actions, even in extreme circumstances. Under Israeli army regulations, there is a procedure for refusing to obey an order when it is "clearly illegal"; that is, when it violates the laws of the state or the values of democracy. For instance, actions such as harming civilians or any form of ethnic cleansing are "clearly illegal." Unlawful orders should not be obeyed; the soldier is fully responsible for the acts he carries out[44] and thus must not implement them. This provides soldiers with a way to control their actions, specifically in extreme situations.

Although military service is obligatory in Israel, there are cases of civil disobedience. The first individual cases of conscientious objection were recorded during the 1950s and 1960s. The first organized movement was set up in 1982 during the First Lebanon War by the Israeli peace movement *Yesh Gvul* (There Is a Limit); 170 people refused to fight in Lebanon, and they were sentenced and served terms in military prisons. During the First Intifada, over 2,000 people refused to serve in the army, and 180 served jail sentences. There were also cases of refusal during the Second Intifada.[45] Conscientious objectors in Israel usually come from the political left wing, but during the disengagement from the Gaza Strip in 2005, a movement of right-wing objectors also emerged.[46]

Although it is possible (but not always legal) to refuse to carry out unlawful acts, or avoid enlisting altogether, numbers indicate that while many declare they will refuse, only a few follow through and are prepared to be sentenced to military jail terms. Out of the hundreds of thousands of Israeli soldiers who protest against military activity, only a few hundred ultimately refuse. The small number of people who in fact refuse to carry out orders, or are objectors, indicates that most conscripts cannot make this choice. Nagel's concept of *constitutive moral luck* can lead to an explanation of this state of affairs. Nagel writes:

> The phenomenon of constitutive luck—the kind of person you are, where this is not just a question of what you deliberately do, but of your inclinations, capacities, and temperament. [. . .] Such qualities as sympathy or coldness might provide the background against which obedience to moral requirements is more or less difficult, but they could not be objects of moral assessment themselves, and might well interfere with confident assessment of its proper object—the determination of the will by the motive of duty.[47]

Constitutive luck stems from one's personality, which is shaped by one's genes as well as one's upbringing. This type of luck reflects a paradox: although individuals lack full control over their inclinations and temperaments, they are fully responsible for their behavior and the actions that stem from their personalities. While Nagel describes this type of *moral luck* by focusing on the individual, collective biography also shapes individuals' personalities. Israeli society is highly influenced by the historical narrative of Jewish suffering in the Diaspora. For hundreds of years, European Jews were seen as an inferior minority, and the anti-Semitic stereotype presented the Jew as weak, miserable, humiliated, and feminine. Toward the end of the nineteenth century and with the growth of the Zionist movement, the need arose to change the image of the Jewish prototype.[48] The

Zionists created a new prototype of the (male) Jew, termed the *sabra*—the prickly pear cactus, a nickname for native-born Israeli Jews. The *sabra* is described as having a strong body, thick wavy hair, and tanned skin from toiling the land. He is proud, undiscouraged by failure, a man of action, optimistic and cheerful, loyal to his friends, and instilled with a powerful sense of ideological commitment and national responsibility. The *sabra* is the perfect warrior; he is brave, devoted to his mission, and willing to give his life to protect the country and its people.[49]

The myth of the *sabra* was born out of necessity, and for years it symbolized new Israeli masculinity. Israel's education system and its socialization process are still imbued with this myth. School field trips impart both geographic information and war heritage; children learn that Israel is a democratic state that yearns for peace, yet fighting is inevitable when striving to protect the very existence of a state that provides a safe haven for the Jews. Thus, it is considered good citizenship to play a significant role in military activity, especially in combat units.[50] Israelis absorb military values from a young age, and military service in Israel is often perceived as essential to a boy's right to belong to the inner circle of adult males.[51] Thus, the militaristic message embodied in state education explains why many Israelis not only want to join the army, but are eager to acquire its "manly" values, and why refusing to serve in the army is unthinkable. This may be what Ron Furer criticizes when he refers to "brainwashing."

As Nagel argues in his discussion of *constitutive moral luck*, individuals have certain personalities over which they have only limited control, which dramatically affects their actions. People may find it difficult to carry out certain acts if they contradict their inclinations and characteristics, yet the responsibility for the act they perform, or refrain from performing, remains theirs. Tamar Libes and Shoshana Blum-Kulka argue that young people in Israel grow up with a feeling of commitment to the IDF, and thus have a sense of personal and voluntary responsibility to military service. This feeling is "the chief condition that must be present under the laws of cognitive dissonance, to enable a sense of dissonance in a situation of 'induced compliance.'"[52]

These literary texts show that soldiers enlist out of feelings of commitment to the county and the army. In Kravitz's *I, Mustafa Rabinovitch*, Yair the sniper believes his mission is to protect the home front; Opher, in Polity's *Roof Rabbits*, is also motivated by the urge to save innocent people in Israel from the next terrorist attack. Only later, during their service, do they discover the moral complexity of military service in Israel. They cannot see the full picture, they cannot judge for themselves, they are subject to the military hierarchy, and they must conduct military actions that often contradict their beliefs. Ron Furer describes the process of military education as brainwashing, which every soldier undergoes from childhood; Holly, in Ben-Ner's *Delusion*, embraces this brainwashing blindly. Yet even Opher and Yair realize that taking part in military activity contradicts the ideals of the Israeli army as perceived though the education process in Israel. These literary examples confirm what Libes and Blum-Kulka claim: that soldiers' sense of responsibility and good citizenship lead them into the "Intifada traps."

Thus, although *constitutive luck* typically addresses personal inclinations and temperaments, it is quite possible to view this concept as involving a national-collective education. Soldiers discover that the situation they were educated on and trained for is actually different, that the Occupation is not enlightened, and when military values transform into something else in the realm of an Intifada, they may feel betrayed, to a certain extent, for having to face such radical and even unfair moral tests, and pay the moral price for their deeds.

Kravitz phrases this situation in lines of poetry:

> Why Daughter of Zion have you gone astray
> Your children vanquish their neighbors in the fray
> They strike with clubs their eyes full of terrors
> Why have they become like the swastika bearers[53]

As depicted in many literary texts, the portrait of the Israeli soldier in the Intifada cannot be praised or justified. The examination of the state of deterritorializaion and the concept of *moral luck* can provide a spatial and ethical model for the pathology of the Occupation and soldiers' moral position of *shooting and crying*, of being perpetrator and victim at the same time. The cases discussed here furnish examples of both *consequential luck* and *constitutive luck*. The nature of the circumstances portrayed in these texts places the characters of soldiers in extreme deterritorialization and forces them to confront tough moral tests. The portraits show that these soldiers have been trapped in a situation that negates the Zionist humanist legacy and are destined to play the villains and be condemned for their deeds. As a result, they do not refuse to shoot and are only left with the option of *shooting and crying*—they are doomed to suffer incurable guilt and disorientation. These literary representations thus relate to the sense of victimhood, but do not dismiss, not even once, the responsibility and guilt of the perpetrators.

CHAPTER 3

The Third Eye

> I am the dead boy / I am the dead boy Ismail/ I am dead / I am Ismail the dead / Two angels walk beside me / One is all good / One is all evil / A jinn and another jinn walk beside me / One of heaven / One of hell / From sickness I die / In my sleep I fell asleep / A gravel truck ran me over / I drowned in the fish pond / Soldiers shot me / Policemen shot me / Citizens shot me / Collaborators shot me / My mother wept and wept for me / My mother wept and wept and struck her chest / My mother wept and wept and struck and pulled and tore her dress / My mother wept and wept and struck and pulled and tore and pinched her flesh.[1]

In Itamar Levy's *Otiyot ha-shemesh, otiyot ha-yare'ah* (Letters of the Sun, Letters of the Moon) published in 1991, the title of each chapter is a different letter of the Arabic alphabet that the narrator, a Palestinian child, is learning. A short summary of each chapter appears in a different font underneath the title. The text above, with its snippets of phrases, is the summary of the final chapter that describes the death of the narrator. It details the "blows the soldiers struck at my head,"[2] the child's gradual loss of consciousness, and the neon lights in the corridors of the morgue when his dead body is washed.

This chapter proposes a counterpoint reflection consisting of a shift from the viewpoint of the soldiers and the occupier, to the imagined point of view of the occupied, using Palestinian narrators located in the Palestinian territories.

While Arab characters have played important roles in Hebrew literature by Jewish authors, since the beginning to the twentieth century, and their depiction has been discussed in numerous scholarly books and articles over the years,[3] only a few texts are mediated through the voice of the Palestinians. This chapter focuses on these texts and discusses the conscious choice of their authors to create literary deterritorialization. It discusses the state of alienation, and the contra-images that provoke rupture and shock readers, through the use of nonrealistic descriptions and grotesque images. These texts can be seen as fashioning a "transversal process that defines the creativity of an assemblage: a nonlinear and nonfiliative system of relations."[4]

The Talmudic tractate *Pirkei avot* (Ethics of the Fathers), states: "do not judge your friend until you reach his place." This concept, presented through various phrases such as "do not judge a man until you have walked a mile in his shoes," is a commonplace ethical view. The basic assumption is that moral judgments are universal, and that in comparable situations people are able to define what is right or good or what they ought to do.[5] Moral philosophy is hence often engaged with the notion of point of view, and examines the claim for objectivity and its problematization. Thomas Nagel, for instance, chose the title *The View from Nowhere* for his 1986 book, which articulates the theoretical claim that ethical questions should be addressed from a neutral point of view. While it is understood that such a point of view is impossible in real life, changing perspectives or imagining ourselves in the place of another is a valuable way to better understand different situations and ethical dilemmas. As Noël Carroll shows, literature provides the opportunity for these kinds of thought experiments, which transport readers to another place and introduce them to "experiences" that are far removed from their own lives.[6] These thought experiments take on a dramatic force when they give the Israeli reader an opportunity to see things from the Palestinian side.

Instances of Jewish-Israeli writers (occupiers) writing a narrative through the purported gaze of Palestinians (the occupied) can have an ethical merit but also raise a series of ethical questions. For writers who are on the powerful side of the conflict, and in a certain respect engage in colonial relationships with the Palestinians, writing in the name of Palestinians can be seen as appropriating their voice and silencing them even further.

Because the language of the texts is Hebrew and not Arabic, it transforms these stories into the language of the master and obviates historical and cultural references. Writing a fictional narrative that is constructed to present the Palestinians' voice is associated with paternalism and orientalism, stereotypes, and hollow representations. By discussing these concerns at length, I also point to the ethical value of these texts.

This chapter explores three main works: David Grossman's *Hiyukh ha-gdi* (The Smile of the Lamb, 1983), Dror Green's *Agadot ha-intifada* (The Intifada Tales, 1989), and Itamar Levy's *Otiyot ha-shemesh, otiyot ha-yare'ah* (Letters of the Sun, Letters of the Moon, 1991).[7] These books were not the first to give voice to Palestinians. A. B. Yehoshua's *Ha-me'ahev* (The Lover), published in 1977, presents the voice of Na'im, and Yoram Kaniuk's *Aravi tov* (Confessions of a Good Arab), published in 1984 under the pseudonym Yosef Sharara, is made up of one long monologue by the protagonist, who is both a Palestinian and a Jew. Though they were written before the Intifada, and are thus beyond the scope of this chapter, it is important to refer to these texts here because they reveal the challenge of presenting the Palestinian voice through a narrative written by Jewish Israeli writers.

Yehoshua's novel, which takes place in Haifa against the backdrop of the Yom Kippur War (1973), tells the story of Adam, a garage owner who discovers that his wife, Asya, has a lover, Gabriel. Gabriel disappears during the confusion of the war (after Adam encourages him to enlist), and Adam decides to find him, driving day and night to search for the missing lover with his young Arab employee, Na'im. The novel is composed of monologues by six characters, including Na'im.

Immediately after the publication of the novel, reviewers argued that its main achievement was to depict an Arab character with a voice.[8] Later, however, critics and readers began to take issue with Yehoshua's depictions. The first had to do with the decision to give a voice to a young boy, a relatively simple character, whose identity is fluid. The universal contrasts in the novel between the village boy and the big city, the menial employee and the boss, and the young assistant who falls in love with the boss's daughter make Na'im empathetic, while blurring and neutralizing his national identity.[9]

The second criticism was that Na'im was not attached to his national identity. For instance, Yochai Oppenheimer argues that for Na'im, "being an Arab is not a way to define his identity, but a handicap."[10] Unlike his brother Adnan, who joins a terrorist organization after being rejected by Haifa University, Na'im does everything to efface his identity. He obsessively washes himself before going to Adam's apartment to make a good impression and uses elegant Hebrew; he refuses to speak Arabic, his mother tongue, even when he could talk with Veducha, Gabriel's grandmother, who has a North African background. He quotes poems by Bialik and steals a book of Alterman's poetry from Adam's house, to memorize.

Fanon notes that "all colonized people [. . .] position themselves in relation to the civilizing language; i.e., the metropolitan culture."[11] The education system in Israel requires Arab students to study Bialik's and other Jewish national poetry, much more than poetry written by Palestinians. Na'im is a radical example of a boy who internalized his place within a minority group, to such extremes that he puts on a "mask of whiteness" he can never remove. While learning the major or colonialist language (the Hebrew language and its national literature), Na'im, as a subordinate, forfeits his native culture to mimic the major culture.[12] As Oppenheimer notes, Na'im's mimicry turns grotesque when he quotes Bialik, and specifically when he recites "The Dead of the Desert," a poem that is used in Israelis school ceremonies to express the Zionist liberation.[13] While Nai'im is proud of being educated and able to recite this poetry, he is unaware of the political aspects of the texts he quotes. He does not have an authentic voice, so he mouths the poetry of Jewish Zionist liberation without recognizing his own status as a member of a nonliberated minority.

In certain ways, the character of Na'im can be understood as a subversive challenge on the part of Yehoshua to the Israeli education system for Arab citizens, and a condemnation of the Israelization process of Israeli Arabs. Na'im's artificial use of the Zionist-Hebrew canonic literature highlights what Deleuze and Guattari call the "deterritorialization of language,"[14] by revealing the cultural violence waged against the Arab minority in Israel. However, as Rachel Feldhay Brenner comments, the text still maintains the Zionist ideology—Na'im is an inferior worker, who serves Adam but is usually invisible and poorly treated; and more importantly, at the end of the narrative, when there is a chance of an intimate relationship between Na'im and Adam's daughter, he is removed quickly from the scene and brought back to his village. Hence, the novel still documents the "absent presence" of Arabs in Israel.[15]

This novel may have entered the cannon because Na'im's character is perceived to be sympathetic and does not constitute a threat to the majority, since he behaves like an *Aravi mahmad* (pet Arab)—an Arab who adopts a mimicking existence of his minority status and does not challenge the power structure. However, Na'im's character continued to disturb critics and authors years after its publication. A decade after the publication of Yehoshua's novel, Anton Shammas, a Palestinian Israeli author, published his renowned Hebrew novel *Arabeskot* (Arabesques, 1986), showing that an Israeli Arab can write perfect Hebrew, but use it to subvert Israel and Zionism.[16] In an interview with Bernard Horn, Yehoshua referred to Shammas's text and also to his naiveté in the 1970s, and confessed that at that time he believed that he "could really describe an Arab from the inside."[17]

Kaniuk's 1984 novel *Confessions of a Good Arab* is another example of a narrative with an Arab voice. Kaniuk deliberately chose a pseudonym—Yosef Sharara—to imply the book was written by an Arab; however, Kaniuk was revealed as the author soon after the book was published. Unlike the naïve construction of the character of Na'im, Kaniuk's protagonist Yosef is both a Jew and an Arab and is fully aware of his complex identity. His mother, Hava, is an Israeli Jew, and his father, Azouri, is a Palestinian intellectual. He is also the grandson of Franz, a respected physician who fled Nazi Germany, and the lover of Dina, the quintessential Jewish daughter of Holocaust survivors. Yosef cannot find himself in either the Israeli or the Arab world, and the novel describes the contradictions he faces and his resentment, and eventually his decision to leave Israel. He tells his story from Paris, yearning to return to a country that rejected him.

Kaniuk's novel did not receive much attention when it first appeared in Israel. It had much better reception outside Israel in its foreign editions.[18] While the fictional world of the novel can be "a densely constructed metaphor for a reality in which Jews and Arabs are welded together in a shared fate of doomed relationships and impassable emotional barriers," as Gilead Morahg suggested,[19] others claimed that the novel still does not paint a full picture of Arabs as authentic moral beings.[20]

Both Yehoshua's and Kanuik's novels played a role in the evolution of Hebrew literature on its path to tell the story of the Other. However, neither deals exclusively with the Palestinian identity, but rather describe it in relation to Jewish Israeli identity. The spatial setting in these two texts is also highly important—in both cases an Arab goes from an Arab village or town in the Galilee to the big city, to an affluent neighborhood (in Haifa or in Tel Aviv), and is perceived as a foreigner. The space is dominated by the Israeli Jewish elite, and the novels are about the relationships between a single Arab and other Jews in "Jewish" territory, enforcing a hegemonial point of view.

The more recent texts discussed in this chapter differ in that they are located within the Palestinian space, and specifically in the Occupied Territories. They provide a double deterritorialization that creates a spatial and an ethical transposition: they reveal the inner life of Palestinians beyond the context of interactions with Jews or Israelis and try to tell the story through Palestinian eyes. In addition, the authors reject a causal and linear narrative and a structured concept of space, in favor of a style of writing that emulates the folktale and the tradition of the grotesque.

A Palestinian Legend

> *What do I expect from a writer? That he is open, takes chances, dares to expose himself to the complexity of the enemy. That is what a writer should do. Not hide behind stereotypes—that's too easy; that's what the papers do, particularly in Israel and Palestine. So, say I was to write about this meeting between you and me, I would write about it from my point of view, from your point of view, from your wife's, from that of the three people sitting over there, and the suicide bomber who, right now, is walking down the street looking for a new target.*
>
> —David Grossman[21]

Though written four years before the outbreak of the First Intifada, David Grossman's novel *The Smile of the Lamb* is clearly part of this corpus, since much of the text is located in a Palestinian village and has to do with the relationship between the Israeli army, the Palestinian population, and the Palestinian resistance. There are many structural similarities between Grossman's novel and Yehoshua's *The Lover.* Both are made up of different points of view that form a kind of Rashomon narrative. Four characters tell their story, not all of them in the first person: Katzman, the military commander, whose father was a Holocaust survivor; Uri, a young, naive Israeli soldier; his wife, Shosh, who is a child psychologist; and Hilmi, an elderly Arab living in a cave on the outskirts of the occupied Palestinian village. The text reveals the unique relationship between Uri and Hilmi and its culmination when Hilmi discovers that his beloved son Yazdi, who joined the Fatah movement, has been killed. Showing love and care for Uri, whom he nurtured practically as a substitute for his lost child but also with the resentment of someone who tries to be stoic but cannot be passive anymore, Hilmi takes Uri hostage as a bargaining chip to demand withdrawal from all the Occupied Territories within twenty-four hours.

Since this chapter focuses on a Palestinian narrator, I will only examine the parts narrated by Hilmi. Hilmi is both a Palestinian Arab, whose tales convey a feeling of life in a Palestinian village, and a mad hermit trying to teach his son the language of nature and urging him to remain uneducated. Nurit Gertz notes that "he belongs to the Arab world and lives outside of it. He hovers above reality and rests within it as well."[22] Hilmi is not a reliable narrator, and the reader does not believe much of what he says, yet his persona is to a certain extent authentic. Although he speaks Hebrew, he uses Arabic at the beginning of his stories by saying "*kan ya ma kan*" (once upon a time) both as an identifier and as the cue for the start of a new tale.[23] His broken and associative language differs from the calculated high level of Hebrew of Na'im in *The Lover.*

The relationship between Uri, who wants to improve the lives of the villagers based on notions of enlightened occupation, and Hilmi gives the novel a new political stance. Uri respects Hilmi and loves to come to his cave hear his stories. He knows that telling Hilmi his son has died will destroy him, and eventually when Hilmi takes him hostage he does not protest or resist, and even enjoys the silence and rest in the cave.[24] To a certain extent, they are both naïve dreamers who eventually have to confront the harsh reality.

Dror Green's collection of stories *The Intifada Tales* (1989), a collection of pseudo-legends that are presumably narrated orally by Palestinian villagers, provides another example of a Palestinian voice. Green's stories use the technique of defamiliarization, since his plots involve strange events, which deviate from any system of reasoning and rationality. The tales all follow the same rhetorical pattern: the story begins by introducing the familial texture, and then a tragedy occurs in the form of injury or death, usually of a child, caused by soldiers who are always described in general terms and not as individuals. This injury or death infuses new powers into the family or village, since the people who were injured or died turn into magical entities and continue to act in the world. For instance, little Arafat, who was shot on the day he received his new bicycle, continues to "walk" among the living, and the sound of the bicycle continues to be heard. Like him, little Ali uses his glass eye to see when soldiers are approaching the village. The disappearances of the dead children are described in a restrained manner, and although they die, more and more children are born, the "children of the Intifada," who are found every couple of days next to garbage cans: "Dr. Fuad found another baby between the garbage bags. This baby also lacked a bellybutton, and his fist was clenched around a green olive branch."[25]

Green's stories are constructed like oral fairy tales told by the elders of the tribe who do not judge or fight an enemy. This lack of explicit judgment and the neutral description of the terrible stories of the death of innocents and the cruelty of the soldiers create unease, since they have no causality or rationalization that can operate as a source of political understanding. Instead they reveal a grotesque picture of society under siege. This is a society that is full of fear and insecurity and is riddled with handicapped or dead children and their ghosts.

The realm of legend is also dominant in Itamar Levy's *Letters of the Sun, Letters of the Moon* (1991), which presents the daily life of the residents of a Palestinian village that is placed almost continuously under full curfew. The narrator is a boy who describes his life as though it were a part of a colorful festival with costumes, games, heroes with supernatural powers, and fairy tales. Jaffar Omar Ismail Zakkut lives with his father and brother and witnesses the power struggles within the village, between his family, the respectable Zakkut family that owns an ice cream factory, and another family that also owns an ice cream factory. Jaffar's daily life is very bleak, but it is brightly colored, at least in the first part of the work, which blurs the line between reality and imagination.

Throughout the novel, the narrator learns how to write the Arabic alphabet, one letter after another. The title of the novel refers to two groups of Arabic letters—sun letters and moon letters—based on whether or not they assimilate the letter *lām* (ل) of the preceding definite article *al-* (ال). These names come from the fact that the word for "the sun," *al-shams*, pronounced ash-shams, assimilates the *lām*, whereas the word for "the moon," *al-qamar*, does not. Each chapter is devoted to a different letter, and in the last lines of the novel he writes his name. The text is written in Hebrew, but the narrator continues to learn the Arabic alphabet and uses the letters to express what he sees. The Arabic text documents his writing, from single words and phrases in the first chapter to much more complicated words in the later chapters, which all appear in Arabic alongside the Hebrew translation. The words that he writes describe the reality around him, from "Jerusalem" and "God" to routine lists of "doors," "shops," and "notebooks," to words that express building a house such as "engineer," "cement," and "water,"[26] and later to words that describe the murder of his father by his eldest son and the helplessness of the narrator,[27] and finally to words that describe doctors in the hospital during the young narrator's last day.[28]

Learning the Arabic alphabet—learning how to write—symbolizes Jaffar's maturation process, which is supposed to lead him to recognize the world and describe it in a rational and organized manner. However, this process brings him closer to his death: with each new letter, another one of the vibrant images of his playful childhood dissolves and is replaced by the bleak image of a weak boy who tends to faint, stutter, hallucinate, and not understand what is taking place before his very eyes. His beloved, clownish brother is replaced by a harsh older brother (the legend that he made his fortune in oil-rich countries turns into a reality in which he was not home for years because he served time in an Israeli prison—"the lands of oil? . . . it is time, brother, that you learned the truth! All these years I was in jail you fool! I murdered Jews"[29]). He then witnesses his older brother killing his father for cooperating with the Israeli army. He barely manages to take one stone from the vast, legendary house before the military destroys it. Eventually, Jaffar also loses his life, but not before he eats three boxes of ice cream and dozens of popsicles, drugged by their sweetness.

In her seminal essay "Can the Subaltern Speak?" Gayatri Chakravorty Spivak argues that the attempt to retrieve the voice of the subaltern is doomed to fail since the "subaltern" cannot appear without the thought of the "elite."[30] In the case where the representation of the subaltern is mediated by a member of the majority, this may be an inherent criticism. As Linda Alcoff phrases it: "There is a strong, albeit contested, current [. . .] which holds that speaking for others is arrogant, vain, unethical, and politically illegitimate."[31] It is indeed clear that "what is said gets heard depends on who says it";[32] however, "the declaration that I 'speak only for myself' has the sole effect of allowing me to avoid responsibility and accountability for my effects on others."[33] Thus, while pointing to the risks of paternalism, speaking for others can also express political responsibility and provide a rare ethical opportunity.

Speaking for the Palestinian Other reveals the two sides of this coin. The shadow of paternalism and orientalism is not easily dismissed in these three texts; however, they have an enormous literary quality that brings their ethical and political importance to the forefront. Edward

Said's *Orientalism* discusses Western culture's binary division between Westerners and Arab-Orientals: "the former are [. . .] rational, peaceful, liberal, logical, capable of holding real values, without natural suspicion."[34] As he shows, many cultural descriptions present Orientals or Arabs as passive, "devoid of energy and initiative," much given to "fulsome flattery," intrigue, cunning, "everything opposed to clarity, directness and nobility."[35] The Palestinian narrators in the novels by Grossman, Green, and Levy appear to manifest these "oriental" attributes in that they are unstable, unreliable, exhibit illogical thinking, are passive, close to nature and the land, and usually not clean. As Philip Metres argues, in Grossman's text, "the only Palestinian character [is] a half-mad, half-blind holy fool who eats soil and rubs himself with lemons to reduce his stink. [. . . This description] is something so excessively Orientalist."[36]

A common attribute of this Oriental gaze is its predilection for the culture of oral stories and legends, as manifested in all the texts discussed here. Amnon Raz-Krakotzkin described this legendary style when analyzing Green's *The Intifada Tales*, as well as two other short stories that appeared in a newspaper.[37] In 1989, the same year Green's book was published, two stories that portrayed characters of young Palestinian women under the Occupation won the annual short story competition of the *Haaretz* newspaper. Yossi Levy's "Avak shel bustanim" (Dust of Orchards) describes a Palestinian girl, who is fascinated by Israeli soldiers and eventually goes out in the middle of night to the soldiers' fence, "climb[s] on the rusted gate with a drawn knife,"[38] until she is struck by a bullet in her forehead and dies hanging on the gate between heaven and earth. Avner Shats's "Te'enim" (Figs) is narrated in the first person by a young woman who tells the story of her beloved village. Since the beginning of the Occupation, only boys have been born in the village, as though someone heard the traditional prayer of women who wish for a boy. No one understands this miracle, yet the narrator often thinks that these occurrences have also happened on the Israeli side, and perhaps this is why Israeli soldiers, who presumably do not have access to women, have decided to go to war. She is the latest woman to be married, but she decides not to follow the traditional custom of going to a holy tomb to pray to have a boy but instead prays for a girl.[39] Raz-Krakotzkin discusses the image of women as exotic and unreal, which is manifested in literature by a "chauvinistic-male longing for quiet women, with long braids and black eyes."[40] He claims that this type of writing does not reveal the Other, but rather distances him or her.

Green confessed that political motivation drove him to write this book—"someone asked me if I wrote this book as an alibi, if and when I would be asked where I was when all this happened. It may be so, I am not sure. I do not feel that publishing a book is enough."[41] However, the Palestinian Druze writer Salman Masalha took a different view. He criticized this writing of fictitious Palestinian folk tales, calling it "Israeli *chutzpah*" (impertinence). When he first read Green's *The Intifada Tales* without knowing who wrote it, he thought it was written by a Palestinian author.[42] However, when he realized who the true author was, he felt uneasy and blamed the Israelis for appropriating both sides: first shooting the Palestinians and then telling their story by appropriating the Palestinian voice. Masalha claims that when these Palestinian stories on the Occupation and the Intifada "are submitted to the Israeli reader in the guise of a legend [. . .] it simplifies the pain"[43] and makes it more abstract. Masalha understood that Green wanted to shock the reader as a form of protest, but the genre actually "distances all these tragedies that happen every day five minutes from Kfar Saba." Eventually, "the Israelis shoot and cry, shoot and tell tales."[44]

The use of an oral folk literature structure is at times erroneously associated with primitive societies with a high rate of illiteracy, thus making it a problematic choice when projected through a Jewish Israeli writer. However, these works can also be read as a part of the 1990s postmodern style in Hebrew literature that deviated from realistic writing. At the end of the 1980s and the beginning of the 1990s, a new generation of young Israeli authors, most famously Orly Castel-Bloom and Etgar Keret, began writing short fiction in a "new style" that deviated from realism and deliberately disintegrated a coherent worldview through a series of rhetorical strategies. These included shifting from an authoritative to an unauthoritative and unreliable narrator; using "slim" language with a deliberately narrow vocabulary, a colloquial style, and basic grammar; "flattening" the psychological and emotional complexity of the characters; relinquishing a clear linear plot; and creating implausibility in the description of the fictional world.[45] This prose also engaged with modern legends, the grotesque, and provocative plastic images.

While the legend genre in Grossman, Green, and Levy can be seen as an integral part of this new trend in Israeli literature, there is a crucial difference between these texts and the new style in Hebrew literature. The new style tends to deal with the reality of youths in Tel Aviv. These youths are usually struggling to find their place in big cities, and are often unstable psychologically, but do not offer implicit political assesments.[46] By contrast, in the case of Grossman, Green, and Levy, the legend genre deliberately describes the political. To achieve a deterritorialization of their natural (Jewish Israeli) point of view, these authors may have needed to find a dramatic and different poetic style. Although clearly the realist genre can be more authentic when describing the realm of the Other, nonrealist writing can grasp the essence of the Palestinians' everyday existence without full documentation.

Nonrealistic writing can also be subversive as Oppenheimer shows:

> The dimension of miracle that intervenes in the destiny of the oppressed and turns death, humiliation, and helplessness into a source of power [. . .]. This dimension circumscribes a territory in which the occupier has no control over the occupied: the ability to fashion a story which is not subjected to the power relations and the representational patterns of the Arab in Israeli literature. [. . .] the structure of the folktale provides an avenue to focus on the Palestinian public's spiritual resistance while also overtly ignoring a military uprising or any act of violence.[47]

Oppenheimer further argues that legends are able to create nonviolent resistance, an attribute that indeed is evidenced in the three texts presented here. These texts show the power of nonrealistic fiction to generate criticism and subversion relating to the Occupation in general and the concept of borders in particular. However, much of their power has to do with another aspect of this genre; namely, their use of the grotesque that shocks the reader. Thus, unlike the stereotypical, flat structure typical of legends, these texts introduce a chorus of conflictual descriptions and attributes leading to an unstable grotesque reality that is constructed in a closed space, which is always watched from above. Salman Masalha acknowledges this revolutionary facet in Green's book and eventually decided not to dismiss the text simply because it was written by an Israeli Jew, but to translate the book into Arabic. The translation appeared a year after the Hebrew publication. However, Israeli martial law banned its distribution in the Occupied Territories.[48]

The State of Exception

In his column "Welcome to the Israeli Arab Ghetto," Sayed Kashua discusses the high rates of violence in the Arab villages of Israel that have been neglected for years by the state and the Israeli police.[49] His main claim is that Israeli Arabs have no place to go. Unlike other people who can leave their birthplaces and move to other villages or cities, most Arabs in Israel are doomed to stay in the same villages, since they are not wanted anywhere else. Karen Grumberg refers to the concept of space in relation to the Palestinians within Israel and in the Occupied Territories. She elaborates on the concept of the *mahsom* (checkpoint) and what it symbolizes as a demarcation of the space and the ultimate siege of the Palestinians. She coined the phrase "shrinking of space" to illustrate both the spatial condition and the mental condition of Kashua's protagonists.[50] This picture of the Arab ghetto becomes much more radical for Palestinians who live in the Occupied Territories. Itamar Levy's text describes this situation in a highly striking way:

> At first, the enemy posted soldiers in every alley, to protect their cars. We pushed them back to the main street, and not even a few hours passed before they returned to block the entrances with welded iron bars. The gates smiled at us, and invited us to throw stones through them at the yellow cars. As the situation came to this, the enemies returned to us, and placed loops of razor wire. They glued rusted barrels one on top of the other. Raised a massive fence to block the slingshot pebbles that belonged to us boys. The wall was so high that the soldiers were forced to stand on the roofs of the red buses in order to tie the iron net to the posts. First gates, and razor wire, and barrels, and stone barricades, and a huge fence. A wall of stones followed in their footsteps, and a steel net twice as high, on which, anyone who climbs, like my beloved brother, can touch a star and cloud. [. . .] The light in the rooms of all the village houses is yellow and faint. Only the soldiers' light is white. The light in all the houses of the village is faint, and the heat emanating from the furnace is faint, and the faucet stream is faint, and the radio sounds are faint, and the voice of the people is faint.[51]

Whether the occupier has a face as in Grossman's text, or whether he is designated by a general reference to "soldiers" (in Green) and "the enemy" (in Levy), his presence is constant, at the gates of the village, dominating the roads, walking in the streets, and entering any house he wishes. The Occupation in these texts creates a closed area in which the villagers live in constant fear, without freedom, and with no clear rights. This space has much in common with Giorgio Agamben's exploration of a "state of exception": "the state of exception, which was essentially a temporal suspension of the state of law, acquires a permanent spatial arrangement that, as such, remains constantly outside the normal state of law."[52] Agamben draws on the theoretical writings of Carl Schmitt on the state of emergency, but he interprets this concept in terms of its birth and vicissitudes from the French Revolution through World War I, the Nazi regime, and finally to contemporary politics and U.S. policy on Guantánamo Bay. Agamben explains that the term is paradoxical, since it enables democratic countries to create a space devoid of constitutional rights, which operates outside of the law after a declaration of a state of emergency or crisis.[53] In Israel, a state of emergency has been enforced for years. The curtailment of certain civil and legal rights was imposed by the government on Israeli Arabs from 1948 to 1966, and since then emergency regulations, which should be temporary, continue to create a "state of exception" that restricts the rights of many Palestinians.[54] Agamben comments: "The state of exception [. . .] becomes now a new and stable spatial arrangement inhabited by that naked life that increasingly cannot be inscribed into the order."[55]

The previous chapters elaborated on the topographical superiority of the Israeli soldier and the metaphor of the panopticon. The Palestinian village or camp is monitored by soldiers who know everything about everybody, including their most intimate details. Thus, the physical features of the lives of the Palestinians under the Occupation are exposed. Agamben's phrase "naked life" can be related to this concept, since the lives of the Palestinians are completely and intimately exposed. With this space, where "everything is truly possible,"[56] only grotesque images can produce a countermovement against the shrinking space.

From Stereotype to Grotesque

Whereas orientalism is associated with stereotypical descriptions that reveal "alertness to resemblance in its lack of sympathy and hyperbole, even as it stays blind to differences within the same delusional dynamic," as Gaurav Majumdar puts it,[57] the grotesque injects the dangerous, unstable, threatening, and transformative, and derails our automatic systematization. In this sense, it clearly complements the concept of deterritorialization. Legends recount fantastic events and strange creatures, but the story is usually based on stereotypical characters that have a concrete role in the plot, who are defined as "good" or "bad," "ugly" or "beautiful." On the other hand, the categories of the fantastic and the grotesque are replete with ambiguities and instability that generate unease in the reader and suspend judgment.

Grotesque was originally restricted to descriptions of the visual arts but was later applied to literature as well. Forms of the grotesque are hybrid combinations of objects, plants, animals, and human beings,[58] which engender confusion, the absurd, and deformation. Grotesque bodies evade coherent definitions and borders[59] and form dismantled and suspended hierarchic categories.[60] Mikhail Bakhtin defined the grotesque body as a body that is "not separated from the rest of the world"; "parts of the body that are open to the outside world, [. . .] the open mouth, the genital organs, the breasts, the phallus, the potbelly, the nose," articulating "pregnancy, childbirth, the throes of death, eating, drinking and defecation."[61] Moreover, the open body is always "in the act of becoming. It is never finished, never completed; it is continually built, created, and builds and creates another body,"[62] and thus "in the grotesque body [. . .] death brings nothing to an end, for it does not concern the ancestral body, which is renewed in the next generation."[63] The grotesque situation, according to Geoffrey Harpham, is located in "the space between, in which perfectly formed shapes metamorphose into demons. This mid-region is dynamic and unpredictable, a scene of transformation or metamorphosis."[64] The space in between creates confusion as it prevents the reader from categorizing and instills emotional disorientation and suspension of ethical decision in the reader.[65]

The grotesque is closely associated with hybridity. Homi Bhabha extended Fanon's *Black Skin, White Mask* to discuss the hybridity of the colonial subject and linked it to the grotesque. He articulates the stage "where the disavowal of difference turns the colonial subject into a misfit—a grotesque mimicry or 'doubling' that threatens to split the soul and whole."[66] According to Bhabha, the colonial subject cannot manifest authenticity, since he lost his original identity while adopting, artificially, the culture of his ruler. This hybridity leads to a grotesque existence.

Majumdar differentiates between two types of grotesque in his analysis of Salman Rushdie's work: the "repressive grotesque" and the "expressive grotesque."[67]

> The "repressive grotesque" asserts a repressive violence, either through the agency of a single subject (in the repression of the self or an unacknowledged aggression), or through the repression exercised by state-power and other forms of institutionalized power.

Na'im, the Arab protagonist in the Yehoshua novel, follows Bhabha's description of the colonial subject and Majumdar's "repressive grotesque." His entire personality is based on mimicry, and thus, has a grotesque quality in that he cites texts with no punctuation, he shifts from quoted high language to slang, he does not know if he is allowed to laugh, and he adopts Bialik as the absolute authority.[68] Na'im internalizes the culture of the Jewish and Zionist majority and acts like a ludicrous marionette. Na'im manifests what Majumdar defined as the "repressive grotesque"—a restrained grotesque, where the violence is hidden. Na'im does not reveal and may not even be aware of the oppression of Israeli Arabs, the poor village, or his family; he accepts everything and tries to please his Jewish Israeli boss. Even the fact that he had to go to work at an early age instead of remaining in school is not emphasized and is eventually resolved at the end of the novel by Adam, his Israeli boss who takes him back to his village. However, the readers are made aware of this disparity that highlights "the space between."[69]

In contrast to the "repressive grotesque," Majumdar defines the "expressive grotesque" as follows:

> [it] overtly signifies difference through "deformation" or a changing, unstable shape. Further, it has no dominant social or political sanction, a lack which catalyzes its designation as the grotesque. To be sure, its categorization as "deformed" and its lack of political currency are often mutually debilitating. However, its forms frequently express a deviance from norms through a systematic strangeness or even an exuberance.[70]

While Yehoshua's novel and the character of Na'im manifest a "repressive grotesque," Grossman's, Green's, and Levy's texts depict an "expressive grotesque." Their hybridity and violence internalize Elizabeth Grosz's concept of the body "as the threshold or borderline." Since the body is "neither—while also being both—the private and the public, self and the other, natural and cultural, psychical and social, instinctive or learned, genetically or environmentally determined,"[71] oppression and violence can be demonstrated through it, in a process of both actual and metaphorical deformation.

The Smile of the Lamb and Abjection

Hilmi, the old Arab character in Grossman's novel, was

> a secret child, sprawling behind tree or rock, cast out of the bustle of life, out of memory, waiting for an older brother to take—Hilmi-el—Kazza—the—dwarf—from—my sight, someone—take—him—to—Dahaisheh—the soothsayer—to—wind—a—*khajab*—around—his—finger—and—cure—him—of—his—idiocy, *'Ya'lla—y'alla.*[72]

His physical and mental disabilities make him a scapegoat, and he has learned to live by himself, close to nature, on the outskirts of the village in a cave. Lital Levy notes that "caves have a rich history in literature and philosophy and in Jewish, Christian, and Muslim mystical traditions. [. . .] The geography of historical Palestine is dotted with caves, many of them man-made shelters that date back to antiquity."[73] While defining the spatial locations of villages and caves in the writing of Anton Shammas, Emil Habiby, and Elias Khoury, Levy shows how these places operate as a symbol and the key for their identity: "Anton (Shammas's protagonist) is told about his name and its place in the family history—in other words, given the core of his identity—while standing on the boulder above the cave,"[74] and later he chooses to return to the cave on his personal quest, but it is already sealed.

The cave on the outskirts of the village is the ideal place for the role Hilmi takes in his society: fathers come to him and ask him to marry their daughters who become pregnant outside of wedlock. He takes care of them until they give birth. Although he is not the father of their children, he is legally their husband during pregnancy and birth. In so doing he makes his living by protecting them from social stigma. Thus, while there is no love in the cave, and the women are usually disgusted by him, they need him just as much as the traditional system needs him.

Hilmi exemplifies a natural-physical "naked life" on the verge of animalism. His stories describe similar protagonists. In his tales, his father, Shakif Abu Sha'aban, was a rich man who held huge feasts for all the people in the village. He had a gigantic body, a mirthless laugh, and an arm that was "swollen slippery as an elephant's trunk."[75] When he was angry, he turned into an animal: he "leaped up on all fours with a bristling mane, drawing a mighty roar [. . .] and flailing them with his tail."[76] The physical relationship with his mother is also described in animal terminology—she appears in his tent like a "golden lioness," "moaning with love under the yellow eyes of a stuffed karakul that hung by its tail from the tent flap," yet afterward he "tired of her and drove her off like a ewe."[77]

Both Hilmi and the characters in his stories deal intensively with bodily functions such as eating, having sex, giving birth, and defecating. These descriptions seem vulgar and exaggerated, creating a grotesque image of a colorful, but extremely unrefined society. Hilmi's physicality and animalism constitute his legacy and his own ethical and political perspective. When he tries to pass his principles on to his son, to educate him to live close to nature, not use human language, and not read or write, he teaches him to "drool from his nose and mouth" and "to shit in his pants at meals," babble, and behave like a blind puppy.[78]

One of Hilmi's typical states consists of sitting in a barrel, "with a slow, winding motion, like a big spider [. . .] letting the flies to over hover around him in a kind of a morning, before they fly to fields to bite the bulls."[79] At every meal he puts some soil into his dish to bless the land and the nature around him. His actions are a declaration, subverting the typical concept of hygiene.

Typical discourse on hygiene expresses superiority and a paternalistic approach toward people who do not belong to the "First World"; they are considered primitive, are compared to snarling animals wallowing in the mire, and are often associated with concepts like dirt, decay, and filth. Norbert Elias's study *The Civilizing Process* suggests that the laws of proper conduct and cleanliness are all part of a broader social order with economic, social, and cultural traits and hence accumulate a wider cultural meaning. Frykman and Lofgren showed that the goal of teaching "simple" people about hygiene is intended to "bring them up to be citizens pure in word, thought and deed."[80] Mary Douglas argues that "dirt is the by-product of a systematic ordering and classification of matter, in so far as ordering involves rejecting inappropriate elements. This idea of dirt leads directly into the field of symbolism and can be connected with more obvious symbolic systems of purity."[81]

Julia Kristeva, in her *Essay on Abjection,* takes the notion of dirt and cleanness further: it is "not the lack of cleanliness or health that causes abjection but what disturbs identity, system, order. What does not respect borders, positions, rules"[82] leads to the removal of basic cultural oppositions such as "life and death, vegetal and animal, flesh and blood, hale and ill, otherness and incest [. . .] food taboos [. . .] corporeal alteration and its climax, death [. . .] the feminine body and incest."[83] Thus the discourse on hygiene and the concept of abjection has much in common with the grotesque, since they both have the power to subvert the modern system and to challenge cultural concepts and norms.

Hilmi took a passive position in relation to the Occupation, until the death of his son. He believes that "the Jews are not stupid and they have probably realized by now that the conqueror is also the conquered, and that injustice has teeth in its tail."[84] Apparently, what he suggests is patience; however, the nature of his stories and his physicality constitute a new kind of protest. When Yazdi blames his father for not seeing the humiliation the army imposes on the men of the village, he tells a story about Saif-a-din, an old Palestinian who was asked by soldiers to get off a bus and produce his identity papers. He refused and said in a clear voice: "I, Mr. Officer, *khadrat eldabet,* I will not stir from here, because you ordered the men off the bus, but there are no men here, sir, only empty shells, not like the men of my day, who were men of flesh and blood, these men are made of paper bound in blue."[85] Saif-a-din is referring to the types of identity cards issued by the State of Israel. The blue I.D. is a card inserted into a blue plastic holder that indicates that the person is a citizen of Israel; a card in an orange holder, with the IDF (Israel Defense Forces) insignia embossed on the cover, indicates that the person is Palestinian and a resident of the West Bank; and a green holder indicates Palestinians who are banned from entering Israel. Saif-a-din refuses to be classified by these documents. After his monologue he grabs the officer's gun and shoots himself, so that the soldier will not arrest him for political resistance. Hilmi burns his I.D. card to reject the authorities that issued it, knowing he has an identity that the army cannot take from him, his direct and intimate attachment to the land.[86]

Finally, Hilmi takes Uri hostage and threatens to kill him if the army does not withdraw from the Territories within twenty-four hours. Yet, his subversion of the Occupation is deeper than this action, and is rooted in his grotesque appearance and his ties to nature. He has been at one with the land from its early precivilized days and will stay there long after any specific conqueror will leave his land—he lives in a cave no army can destroy. His way of life and its grotesque features are a declaration of war against any colonialist occupation, and against any spatial boundaries. This is why he is patient.

The Living Dead in *The Intifada Tales*

Dror Green's *The Intifada Tales* (1989) also depicts "naked lives," and suggests a way of coping with the unbearable situation of the Occupation, but takes a different approach to the grotesque. At the beginning of the story of little Ali, the narrator describes how he ended up with a glass eye. There is no reason or guilty party in this description, no context or circumstances, no justifications or reprieves.

> Little Ali had a glass eye. When the sunlight fell on his face, his one eye would almost completely close from the blinding light, and his second eye would remain open to the sun and shine with a thousand golden sparks. [. . .]
>
> Little Ali did not always have a glass eye. At first there was a regular eye there, like all the other children. Then, there was a rubber bullet there, when the soldiers shot him, and only when little Ali's screams were heard throughout the street, did they take him to the hospital and the doctors, who pried the rubber bullet out of his eye, placed a shining glass eye, in place of his black eye.[87]

Like Bakhtin's concept of the grotesque, in which body parts become autonomous,[88] in this story with its ironic title, "What Little Ali Saw with His Own Eyes," the eye is the protagonist and the whole process is described through a very thin binocular. It was an ordinary eye, hit by a rubber bullet, which is later replaced with a glass eye, and is endowed with supernatural power. Ali now has the ability to know when soldiers are coming. Although the eye cannot see anything, it can observe things far away, beyond the outskirts of the village. Like the blind prophet Tiresias in *Oedipus Rex,* in certain moral situations a blind eye can see more than a seeing eye. Thus, Ali has the power to protect the people in the village by warning them that soldiers are coming.

In the story "The Sand Boys" Daud, who worked in a quarry before the Intifada broke out and owns a bulldozer, is asked to cover his children with sand after they were blamed by mistake for taunting a soldier. Daud refuses, but after a rifle is pointed at his wife and daughters, he begins to comply. After he covers the children and the solders leave, he gently uncovers the children but sees that they have disappeared. He later discovers two trails of sand that lead to them and sees them apparently healthy, hiding behind the house. He puts them to bed and sees that they are full of sand. As a matter of fact, they are leaking sand, and "since that day, Daud's sons have lived in the yard, and as the evening descended they would sleep between the pillars under the house. In the morning Daud would crawl into the bulldozer and shovel the sand into big piles behind the house."[89] The sand they produce is important for building houses, since bricks and other building materials are forbidden, and Daud is able to continue his work. Thus, in this story, as with Ali, the children acquire new abilities that help the villagers live under the Occupation.

Another supernatural baby is the dead fetus of Hamdan's mother. When Hamdan's mother was five months pregnant with her first child, Israeli soldiers detained her, and after they pushed her to the ground, she fell on her stomach and lost her unborn child. However, the role of the dead fetus, her eldest son, did not end there. Hamdan's father placed his dead unborn child, his tiny perfect little angel with his smooth legs and thin arms, in a clear glass jar with salt water, sealed it with waxed paper, and put it on a chest in the living room. Friends were invited to congratulate the family on the birth of their first son. Every day, the mother would take the jar out of the chest to look at him, and she was the first to see that the baby was continuing to grow in the jar.[90] The story disturbingly describes how the dead fetus continues to grow, first in the jar, and later when the jar can no longer contain him, he breaks it and disappears, leaving behind him a trail of little footprints, as he, like the other dead children, finds ways to challenge closed spaces and expand them.

Green's stories illustrate the essence of the grotesque as a space between life and death, and show that "death brings nothing to an end."[91] The disappearance of the dead children and their strange reappearances, along with the new babies that are born and found in the garbage with no bellybutton by Dr. Fuad, are a new twist on the "living-dead," which undergoes a chilling transformation from the Zionist territory to the Occupied Territories.

In Hebrew literature written about the 1948 war, the notion of the living-dead symbolized the myth of national sacrifice. When many young soldiers lost their lives in battle, they were symbolically linked to the biblical story of the *akeda* and were portrayed as courageous young men, who risked their lives for the sake of the homeland. The phrase "in their death, [the fallen] ordered us to live," taken from Bialik's 1898 poem "Im yesh at napshekha la'da'at" (If your soul would know), gave expression to the feeling that there is a close link between death and life. The ceremonies for the Memorial Day for the Fallen Soldiers of Israel end on the eve of Israel Independence Day. The juxtaposition of the two draws on the symbolic meaning that the fallen gave their lives so that others could live.[92]

The link between the *akeda* and the bond between the dead and the living suggests seeing these young men as *akudim* (bound), or as living-dead: the dead soldiers remain beautiful, ever present and intact in the memories of the living; their male image remains untouched. Green's "living dead" are also perceived as heroes, who implore their family and people to continue living. However, unlike this motif in Israeli literature, the Palestinian "living-dead" is not a fighter, but a child who loved to live, play outside, climb trees, ride a bicycle, and whose circumstances caused him to be killed. He is an innocent victim, who has not known another reality, who did not understand the situation, who did not have the ability to change his destiny. He is a child who will forever remain in his family's memory as a reminder of unconditional love and happiness, and he is also a grotesque entity, which, unlike the purity of the Israeli mythic living-dead, exposes his deformation that was caused by the Occupation.

Green does not hesitate to associate Zionist literature and history with tales of the Intifada. This is most evident in the only story in the collection that has a Jewish protagonist. Raaif's young daughter has epilepsy. Every morning Raaif accompanies his daughter on the bus to her special education school, and her tongue always protrudes from her mouth. Every morning the soldiers check the bus at the checkpoint and wave it on through. One day, however, one of them notices the little girl with her tongue sticking out and is convinced she is mocking him. The commander orders the driver to drive to the police station; in the station all the passengers are detained for hours in the bus with its windows closed by military order. David Green (whose name may refer to David Ben-Gurion but also has a surname identical to the author's), Raaif's employer, sees that he is late for work, drives to his home, and then locates the bus. He tells the officer about the child's illness and asks to board the bus.

> As David Green walked into the bus, he was hit by the stench of urine and feces and by the sight of the naked people rolling in the god-awful dirt, and his vision grew dim. After a time, he awoke and found himself cast amongst the heaving bodies. He heard the sound of his childhood's model train and at the end of the car he saw the SS soldiers walking in.[93]

In this episode David Green associates the situation on the bus to a flashback from the Holocaust. This explains why he cannot remain indifferent to the distress of his worker. After Green intervenes, the commander of the police station orders the release of the bus; however, to everyone's astonishment, Green disappears. An investigation reveals that David Green was last sighted "getting on a train to a death camp, over forty years ago, never to be heard from again."[94] In this tale, David Green, a Holocaust victim, is called upon to return to the world of the living, not to save his Jewish brethren or strengthen the spirit of the Hebrew fighters, but to help a Palestinian victim. Here, the Holocaust victim and survivors are the ones who can understand the misery of the Palestinians and save them.

Human Organs in *Letters of the Sun, Letters of the Moon*

Chilling descriptions and grotesque images play a major role in Levy's novel. The opening lines of the novel refer to a classical form of the grotesque—the carnival.[95] The setting is the Jewish holiday of Purim, when Palestinian children look forward to the "enemy's masks holiday," and even choose their costumes from among the classical Pinocchio, Snow White, Charlie Chaplin, and Mickey Mouse or choose to dress up as Israeli figures such as Moshe Dayan and Israeli soldiers. All the children and teenagers dress in costumes that were prepared by grownups, and happily go down to the military base to harass soldiers.[96]

Bakhtin argues that in addition to the way in which it emphases people's physicality, the grotesque shares an intimate affinity with the carnival and the timeless ability to throw the hierarchical system into chaos. Medieval carnivals took place for a predetermined length of time of one day or several days, in which the social structure of values and classes was inverted. The donning of costumes, the degradation, and the reversal of the social structure constitute the foundation of the grotesque: "the temporary suspension, both ideal and real, of hierarchical rank, created during carnival time a special type of communication impossible in everyday life."[97] In Levy's text, for a few precious minutes, until he hears the soldiers' gunshots, the protagonist of the novel can believe in this inversion of the norms, and pretend that he is Moshe Dayan "with the General's stripes, with a black plastic eye patch." He imagines he belongs to the strong ones, yet this fantasy is cut brutally short. They rip the General's stripes off him and "order everyone who was not captured to progress towards the 'urination wall.'" The children hold hands as in "a race of beggars, a race of Dabkas, a race of kings, a race of fruit. [. . .] a thousand Moshe Dayans. Among the dancers, I also saw my beloved brother, and glasses of blood painted on his eyes."[98] The brutality of the soldiers is described in color, like a hunting game, while articulating the grotesque images of the children with their ripped costumes and blood. However, these images do not only refer to Palestinian children. Grotesque images characterize the grownups in the novel and endow them with the power to challenge the shrinking space.

Two of the novel's most grotesque characters are the grandmother, who grows roots into the ground and the grandfather who is buried under stones and still exists in the house. The grandmother, Suad Muhamad Zakkut, lived in a shed near the house where the food was kept and constantly ate huge quantities of fruit, vegetables, meat, bread, cooked and uncooked meals. After the death of her beloved grandson, the narrator's brother, she moved to the backyard of the house, near his grave, and continued eating. However, a few days later the family members discover that she has grown a physical connection to the ground, and so cannot return to her room, where the food is kept. With her roots connected to the ground she continues to eat—lentils, peanut butter, chocolate spread, hot dogs, coleslaw, egg salad, pickles, and tahini.[99] And as the narrative unfolds she gradually loses her human appearance, first her sight and then her body, whereas the ground around her flourishes, making a nice garden around the brother's tomb.[100]

The confusion between humans, plants, and inanimate objects, and specifically the representations of a human being whose arms turn into a plant are the key features of the grotesque, which depicts characters in a constant state of becoming and change. This instability is also a key concept in Deleuze's and Guattari's theory, which refers to the state of becoming as a characterization of the minority.[101] This becoming turns out to be a source of power and protest, where the minority can challenge its rulers.

The grandmother blends into the ground. She is in a state of continuous becoming and her roots nourish the soil around the grave, helping it flourish. Like Hilmi, she seems passive and looks upon all of these horrific events with tranquility, but she physically embodies resistance. She anatomically merges with the ground, she is free of the marked spaces above the ground, because she has roots that grow beneath the ground, and she is free of the military decree to destroy the house as punishment for the activities of her grandson, since she cannot leave the area. Eventually she is bound to the territory by her becoming, by her physicality.

While the grandmother is a combination of a human being and a plant, and thus has the ability to challenge spatial boundaries, the grandfather is a mutation of a human being and a rock. The grandfather has a room in the house, and in the room "lies a giant piece of limestone. A lump of plaster, in which he is hiding."[102] People called him a dwarf: "The man was a painter. A painter and a drunk. They say he was smaller than a baby."[103] After crashing his car transporting two hundred and thirty liters of white paint, he became a huge rock: "They carried this huge, silent, unfamiliar, obedient, submissive, beautiful, snow-white, expensive, exotic, smooth limestone. In it lay the body of a man, covered with two hundred and thirty liters of paint."[104] This image of the grandfather illustrates another form of resistance. The grandfather was a little man who used to drink, but he is changed into a dignified rock, which symbolizes stubbornness and power.

Aside from people who become plants and merge with the soil, the narrative refers frequently to independent human organs that fight oppression: "Ibrahim Abu Khaled's hand held the stone, Abed al-Majid's right hand waved the flag of Palestine, it is the speaking tongue, and the hearing ears, and Said Regev's two fingers that made the victory sign."[105] In a much darker reality, when power relations are imbalanced, resistance finds different venues; thus, without referring to people who are always weak when facing the enemy, arms hold a stone and not the person, eyes look at the soldiers in contempt, and fingers signal victory. Like the characters of the grandfather and the grandmother, and as in Green's stories, these grotesque organs have the power to resist the enemy.

In his stories, Jaffar frequently depicts images and independent human organs. He insists on describing the events he witnesses as a fascinating and amusing playground. Whether this stems from his mental disability or is a way to cope with the terrible reality, the disparity between the way the event is narrated and the reader's understanding of the concrete situation creates not only defamiliarization but also a disturbing effect.

The character of Taha, Jaffar's beloved brother, who appears throughout the work, leads to unresolved tension between the comic element and incompatible elements, like the horrific and the terrible, and creates a typical grotesque disorientation, which follows Philip Thomson's definition of the term.[106] Taha is an acrobat and clown who finds different ways to challenge the state of siege and the spatial borders. Taha performs tricks and complies with the soldiers' orders in an unconventional manner. His little brother Jaffar admires him and often does not understand the rationale for his actions, but nevertheless sees him as a source of joy and perceives him as someone who actually conquers the enemy. For example, when the army asks Taha to remove the Palestinian flag, which involves climbing to a dangerous height, Jaffar interprets it as an acrobatic performance. After Taha reaches the flag, he begins to wave it while singing the "Color of the Nation" song. The soldiers cannot catch him, and he walks with the flag as his balancing pole: "Higher than the houses, above the lighthouse mosque. Higher than the army antennas. Higher than the helicopter, and the smoke, and the electricity lines flowing under his feet. Higher than the dead."[107] He dances in the air; he takes stones from his pocket and begins to juggle them.[108] His athletic, almost inhuman body enables him to overcome the enemies, since he can go beyond the walls.

However, Taha's victory is only temporary, and his resistance, although comic, is not accepted. Eventually he is killed:

> My brother did not jump that day, he did not juggle back and forth, did not drink sewage [. . .] my beloved dreamed forever of how he would catch the bullet with his teeth. [. . .] My beloved stood before them, made up like Riga's national circus. [. . .] He ripped his shirt and revealed the painting placed on his chest. [. . .] A target made of a circle within a circle . . . the clown opened his mouth and said "shoot me." [. . .] Taha fumbled for minutes, tumbled backwards, and stared with astonishment into the heavens. A painted tear ran down his left cheek.[109]

The novel presents Taha's death as an unnecessary, stupid demise that is almost accidental, but the reader, who is aware of the disparities between the way Jaffar tells the story and the reality he lived in, assumes that the circumstances were different. In fact, Taha is a political activist (like his older brother), but the viewpoint of the narrative changes the reader's perception altogether and upends the concept of Palestinian resistance in the novel. Taha the acrobat, the admired brother, is a hero in life and in death. He chooses to construct a death scene for himself "to the sound of the cheering crowd, to the beat of the band, to the light of the white spotlight."[110] He asks the soldiers to shoot the target he painted on his chest, and as he is dying, a painted tear runs down his cheek. Later, when he is buried in silence in the backyard, his friends honor him. "His friends lay him in the backyard in the ground, his face still colored like a Russian circus clown, and a tear of pain gaping under his eye."[111]

Up to a certain point in the novel, Taha is depicted as an immortal marionette, who can escape the soldiers whenever he wishes, whether by walking on an electric wire or by spitting fire. Later he is associated with the character of Lockman the storyteller, who is also going to be buried. His death is reminiscent of what the narrator states at the very beginning of the novel: "a man stays a man, even if he disguises himself in a Moshe Dayan costume."[112]

> My respectable father and my beloved Taha have always said that I am fanciful. But here, the alley is an alley, and the street a street, and the curfew a curfew, and the soldiers are soldiers with gas masks, and they look like deep sea divers, and a stone is a stone is a stone, and the bullets hit, and the pain is pain.[113]

Thomson argued that the grotesque creates shock in the reader when it is unclear what the correct reaction should be,[114] and Reuven Tsur's theoretical work on poetics stresses the impossibility of escaping a sense of angst.[115] This disorientation stems from choosing unrealistic narratives and adopting a deterritorialized perspective. It also emerges from the distorted and deformed characters and the bizarre events in all the texts that make it hard to implement mechanisms of rationalization or formulate rational political, historical, or ideological considerations. Levy takes the description of the Intifada into extremely difficult terrain. The reader, who is introduced to this bleak Palestinian circus, oscillates between laughter and horror and remains powerless in the face of the image of the Other, painted in colors that can never fade.

On Storytelling

In the last story in Green's *The Intifada Tales*, after the army demolishes Jamal's house, he asks his brother, the painter, to paint it:

> Day and night Samir toiled to paint his brother's home again. When he finished, the entire family stood before the painted wall, and for a moment, it seemed as though their home had risen from the ashes, that the door would open again and everything would return to the way it was.[116]

When the soldiers order them to demolish the painted wall, Samir "walks to the wall, opens the painted door of the house he had just finished painting, and nods his head as an invitation to his family members to walk inside."[117] This story is about the power of the artist and the power of representation within the unrealistic description. It shows that art and narrative can demolish walls and liberate the protagonists from a shrinking and suffocating space.

Amal Amireh points out that Palestinian nationalism has "consolidated itself in defeat."[118] This is both a loss of identity and a loss of narration. According to Edward Said, Palestinian national recognition and self-definition are inexorably linked to the right and the duty to tell the Palestinian story.[119] The Israeli authors discussed in this chapter took it upon themselves to tell a Palestinian story. Though they appropriated the voices of the Other, their use of grotesque images creates an opportunity to recognize and acknowledge the suffering from within, and hence presents an interesting mode of resistance. They turn familiar concepts upside down, and thus avoid the familiar militaristic terms of Palestinian terrorists, stone throwing, and other forms of Palestinian confrontation of their substance.

In Grossman's *Ha-zman ha-tsahov* (The Yellow Wind, 1987), which documents conversations between Palestinian and Israelis about the Occupation, he highlights this role of storytelling as an act of remembering. In one conversation, an old woman tells him that "Our water was so clear and healthy [. . .] we had a field there. A vineyard. Now see what a flowering garden we have here."[120] Her story "reminds me of my grandmother and her stories about Poland, from which she [was] expelled. About the river, about the fruit there."[121] In another conversation he realizes that "It is grandmother who preserves the family tradition" since even the "mother has no memories from there."[122]

Oppenheimer discusses the metaphor of the yellow wind in Grossman's text. Grossman describes it as a "horrid hot east wind, which comes and heats up the area once in several generations, and the people run away from its heat and take refuge in caves and crevices, but even there it reaches those it wants to reach, those who do deeds of evil and injustice."[123] Oppenheimer states that "this story grants the Arab a living dimension beyond the range of his grievances. [. . .] The yellow wind is perceived here as a political symbol, although it suits any context involving an affliction that requires a solution."[124] The wind offers a solution to the distress of the Occupation in an almost supernatural way. Until this takes place, the storyteller gives the community the power to deal with this reality through legends and to resist it through grotesque images.

The freedom to narrate is a major theme in both Green's and Levy's novels. It is associated with the concept of the grotesque in that it endows the narrators or the storyteller with unrealistic attributes and unnatural powers. The first story in Green's book is about a storyteller who is a kind of magician. The storyteller is arrested by the soldiers after he narrates "a cruel fairytale growing out of life itself and the ongoing occupation";[125] however, in jail he discovers that he can walk through walls:

> His hand did not feel the wall and passed through it. Like a magic show. Azmi quickly pulled his hand out and found it as complete as it was. [. . .] Thereafter Azmi Shahin would wait until twilight and walk out of the wall into the street. He would walk past fences and rocks, trees and cars. [. . .] He would come up to a group of people huddling in the street corner and tell them his stories.[126]

The story cannot be silenced and neither can the storyteller; moreover, the story has the power to remove walls, borders, checkpoints, and barriers. Levy ascribes supernatural attributes to Lockman, the storyteller in his novel, as well. Lockman wanders through the villages and tells stories. He is saved by his stories like Scheherazade, in that the wonderful tale he continues to tell overcomes the devil and saves his life.[127] Lockman dies but is resurrected. When he dies for the second time he seems to merge with other characters, such as the narrator's brother Taha. After Taha's death, the family receives a box with his belongings. Among his personal effects the narrator finds Lockman's original notebook.[128]

The narrators/storytellers are safe and immortal; they are free and can cope with hard questions like the one Jaffar asks: "how can we understand a home that turns to dust?"[129] The power of the narrative is to strengthen the people when body and home are destroyed. The more the Israeli army tries to vanquish it, the stronger it grows; when they try to lock the madman away so he will not be able to tell the stories, he escapes by walking through the walls, since the stories are not physical entities that can be conquered or silenced.

PART 2

Does Literature Matter?

In 2004, David Grossman described the "Israeli condition" in the era of the Second Intifada as follows:

> In recent years, the years of the second Intifada, Israelis have been living in a world in which people are, quite literally, being ripped apart. Entire families are killed in the blink of an eye, human limbs severed in cafés, shopping malls, and buses. These are the materials of Israeli reality and the nightmares of every Israeli, and the two are inseparably mingled. Much of daily life in Israel now occurs in the pre-cultural, primitive, animalistic regions of terror [. . .] To be an Israeli today means to live [. . .] in a dismantled state, in every sense—the dismantling of the private, human body, whose fragility is exposed over and over again, and the dismantling of the public, general body.[1]

Grossman's passage on the Second Intifada refers to the experience of what he calls "a dread of calamity and dissipation"; the reality of having to face the death of relatives and loved ones that has become a collective trauma in the Israel. Indeed, the Second Intifada was characterized mainly by terror attacks in the heart of Israeli cities. Whereas lives in Tel Aviv or Jerusalem did not change much during the First Intifada, in the second half of the 1990s and in the early 2000s, specifically after the failure of the negotiations led by Ehud Barak and Yasser Arafat, the conflict became part of people's everyday lives, in every part of the country. A study conducted at Tel Aviv University in 2004 by researchers from the School of Medicine and the School of Social Work found that about one-third of all Israelis had personal experiences of a terror attack either directly (11 percent) or indirectly, through family and friends (20 percent), and that one out of ten Israeli suffered from posttraumatic stress syndrome as a result of the attacks.[2]

Yaron Peleg notes that "as the momentum of peace slowed after the assassination of Rabin in 1996, and the relations with the Palestinians cooled and soured [. . .] the country's euphoria [. . .] gave way to a deep melancholia, exacerbated by the rising death toll of both soldiers and civilians." He claims that the year 2000 constituted a crossroads in Israeli literary history, marking the shift from escapist-romantic short prose to more realist long novels, whose authors developed a new a sense of unity and a "renewed form of tribalism."[3]

Part II of this book deals with literary works that describe the lives of Israelis in the era of the Occupation, and specifically the social and cultural atmosphere following Rabin's assassination and the Second Intifada. Rather than concentrating on the Israeli soldier and his Palestinian counterparts or the reality of the Occupied Territories, these works examine the effects of the Intifada on everyday life in Israel by exploring the relationships between the battlefront and the home front. The four chapters in this part analyze well-known Israeli novels, which have been translated into English. Each chapter discusses two texts through the prism of topics such as bereavement, motherhood, suicide bombings, borders, and identity.

While not every literary work in the first decade of the twenty-first century fully corresponds to Peleg's description of that "renewed form of tribalism," I agree with Peleg's notion that a sense of change is palpable, and is expressed not only by changes in themes and attitudes but also in the questions raised regarding the role of the Israeli author as prophet or critic. Chapters 4 and 5 present a comparative reading of the early and late works of two prominent authors, A. B. Yehoshua and Orly Castel-Bloom, which clearly reveal the changes in public discourse in Israel and the literary arena after the Second Intifada. Both chapters refer to intergenerational relations between parents and their sons, who are soldiers or are supposed to be in the military. They analyze how the changing political mood in Israel affected these authors' works and the role of canonic Hebrew literature in a swaying public opinion.

Chapters 6 and 7 discuss works by Shifra Horn, A. B. Yehoshua, Ronit Matalon, and Michal Govrin, which depict powerful ethical and humanistic endeavors in which the Other can be seen and the land can be free. They depict journeys in which spatial movement is linked to new ethical possibilities. In so doing, they highlight the power of literary representations to provide a new, sometimes radical, spatial and ethical perspective on this bloody conflict.

CHAPTER 4

A. B. Yehoshua and the Moderation on the Left at the Turn of the Millennium

In an interview with Harry James Cargas in 1994, A. B. Yehoshua argued that Hebrew literature and Zionism have been inexorably linked, since the first days of Zionist thinking. From Herzl to Jabotinsky, the fathers of Zionism were writers, and the connections between Hebrew literature and political activity were an integral part of the specific identity of Hebrew and Israeli culture. Yehoshua acknowledged this in his literary and political activity and noted that while "the public wants to hear us and demands answers" we "are not just *entertainers*. You are not writing for [. . .] you have a kind of moral relationship to the public [. . .] we have this *responsibility*."[1] Yehoshua claimed that although he took a cultural-political role upon himself, that did not imply that he would endorse official or consensual opinion. Rather, his responsibilities entailed raising moral issues and adopting a critical eye.

In 2003, less than a decade afterward, Hannan Hever describes what he considered to be the failure of canonic authors during the Occupation.[2] Like Yehoshua, Hever does not see national writers as mouthpieces for official opinion, but rather as intellectuals who engage in self-examination and criticism, and who accept moral responsibility while writing in aesthetically complex and uncompromising codes.

Hever argues that the Occupation influenced Israeli literature so profoundly that many contemporary works have been radically altered:

instead of producing texts that call for moral and political scrutiny, authors endorse the dual morality of the Occupation, which reflects the dichotomy between national liberal ideas of morality and their violation in the Occupied Territories. They collude by associating themselves with political interests to minimalize or conceal the horrors of the Occupation and strengthen national symbols and ethos. Thus, they have relinquished their role as canonic authors and have become merely *entertainers*.

Hever is not alone in his harsh criticism of A. B. Yehoshua and other major writers of contemporary Hebrew literature. In recent years, many have claimed that Yehoshua was tempering his critique of Israeli politics and moving closer to the political center and the social and cultural consensus. This commentary focused on his representation of Arabs and the Arab-Israeli conflict, as was shown in the third chapter on *Ha-me'ahev* (The Lover, 1977), but specifically in relation to his 2001 novel *Ha-kala ha-meshahreret* (The Liberated Bride).[3]

This chapter examines this claim both historically and in terms of style in light of two powerful images in Zionist ideology: national bereavement and the bereaved father figure. It explores the use of the bereavement myth in several of Yehoshua's works and compares his early novella *Be-t'hilat kayits—1970* (Early in the Summer of 1970) and his later work, *Esh yedidutit* (Friendly Fire, 2007). It shows the evolution of this image and its political and ethical context and more broadly illustrates the ways in which the literary milieu can reshape the national myth.

Fathers, Sons, and the Myth of the *Akeda* in Yehoshua's Works

In 1992, during a lecture on his novel *Mar Mani* (Mr. Mani), Yehoshua referred to the issue of the *akeda* in his works. Yehoshua commented:

> From my earliest childhood, I have had a problem with that story, which is one of the key narratives of the Jewish people [. . .] the *akeda* is a test that the founding fathers set. It is a hovering presence in our history, like a dark bird. For believers in the objective existence of God and His concern for humanity, the *akeda* must be morally intolerable. What moral authority supports God's demand from Abraham to take Isaac and sacrifice him? Even if it is an ultimately unfulfilled test, the divine authority for demanding it is a moral outrage. But for Abraham, the moral failure is compounded. He is incapable of complying with

> the arbitrary, immoral demand to sacrifice his son—and neither does he receive any grounds for it. What does Abraham's unconditional loyalty mean? Blind loyalty of that kind has led humanity to the worst horrors [. . .] yet it is precisely from the secular perspective that we can, to a certain extent, accept the story of the *akeda*. And that is the perspective from which I engage with it, and can grasp a certain degree of moral coherence in it. Simultaneously, I see the accumulative damage it causes, and so it is well worth being more aware of its negative implications and its intensifying damage, in terms of our self-perception as a nation.[4]

Father and son relationships, the image of the bereaved father, and the biblical story of the *akeda* combine to form a central theme in Yehoshua's writings. Yehoshua says that although in religious terms one must absolutely discard the *akeda* narrative, in the national sense the narrative may be acceptable "to a certain extent." Nonetheless, he warns of the negative ramifications of this story. As a Zionist writer who perceives himself as having moral responsibility, Yehoshua is aware of the ambivalence of such a myth in the context of Israeli culture.

From his early writings to his latest novels, Yehoshua's works have dealt with the familial sphere and focused particularly on the loaded issue of father-son relationships. In the story "Mul ha-yearot" (Facing the Forests, 1963), a son is estranged from his father; in "Shlosha yamim ve-yeled" (Three Days and a Child, 1965), the protagonist plots to murder his "foster son"; the father in "Shtika holekhet ve-nimshekhet shel meshorer" (The Continuing Silence of a Poet, 1966) does not expect that his son will follow in his footsteps; in *Early in the Summer of 1970* (1971), a father fantasizes about his son's death; in *Ha-me'ahev* (The Lover), Adam is fraught with guilt about his son's death and attempts to find a substitute; *Mar Mani* (Mr. Mani, 1990) revolves around rescuing and sacrificing sons; in *Ha-kala ha-meshahreret* (The Liberated Bride, 2001), the father is overly inquisitive about his son's life; and *Friendly Fire* (2007) features a father and his dead son. All these texts compulsively delineate the intricate and difficult relationships between fathers and sons.[5] They are characterized by intergenerational silence, alienation, and a lack of communication that leads to violence, which are manifested both in the domestic sphere and on the political level.

Father-son relationships are directly connected to Yehoshua's place in the chronology of literary generations. As a young author, Yehoshua was considered a member of a new generation of writers who sought innovative modes of expression and hoped to liberate literature from its social function. This new approach reflected the intergenerational tension between the 1948 *Palmah* generation and the *Dor Ha-medina* (the statehood generation). The *Palmah* generation was wholly absorbed in the experience of the 1948 war. In most cases, literary texts by members of this generation were attentive to the Zionist endeavor. Even when their texts were critical, (like those of S. Yizhar), the theme of war was ubiquitous and the Eretz-Yisrael experience was central. During the 1960s, in the statehood generation, Israel became a solid fact and the ideological drive gave way to other topics. The new literature written in the 1960s viewed the individual as unconnected to any given place or time. New poetic and philosophical approaches, such as existentialism, began to permeate literary texts. Yet the 1960s did not break entirely with place and time; rather, distance and skepticism were reflected in an almost obsessive engagement with the intergenerational question. Israeli authors in the 1960s were thought of as "sons," rebelling against the ideals of their parents' generation. [6]

Intergenerational conflict, specifically the divergence of the Israeli born sons from their parents (the 1948 generation), is also a defining conflict in Yehoshua's work. In the literary texts he wrote during the sixties and seventies, the protagonists are fathers from the *Palmah* generation, and the sons belong to the statehood generation. The fathers are world-weary, lonely, and are threatened by their sons. The sons are detached from the values that the older generation wishes to instill in them, and defy their parents' attempts to uphold the old myths and anachronistic ideals. The fathers are depicted as shallow and fake, clinging to obsolete, empty ideas, but still controlling institutional strongholds. Though the sons seek a different path, they find themselves trapped in a web that turns into an implicit or explicit *akeda,* characterized by a bitterly critical clash with the myth of national sacrifice.

The link between fallen soldiers and the myth of the *akeda* crystallized during the early decades of the twentieth century, primarily around the period of the 1948 war, and was part of what may be termed the "hierarchy of bereavement," in which the dead soldiers, as Rachel Harris points out, "are used [. . .] as a tool for building a national ideology and for encouraging citizens to identify with the national landscape."[7] Thus, while the *akeda* myth reinforces the tie between the individual believer or community and God, in the modern rite of fallen soldiers, God's altar is replaced by worship of the homeland.[8] Soldiers are portrayed in the Hebrew literature of the first half of the twentieth century as courageous youths who risk their lives for the sake of the homeland. A government memorandum on Israel's first Independence Day contained the following statements that show how the *akeda* was embraced as a framework for national bereavement:

> Today Israel will remember with a shiver of pride and appreciation its sons and daughters, the nation's heroes, who risked their lives in the battlefields and with their young, precious, pure and courageous lives, gave us our liberty. The nation will venerate their *memory, bask in the glory of their heroism, and comfort the bereaved parents who were fortunate enough to witness our acceptance of their sacrifice.*[9]

Many writers from the Palmah generation who adopted this model describe these young men as *akudim* (bound), or as living-dead: the dead soldiers are presented on a silver platter and remain beautiful, ever-present, and intact in the memories of the living.[10]

As Yael Feldman and Avi Sagi show, the national sacrifice myth during the 1940s and the 1950s differs from the biblical story. Three major features typify the *akeda* myth in its *Palmah* generation version. Unlike the biblical Isaac who passively let himself be bound, the Isaac of the War of Independence was perceived as an active fighter, consciously assuming his military commitment: discourse in the 1940s and 1950s featured "Isaacs" who willingly sacrificed themselves, whereas the biblical Isaac is replaced by a ram and does not die. This discourse emphasized cooperation between fathers and sons, working together toward a common goal. Furthermore, Isaac was not viewed as an individual but as embodying the pioneer spirit and the *sabra* (native Israeli) outlook in general.[11]

The myth of the *akeda* and the role of "sons" in this scheme, with or without the active cooperation with their "fathers," is related to the impact of the spatial settings in which Israeli soldiers are located, and thus to the concept of *moral luck*. The idea that the parents (or more precisely the fathers) place the soldiers in an ideological structure that turns them into the potentially fallen from the first day they enlist, creates a trap that eventually leads to disorientation and deterritorialization. It also positions the soldiers as initially moral, good citizens. Yehoshua's writing was actively engaged with this scheme and its ethical burden but focused mostly on the characters of the fathers.

In the sixties, when Yehoshua started writing, criticism of the *akeda* myth was already being voiced. This was true even during the 1940s and 1950s, for example S. Yizhar's book *Yemei tsiklag* (Days of Tsiklag, 1958)[12] and Haim Gouri's *Shoshanat ruhot* (Compass Rose, 1960).[13] Attempts at subverting the myth intensified during the 1960s,[14] and it is very clear that they influenced Yehoshua. But unlike the criticism leveled by the members of the *Palmah* generation (such as Yizhar and Gouri), for Yehoshua, subverting the myth was interwoven with descriptions of the gap between the parents' *Palmah* generation and that of their children, the 1960s generation.

The novella *Early in the Summer of 1970*, published in 1971, is the best example of Yehoshua's attitude toward the *akeda* at that time. The father, a Bible teacher in a school, represents the *Palmah* generation; he believes in Zionist ideals and feels truly invigorated in times of war. In contrast, his son, who has returned from the United States with a foreign wife and child, who do not speak Hebrew, believes in peace and rejects the concept of going to war and doing reserve duty.

During the 1970s Yehoshua's attitude to the theme of fathers, sons, and *akeda* progressed in tandem with developments in his work, which turned to more complex realism and forms of polyphonic writing.[15] *The Lover*, written in 1977, is an interesting way station. *The Lover* has a tri-generational rather than a bi-generational structure in which corruption is rooted in the mid-generation of the 1960s. It tells of the 1948 generation—the parents of Asya and Adam, and the character of Veducha; its main protagonists are Adam, Asya, and Gabriel, her lover, and Dafi and Na'im, the younger generation in the novel. Unlike the grandparents—the 1948 generation who were industriously engaged in national projects and endeavors, whether by joining the security forces (Asya's father) or contributing to Jewish labor (Adam's father)—and in contrast to the figure of the grandmother Veducha, who represents the entire history of Zionism, Adam and Asya's generation discards the old values and becomes engrossed in their private lives and economic well-being. This generation came of age after 1948 and sank into the euphoria of the 1960s, a generation more intent on financial gain than relationships or ideologies. As in the novella *Early in the Summer of 1970*, here too the solution to that generation's problems is war, which makes various encounters possible and revives the dead.

The clear-cut picture of father and son in the earlier novella fades in *The Lover* to allow for a gallery of characters. Gabriel, the lover, is younger than Adam and Asya, and his opinions are closer to those of Dafi and

Na'im. His character does not fit the generational tree, yet he can be seen as the missing son, since he is sent into battle and is compared to a fallen soldier when he disappears: "In the last war we lost a lover. We used to have a lover, but since the war he is gone. Just disappeared."[16]

Gabriel, who is not quite a father and not quite a son, symbolizes a rebellious ideological outlook; like all the sons in Yehoshua's works, he reveals the decline of the fathers' generation. His mother was killed during the siege of Jerusalem during the 1948 war, when he was a little boy, and though he hiked around the country with his grandmother, Gabriel decided years earlier to leave Israel, a step condemned by those around him. When he returns to Israel, he is recruited to the war. His officer is determined to ensure he sees battle: "Make sure he fights properly. [. . .] He's been out of the country ten years [. . .] he tried to run away."[17] From Gabriel's point of view, he is confronting a generation of fanatical commanders who cling to war like a life buoy. Gabriel feels that the officers want him dead: "I say it again—they simply wanted to kill me."[18] He understands that the war is emblematic of Zionism's failure: this is "a nation ensnaring itself."[19] He refuses to take the bereavement myth upon himself and goes AWOL.

Mr. Mani (1990) is one of Yehoshua's pivotal works in which he charts the fate of a long series of fathers and sons who differ ideologically. Throughout the text many parental figures in the novel are obtrusive. The novel is organized in reverse chronological order, starting from the present generation. In the first episode, Effi Mani (b. 1958) vanishes while on reserve duty, and Gabriel (b. 1938), his father, tries to commit suicide. In the second episode, Gabriel, as a young boy, is about to face death. Efraim (b. 1914), Gabriel's father, drags him to a labyrinth in Crete, where a German paratrooper awaits him, and Gabriel witnesses the confrontation between the two. Eventually, Efraim offers himself up as a victim in exchange for his son's life. In the third episode, Joseph Mani (b. 1887), Efraim's father, is the fourth child in the novel who is condemned to death and is then rescued: as a child, he was destined to die because of his parents' "incompatible blood."[20] As an adult, he is again miraculously saved after having been sentenced to hang for spying. Moshe Mani (b. 1848) was not supposed to be born at all, and had the *akeda* been carried out in the final chapter of the book (which is the earliest chronologically), he would never have seen the light of day. Moshe Mani may have known his biological father, but he knows nothing of the drama that unfolded before he was born. As an adult, he becomes a physician, but eventually commits suicide.

In the final episode, when all these themes converge into a full-blown *akeda*, the intergenerational conflict is staged in all its tragedy. Abraham Mani (b. 1799) binds his son, Joseph (b. 1826), on Mount Moriah, using a knife and ropes: "He had his throat cut, madam: like a tender lamb, or a black goat in the dead of night."[21]

As in the other works discussed here, in *Mr. Mani* the crux of the crisis between fathers and sons is ideological.[22] In the last episode, Abraham the father needs to bring about his son's death and impregnate his son's wife, since he opposes his son's ideological stance and bizarre revolutionary ideas. The son, Joseph, wants to forfeit his sperm, the continuation of the dynasty, to unite the country's inhabitants into a cohesive national whole, based on affinity to the country. The father understands that his son's radical ideas could bring disaster not only on himself, but on the entire Jewish population of the Old City, and so he takes his son's place, assuming responsibility for the dynasty's continued existence and growth.

In his essay on the *akeda* in *Mr. Mani* Yehoshua stated that in this novel he wanted "to revoke the *akeda* by performing it." He argued that the only way to get rid of the myth entailed realizing it in full, and this is what he decided to do:

> Here, the question of the *akeda* that occupied me for years in many works, finally reaches, I hope, its ultimate realization. And I feel that this time, I've really freed myself from it. Not only my personal self is freed from it, in fact with this novel (what a terrible pretension!) I wanted to free the collective self from this important, powerful and awful myth that hovers so strongly over our history and culture.[23]

Did Yehoshua manage to get rid of this frightening myth? Apparently not. Rather, the myth that was so dramatically honed in *Mr. Mani* emerges in a different form, in his later works. In *Friendly Fire* (2007), fathers and sons are a central theme and like *Mr. Mani,* this work is also polyphonic since it deals with several fathers and sons and is based on duets of voices. Nevertheless, the intergenerational conflict in this work is virtually non-existent, and the text conveys a new stance on the figure of the bereaved father and a different concretization of the *akeda* myth. Both *Early in the Summer of 1970* and *Friendly Fire* focus directly on sons, who went to war and fathers, who are mourning. However, the comparison reveals that despite the numerous links between the two texts, attitudes toward the myth in the later work seem to have become more forgiving.

Two Kinds of Sacrifice

The protagonist of *Early in the Summer of 1970* is a lonely elderly teacher, whose life is upended by the news that his son was killed on reserve duty during the War of Attrition, a notification that later turns out to be erroneous. From the moment the protagonist receives the news that turn him into a bereaved father, all his former acquaintances, who consider him a tedious old man and have abandoned him over the years, now swarm to see him. At his school, the principal, teachers, and students seek his company. His previously alienated relationship with his son's family—his daughter-in-law and grandson—is transformed into a new bond based on their shared loss. He becomes frantically active, hoping to find his spiritual vocation, and plans to continue his son's research work.

The story is constructed cyclically. The father, who narrates the story, re-lives the moment he received the news of his son's death and describes it over and over again. In between the reconstructions, he reminisces about events connected to his work at school and his relationship with his son. He also depicts the process of searching for his son, first at the morgue, where it becomes clear that the corpse shown to him is not his son, and then during the trip to the army base where he finally meets his son, alive and well, and oblivious to the mistake that has been made. The story ends with another reenactment of the announcement of his son's supposed death, in a kind of desperate attempt to cling to the calamity.

Early in the Summer of 1970 has clear ties with both the biblical story of the *akeda* and its modern myth. Like the biblical Abraham, the father in the novella agrees to sacrifice his son. Although he does not directly cause his son's death, clues in the text link him to it; for example, he is portrayed holding twigs as though taken from the altar: "It is the branch that makes me so suspect."[24] The son is considered dead, almost dies, or is expected to die, but in the end is saved. In the Bible, Abraham is rewarded for proving his belief in God. In *Early in the Summer of 1970* the father also benefits from the alleged death. He is redeemed from distress and solitude, and he enjoys social recognition and attention. In addition, the connection to the *akeda* is present in the language of the text: the father mentions his age in the style of biblical genealogy, and the description of the son's death borrows from the scripture's triple-layered sentence: "Take your son, your only son Isaac, whom you love." The narrator always uses a three-part structure when relating to his son's death: "thirty-one years old. An only, beloved son."[25] There is also a clear reference to "shed blood,"[26] and the biblical text is mentioned explicitly as the "mumble" of "the morning's tidings in an ancient, biblical Hebrew."[27]

The father in this story both kills and revives. In his imaginary address at the school's graduation ceremony, he emphasizes the responsibility of parents who send their sons away to die, thus ascribing a sacrificial role to himself. As a representative of the *Palmah* generation he is also perceived "as though in some furtive manner [he was] enjoying this war,"[28] "and as if it [was he] who issued call-up orders."[29] But just as the father sacrifices the son, he ironically describes how he also resurrects him (since he was not dead in the first place), "as though by my power I had killed him, as though by my power brought him back to life."[30] This takes place entirely under divine protection: "and to look at once for signs of a dead, distant, biblical deity among the arid hills flanking the road."[31]

The story delineates the rift between father and son in detail. The apparent physical likeness between the two is described first: "they are amazed by the resemblance between us,"[32] yet there is no sign of intimacy between the two men. Silence and gloom characterize their encounters. The son returns from the United States but shows no special interest in his father's life, while the father does not understand his son's academic research and finds it difficult to converse with his daughter-in-law and grandson.

After his son's "death," he reports: "[I] cleanse myself, put on fresh linen, find a heavy black suit in the wardrobe and put it on."[33] He takes advantage of his son's death in all possible ways—relishing his tragedy, reconstructing his future. After he hears the news he falls down "sobbing on the rug where they [his son and the son's wife] lay that night."[34] He seeks out his son's wife, admitting that she is "of the kind who many years, ages ago, I might have fallen in love with, pursued in my heart, year after year."[35] He also becomes a stand-in father for the grandchild and collects him from nursery school. Professionally, he is willing to try to understand his son's new ideas, and rakes over his papers trying to see whether he can continue his research, "[I] will have to try and read these as well."[36] He even plans to publish a collection of his son's works.[37]

The status of bereaved father not only benefits him on a personal level, but in the public sphere as well. People want to be near him and show their respect. He imagines himself giving the keynote address to the graduates. His pride is restored, and paradoxically, through death, his son returns to him. "I was prepared for his death in a manner, and that was my strength in that fearful moment."[38] Apparently, he was not only prepared, but even consciously or subconsciously desired it.

In his essay on the *akeda*, Yehoshua's outlines his interpretation of the biblical story. In his final years, Abraham was not convinced that Isaac would abide by his faith. How could he ensure that his son would not only continue his lineage but also reject the new belief? According to Yehoshua's analysis, through the *akeda* Abraham shows Isaac a redeeming God, to whom Isaac now owes his life. This interpretation is echoed in Yehoshua's *oeuvre*. To secure their sons' faith, fathers (like the ones portrayed in *Mr. Mani* and other texts) must steer their sons toward a perilous situation, in which a knife is placed dangerously close to their hearts. After an act of rescue is staged at the very last minute, salvation can be attributed to a higher power.[39]

In *Early in the Summer of 1970*, the father invents a slaughtering-knife game, hoping to draw his son closer to his own world of values, even at the price of his death. The novella pushes the father's ideological loyalty to the extreme. Yehoshua's criticism is not directed solely at the character of the father, but at all agents of sacrifice and bereavement. The society reflected in this text worships disasters and wars, and endorses sacrifice for the sake of rejuvenation.

Writing about the novella in 1976, Haim Gantz noted the way the text embraces the myth of sacrifice:

> The shift from private pain to public generalizations, to creating grief-related norms, and particularly assigning a historiosophic value to a reality that one can only cry about, gives something of a justification to this reality. [. . .] When I invent customs connected to bereavement this implies I expect that bereavement will continue to occur. Otherwise I would never formulate such a code of behavior since I would simply not believe that it would be necessary.[40]

Gantz argues that bereavement mechanisms actually create an acceptance of the *akeda*. In Yehoshua's novella, he claims, the willingness to sacrifice and the anticipation of bereavement are tantamount to a total acceptance of the myth of sacrifice and the death of the sons. However, acceptance in the novella is clearly a parody, since the father who accepts the myth is presented as a twisted, semi-pathetic figure, and the criticism of the values he represents stems from the irony that incessantly undermines his worldview. Yehoshua depicts the acceptance of the myth as part of a critique that renders ludicrous the whole worldview of fathers who are ready to sacrifice their sons.[41]

Early in the Summer of 1970 and the later novel *Friendly Fire* share many themes: father-son relationships, the bereaved father, and the myth of sacrifice. Yet the two works reflect different views on these issues. While the earlier work is a short novella with schematic irony and biting criticism, the later offers its readers a more complex gaze that is achieved by doubling the fathers and the sons. Nevertheless, alongside the marked differences in textual complexity and maturity, the later text abandons Yehoshua's critical stance and internalizes a moderate approach to the issue of bereavement by addressing it without a trace of irony. The more recent text proposes a modern yet conservative alternative to the myth of military heroism that establishes the morality and hence the legitimacy of the army and state.

Friendly Fire interlaces the stories of three fathers, two of whom are bereaved. Yirmi lost his son Eyal, who was killed while serving in the occupied West Bank. After his son's death, he leaves Israel with his wife and settles in Africa, first as a member of a diplomatic delegation and then, after his wife's death, as part of a scientific mission. When his sister-in-law travels to Africa alone to mourn her sister, Yirmi reveals the circumstances of his son's death and his perception of the world as a result of his bereavement. Amotz Yaari, Yirmi's brother-in-law and the novel's main protagonist, is the second (nonbereaved) father. He too is concerned about his son, Moran, who works with him in his elevator engineering office and has been called up for army reserve duty. The novel describes the seven days of the Hanukah holiday, during which Amotz, abandoned by both his wife (who went to Africa) and his older son, alternates between the office and the tasks of caring for his children and grandchildren. Alongside these two men who are so closely involved with their sons, who are presented most of the time as serving in the army, the novel describes a third father whose son was killed in combat. Mr. Kidron lives in a lavish Tel Aviv residential tower and complains about the winds[42] that haunt the building and whisper through the elevator shaft.

The state of bereavement is at the core of this novel. It is expressed through the characters of all the fathers and sons but particularly through Eyal ("deer" in Hebrew), Yirmi's son, who was sacrificed, like the ram in the *akeda* story. Eyal is accidentally killed by a stray bullet that was shot from his commerade's weapon. Amotz calls it "friendly fire" and Yirmi, the bereaved father, adopts the term:

> But then suddenly, amid all the shock and anger, I also understood that inside this stupid oxymoron, this friendly fire, there was something more, some small spark of light that would help me navigate through the great darkness that awaited me, to better identify the true sickness that afflicts all of us. And from then on, I fell in love with the expression, and started using it a lot.[43]

The concept of "friendly fire" signifies the idea that Eyal is a son sacrificed by his people and emphasizes their responsibility for his death. Yirmi reads the Books of the Prophets, including the book of Jeremiah (Yirmi's namesake). He understands that grim decrees and suffering seem internal to the nation, rather than external (caused by the enemy).[44] Yirmi claims that this suffering is something the Jewish people anticipate and is part of the identity of the Jewish identity:

> Death, destruction, exile, punishment, more punishment, devastation, plague, and famine [. . .] and this we have drunk with our mother's milk, we've been fed it like baby food. So it's no wonder that we're all set for the next destruction that will come, yes, speedily in our own time, maybe even yearning for it, look, it's already right here, we've been hearing about it, we've read it word for word in wonderful language.[45]

Like Gantz's analysis of *Early in the Summer of 1970*, the expectation of disaster, in fact, implies accepting it. Yirmi tells Daniela about a memorial service he attended, where

> they brought some sort of lecturer, an author or poet, who rebound the binding of Isaac, and then I saw how it's possible to find new ore in texts that have been mined over and over. This lecturer tried to describe what the whole story of the captive son and the big knife

> looked like from down below, from the point of view of the two youths who were guarding Abraham's donkey at the foot of the mountain.[46]

Yirmi, in fact, makes a similar move: he tries to find new approaches to the text of the *akeda*. In the investigations he conducts in Tulkarm after his son's death, he constantly demands to see the place where his son was killed, and asks to climb up to the roof rather than remain on the street (to climb the metaphorical mountain of Moriah). Eventually, he is disappointed by the results that reveal no details that are able to diminish his sense of loss, and escapes to Africa.

Yirmi's decision to leave the country can be interpreted as a manifestation of criticism of the bereavement myth. He refuses to play the role of a bereaved father, so he abandons everything, including his natural environment. Yet this escape is a denial of his guilt, since it acknowledges that the kernel of "friendly fire" is a tragedy that stems from the people, from society. Guilt should not be directed toward the specific soldier who fired by mistake (and indeed Yirmi tries to find the soldier to absolve him of guilt), but toward the nation and the fathers. Yirmi rejects and diminishes this guilt. He tells Daniela, "I am warning you, grieve, but do not preach."[47] Yirmi must exhaust the examination of the circumstances of his son's death, but then he declares, "I milked his death dry [. . .] but my responsibility is over."[48]

The character of Amotz Yaari represents another perspective on bereavement through a character who experiences it indirectly. He is the work's most dominant character, who becomes the focus of the text, both in his private life and in the way he investigates the story of Yirmi's bereavement. In many respects, Amotz Yaari, the non-bereaved father, is a kind of evolved, more normative version of the father in *Early in the Summer of 1970*. Throughout much of the novel, his son is on army reserve duty. Since his wife is in South Africa visiting Yirmi, he is lonely and seeks something to lessen his boredom. Yaari is engaged with bereavement a great deal. He is preoccupied with the family's bereavement and takes advantage of it: during his son's attempts to evade reserve duty, Yaari remembers a deceased cousin "after all, your cousin . . ."[49] When his wife hints that Moran, his son, may be afraid of being conscripted, Yaari appropriates his brother-in-law's bereavement: "Can't a father with two children, whose family has already paid its debt to the homeland, ask for a little consideration?"[50]

Moran is taken from his home after failing to report for duty and is kept under arrest in the reserve army base. At this point, his father's behavior becomes implosive: "It's hard for him to accept the fact that his son's cell phone, ever ready for his calls, has suddenly become a mere answering-machine, indifferently storing messages."[51] The personification of the cell phone implies a kind of death message.

When visiting Moran at the base, he impersonates a bereaved father so he will be allowed to enter: "Now listen, you're new recruits, I am a bereaved father. Seven years ago my oldest son was killed in a military action in the West Bank, in Tulkarm. So please, don't be hard on me now. It's already late, and the one son I have left is here with the reserves, a combat officer who needs warm clothing."[52]

While dealing with the problem of the winds in the tower, Yaari approaches the bereaved father, Mr. Kidron, and exploits his familiarity with bereavement to convince him that he wants to help: "I may not be a bereaved father like you, Mr. Kidron, only a bereaved uncle, but I have insider knowledge, family knowledge of your grief, and I respect it a great deal."[53] Thus, for Yaari, bereavement is a tool facilitating an individual's integration and approval by others in society (just like in the early novella). It opens doors and connects people, and therefore at times is seen as desirable.

Like the father in *Early in the Summer of 1970,* Yaari takes care of his son's family, particularly when the son himself is away. "The absence of a father automatically raises the grandfather's stock. He hugs and kisses them, then lightly hugs Efrat and brushes her cheek."[54] He looks at his daughter-in-law, who "surrenders trustingly to his driving and sinks deeper into sleep. This gives him the opportunity to examine from close up just what her beauty is made of."[55] While visiting his son's base, he tells his son and his wife to get away and enjoy some privacy while he takes care of the grandchildren, but even then he feels an imagined bereavement. When the son and his wife do not return to the base on time:

> his practical engineer's mind churns through the outcomes of all possible situations, [. . .] In his imagination scenes of horrible catastrophe mingle cruelly with practical considerations. How he will have to ask Daniela to quit teaching to devote herself to the grandchildren; how Moran's apartment will have to be rented out, and for how much; how his firm's lawyer will examine the life-insurance policy; and who will

> argue in court over the extent of the damages. He makes a mental note of which architect could best add a wing to their house for the children, and considers how he might persuade Nofar [his younger daughter] to become legal guardian after he and Daniela have passed away.[56]

On Winds and Responsibility

In *Friendly Fire* bereavement affects fathers and is conveyed to society as a whole in the form of winds/ghosts.[57] Yaari speaks of winds, and Mr. Kidron from the Tel Aviv tower states that "when we get home and get near the elevator, we don't hear the wind but howls of pain."[58] The winds represent the fallen sons who do not leave the fathers in peace. They demand accountability. But accountability always refers to others, not the bereaved fathers. While Yaari's father, who despite his ailing health still insists on going to his friend's house in Jerusalem to repair the elevator as he promised he would, in the office of his son, Amotz Yaari, a specialist is called in to "free you from responsibility."[59]

The novel *Friendly Fire* portrays bereaved fathers and shares many themes with *Early in the Summer of 1970*. Yet *Friendly Fire* does not criticize the bereavement myth in the same vehement manner as *Early in the Summer of 1970*. Three factors help explain this difference. The first is related to the differences in the characters and the narrator. As noted earlier, the short and concentrated structure of the early text produces focused criticism, while the intricate structure of the dialogic novel produces a fuller picture. The novella's narrator is the father himself, who is under the sway of a complex mental and emotional state. In his descriptions, he alternates timeframes, creating improbable links and describing his fantasies. Over the course of the text, he depicts the moment he received the news of his son's death three times, yet differently each time. He interprets his relationships with those around him—the principal, the pupils, his son's wife and students—in an implausible way. Sometimes he appears to be suffering loss of memory, for example when he finds it difficult to recall verses from the Bible, or when he hallucinates situations that never happened, like the commencement address to which he returns from time to time. The father in *Early in the Summer of 1970* is an unstable character, recounting events from a subjective viewpoint. Although he seems authentic, he gives the impression of being odd and emotionally imbalanced. His peculiar attitude to bereavement and his cultivation of his imaginary state as a bereaved father function in the novella as a kind of parody of Israeli mourning customs and the way that Israeli society has integrated the myth of the *akeda*.

In contrast, in *Friendly Fire*, the narrator is external and the characters are normative. Yaari, who works in an elevator engineering office, is a thoughtful grandfather, a man with both feet on the ground. He is a very human, likeable, warm, and supportive character, always willing to help. His obsession with bereavement and his impersonation of a bereaved father is often ironic, but also empathetic. Yirmi, who left for Africa, is also reliable and tries to make sense of the occurrences and find a way of dealing with his loss. Both fathers represent average families in Israel, and the attitude toward them is generally positive, without criticism or disapproval.

Unlike the situation in *Early in the Summer of 1970* and other works mentioned (such as *The Lover* and *Mr. Mani*), in *Friendly Fire* there is no major generational divide between fathers and sons, and the closeness between fathers and sons is striking. In fact, both generations are in a state of ideological flux that attests to the vast evolution in Yehoshua's writings, which no longer attribute unequivocal positions to each generation. By contrast, in all the early works there are traces of crisis and intergenerational conflict reflecting Yehoshua's own interpretation of the *akeda* story as a narrative aimed at establishing the fathers' world of values. Thus, the conflict between fathers and sons was central to Yehoshua's criticism of bereavement. Once the conflict is blurred, or even disappears, criticism of the *akeda* myth evaporates.

The description of the "work accident," as the Palestinians nominate Eyal's death, is a major factor, which soften the book's critical stance, and in fact reaffirms the function of bereavement and offers a modern alternative to the myth. "My precious innocent son, [. . .] is ashamed to leave behind the bucket they gave him,"[60] states Yirmi, but when he talks to the Palestinian family, he realizes that Eyal's gesture has not earned him their gratitude: "What do you want from me?" asks a student family member. "For me to offer you compassion for your soldier?" Does he think "that if he does us a favor and leaves us a clean bucket, washing away the evidence of his fear, we'll forgive him for the insult and humiliation? But how can we forgive? Can we be bought with a clean bucket?"[61] The Palestinians' words contrast with the text's choice not to refer to any warfare or the Occupation. As with the well-crafted scene in Ramallah, in Yehoshua's novel *Ha-kala ha-meshahreret* (The Liberated Bride), the horror of the

Occupation disappears altogether and yields to the glorification of the Israeli army.

The house where Eyal meets his death is described in a sterile manner, which obfuscates its military mission and emphasizes his humanity. In the novel in general the soldiers are depicted in noncombat activities, and even Moran, who is taken into custody, is portrayed as playing chess at the training base with the officer who arrested him. Eyal is described as a physician who served as a reserve officer, and the circumstances of the death of Mr. Kidron's son are not mentioned, only the upkeep of his tombstone. Although the novel is related to the Occupation and the soldiers' personalities, the sons are always shown in a civilian context. Thus bereaved fathers are glorified, while the Occupation and the fighting that led to the bereavement are portrayed in terms of values and morality.

Moreover, even the desire to investigate the circumstances of the son's death, which could have resulted in ground-shaking revelation, actually reinforces societal values. By ignoring the Occupation and its ethical implications, the text "obscures the moral contradiction and pretends [Israel is] a united national society," as Hever put it (in another context).[62] This may be the reason why the novel refrains from grappling with questions of guilt and responsibility, and avoids any discussion at this level. Here, in complete contrast to other works by Yehoshua, the fathers are not found guilty.

In a generation where people no longer talk about heroism during combat on the battlefield, or about young men sacrificed on the homeland's altar, Yehoshua supplies an alternative to the myth, a new variant of the sacrificial myth, not on the homeland's altar, but on the moral altar of the Israeli army. This is what Eyal represents in the novel, a sort of heroism that reflects a certain consensus between the fathers' generation and the sons'. Indisputable sacrifice is thus justified for the first time in Yehoshua's *oeuvre*.

The Larger Picture

Yehoshua and several other authors of his generation, who burst onto the literary scene during the 1960s, challenged the dominant literary norms of the time and sought new modes of expression. When their first stories were published, they constituted a genuine literary earthquake—a breakthrough and a new trajectory. According to the norms that prevailed among the *Palmah* generation and during the 1950s, literature had to contribute to structuring Israel's nascent society by describing reality faithfully and realistically. This assumption was tied to the desire to produce a native-born, authentic literature rooted in the collective Israeli experience. The generation that started writing in the 1960s, and whose main representatives are Amos Oz and A. B. Yehoshua, was alienated from this societal role and its commitment to shape reality through a specific character that reflected a clear-cut, optimistic stance toward society and values. Oz and Yehoshua, as well as others, continued the Zionist tradition of self-scrutiny. They used their work to call for Zionist soul-searching through new forms of symbolic and ironic writing that reveals the psychological experiences of individual protagonists, the fashioning of passive protagonists, and a tendency toward existentialist thematic. They sought to replace realistic optimism with "worlds of shadows" that depict individualism, skepticism, pain and trauma, and ideological criticism.[63]

However, with time, these authors became part of the Hebrew literary mainstream. Yehoshua is a cultural and political persona aligned with the Left. Like Amoz Oz, Yehoshua appeared on the list of public figures and intellectuals who support Meretz, appearing symbolically in slot 109.[64] Nevertheless, in his prose and essays, he targets a broader consensus.

As will be argued in the next chapter in relation to the novels of Orly Castel-Bloom, after the outbreak of the Second Intifada in 2000, the Israeli Left experienced a political-ideological crisis. Many cite the embarrassment among the ranks of the Left, who believed in peace and could not explain this failure. In the introduction to a volume of essays written by Israeli academics and intellectuals aligned to the political Left, Adi Ophir argues that this crisis encouraged people to put the Occupation aside:

> Some Israelis, who see themselves as people of the left, are already talking and writing about a new civic agenda, the need to preserve the chances for a civic Israeli society within the boundaries of the Green Line. These Israelis want once again to forget the occupation quickly. In fact this is how they lived their lives before the first Intifada, and after the Oslo Accords, and up to the Second Intifada.[65]

Ophir argues that by putting aside the Occupation the left-wing parties eventually gravitated toward the center of the political spectrum and curbed their criticism of the establishment and its policies. As in times of war, the rise of terrorism in major Israeli cities caused Israeli discourse to revert to positioning Israelis as an enlightened people who wish to live in peace, as compared to the Palestinians who are violent and primitive.[66] Thus, a new national solidarity emerged, and the optimism engendered by the impending peace agreement yielded to a new consensus as to the role of the Israeli defense forces. A good example of this change can be found in an interview with Yehoshua in 2008, a year after the publication of *Friendly Fire* and shortly after the publication of his collection of essays *Ahizat moledet* (Homeland Grasp), where he presents his views on the Palestinians' morality. "We have our own moral codes, they have their own moral codes [. . .] they can send people to blow themselves up. [. . .] they kill their brothers, they kill their own people,"[67] stated Yehoshua, and painted an unoptimistic picture of a two-state solution. Yehoshua naturally wants to end the Occupation, and he calls for efforts to find a political solution that will divide the land between Jews and Arabs; however, he admits that "I do not know if this is a cruel occupation [. . .] in my view there is proportion to the occupation. I will not refer to the occupation in Nazi terminology."[68] Thus, while Yehoshua criticized the Zionist solidarity in times of war in his early writings, in *Early in the Summer of 1970* but also in *The Lover* (1977), he later tempered his criticism both in his writings and in the mass media.

Yehoshua was not the only author to temper his ideological position, and he can be compared to the two other most important authors in this context: Amos Oz and David Grossman. Since Yehoshua and Oz belong to the same literary generation, it is useful to examine the similarities with Oz's current writings. Like Yehoshua's text, Oz's latest works contrasts with his earlier writing, which was highly critical of the Zionist project in general and the father-son relationships in particular, as can be seen in "Navadim va-tsefa" (Nomads and a Viper), "Derekh ha-ruah" (The Way of the Wind), which both appeared in *Artsot ha-tan: sipurim* (Where the Jackals Howl, 1965), and *Michael sheli* (My Michael).

Literary criticism of Oz's most recent texts follow the same lines as critics raised against Yehoshua. These accusations reached their peak with his novel *Sipur al ahava ve-hoshekh* (A Tale of Love and Darkness, 2002).[69] Oz's 2002 novel portrays a dialectical relationship between the two narratives. The first is an autobiographical narrative that describes his parents' lives, his attempts to understand his mother's suicide, and his examination of his personal struggle for identity. The second is the national narrative, which, as Oz himself noted, tries to understand "who brought us here. Why we came here. What would have happened if we had not come here."[70] However personal, Oz's text presents pivotal facets of the Israeli experience, including the Holocaust and the events of 1948 war, as well as extensive details on Jewish-Palestinian relations that reflect the new consensus in Israeli culture. In one of the scenes, for instance, in the midst of the celebration after the United Nations' vote to create the State of Israel, Oz's father pleads persistently with his son to look, to remember, and to tell the next generations about the national miracle:

> Just you look, my boy, take a very good look, son, take it all in, because you won't forget this night to your dying day and you'll tell your children, your grandchildren and your great-grandchildren about this night when we're long gone.[71]

Oz's text, despite its description of the traumatic past and the alienation of his parents' generation, eventually fulfills its mission and internalizes national solidarity.[72] However, like Yehoshua, Oz's transition, from a critical to a more accepting position, does not imply a return to the fathers' generation (to values espoused by the *Palmah* generation), but rather a different approach to solidarity. In their later works, both authors prefer to shore up solidarity, as fathers or grandfathers of Hebrew literature, and seem to have taken on a social, national role.

David Grossman is another excellent example, though more controversial. Grossman is a member of the interim generation (between the literary generation of the 1960s and the literary generation of the 1980s and the 1990s). In his book *Isha borahat mi-bsora* (To the End of the Land, 2008), Grossman criticizes the myth of sacrifice. In this novel, Ora, the mother, prefers to flee rather than wait for the bad news that she is convinced will soon be delivered to her doorstep about her son's death. She believes that only those prepared for sacrifice, who are anticipating it, will actually receive the dire news. By taking flight, she hopes that the message will not find her (unlike Yehoshua's protagonist in *Early in the Summer of 1970*, who was very willing to receive the massage).

Grossman thus introduces the mother figure, who refuses to be complicit, into the masculine story of the *akeda*. She flees from the national demand of sacrifice but her flight takes her to the Israel National Trail (a hiking trail that extends the length of Israel), which symbolically suggests conquering and reconquering and, in fact, stakes her claim to possession of the land, a Zionist possession. Furthermore, the whole complex family, the dual fathers, the circumstances of childhood and adolescence, are tied to Israel's wars and actually stem from them. Thus, Grossman's text has an inherent unresolved tension: on one hand, he takes issue with the sacrificial myth, yet on the other he shepherds into being a powerful validation of nationalist values through the furrows of the land and the solidarity of its citizens.[73]

The myth of national bereavement, which is one of the pillars of the history of Zionism, can thus serve as a motif for illustrating literature and cultural phenomena. In the case of Yehoshua, it provides an aesthetic, social, and political mirror for the changes that have taken place over the four decades of his writing and serves as the core for a broader analysis of fathers and sons in Israeli literature, and the unsettled role of being an Israeli writer. These changes may have led Yehoshua to adopt different stances when writing about the Israeli condition, as is discussed in chapter six on *A Woman in Jerusalem.*

CHAPTER 5

Orly Castel-Bloom between the Two Intifadas

Elizabeth Grosz is often quoted for her comment that "the body must be regarded as a site of political, cultural, and geographical inscriptions, production, or constitution. The body is not opposed to culture, a resistant throwback to a natural past; it is itself a cultural, *the* cultural, product."[1] Grosz argues that metaphor can bring this notion to the forefront better "than the mechanistic ones which have dominated the history of philosophy."[2]

Orly Castel-Bloom is a prime example of an author who implements these kinds of metaphors in her writing. Her "extreme poetics," which turned her into one of the leaders of the "new style" of contemporary Hebrew literature in the 1980s and 1990s,[3] radically violates harmony, unity, and value and provocatively raises social and political questions, by depicting controversial relationships between the body and its physicality, and the political and ideological.[4]

Castel-Bloom's works have been examined intensively in scholarly literature. This chapter presents her unique literary take on the concepts of borders, occupation, militarism, and terrorism, and outlines the manner in which she deterritorializes the Zionist space and uses the body as a metaphor to illustrate political perplexity, questions core values, and voices virulent criticism during a critical time in the nation's history. Specifically, it presents a parallel investigation to the previous chapter, which compared two works of the same author to reveal a shift in political and ethical attitudes. I discuss *Dolly City*, published in 1992, which examines motherhood and its role in the Zionist narrative, and *Halakim enoshiyim* (Human Parts), published in 2002, whose title describes both the bloody result of a suicide bombing and the fragmented lives of the individuals in the story. The differences between these two novels reflect a change in general attitude, and prompt an analysis of the role of the author in society.

Dolly's World

The world of *Dolly City* is constructed from bits of cultural images, pieces of modern myths, and shards of decontexualized signs. Dolly the city does not refer to an actual city, but to a twilight zone of the Western urban-grotesque experience, which alludes to places that may be found in Tel Aviv such as the Carmel Market and Hilton Beach, along with places such as the Thames River, fountains that urinate in an arc, and a memorial called Dachau. Dolly City suffers from extreme weather. Sometimes it is scorching hot, but at other times the cold is so bad that "birds froze in mid-flight and fell down like a stone."[5] It is a futuristic city, in which "cable cars, steam engines, express trains, ships, trams, airplanes, automobiles, trucks, motorbikes—they all crisscrossed each other, collided with each other thousand times."[6] *Dolly City* pushes the reader's doubts to the extreme, since there is no certainty in any single sentence. As Smadar Shiffman notes:

> We do not know what, if anything, "actually" happens in the novel, and what is simply a figment of Dolly's hyperactive imagination. We do not know which events are parts of the plot, and which of them are to be read symbolically. [. . .] The plot is deconstructed time and again when it takes impossible turns; [. . .] innovative uses of language create doubts concerning its function and authority.[7]

Dolly City is a limitless example of the grotesque, since it focuses on the body and its organs, blurs the boundaries between the body and its surroundings, and invokes emotional disorientation by the unresolved clash of the horrid and repulsive with a comic element.[8] The nightmarish events and the extreme violence in the text have the same status as the everyday, normal, possible, justifiable, and even obvious narrative elements.[9] The many horrific descriptions and the banal language depicting them lulls the reader into a sense of complacency, since these acts have no apparent repercussions.

Despite Baruch Blich's claims, this trivialization of horror should not be seen as "permission to prefer anarchy, cruelty, disgust, a shattering of borders, randomness and a great deal of pointlessness in everyday behavior."[10] Nor is it the case, as Tzvia Ben-Yosef Ginur argues, that Castel-Bloom prefers the grotesque over writing satirical concrete criticism.[11] Castel-Bloom's distorted and impossible worlds, with their collapsing oppositions between real and imagined, sanity and insanity, human awareness and robotic behavior, may seem devoid of meaning and values. Yet these worlds are the vital condition for any form of moral inquiry. Adi Ophir points out that the constant disruptions in the text and the neutralization of its authoritative dimension create a constant subversion that enables active reading and criticism.[12] In an ideological context, Karen Grumberg notes that "the aesthetics of the grotesque offers interpretive possibilities for acknowledging the violence of contemporary society."[13]

The Mother and the Map

Dolly City plays with geographic and historic images and symbols to create deterritorialization so as to create a rift between map and identity, and to reveal the hollowness and the misuse of the map. In order to do so Castel-Bloom engages with Jewish history and the *akeda* myth. The bonding between people and God appears from the first pages of the novel when a goldfish dies. Following its death, Dolly, the narrator, fishes it out of the tank, slices it into strips (though it keeps slipping from her fingers on the kitchen counter), cooks it briefly, and eats the pieces. The cooking and eating of the fish in the first scene of the novel immediately take on symbolic significance:

> Then I looked at the pieces. In very ancient times, in the land of Canaan, righteous men would sacrifice bigger animals than these to God. When they cut up a lamb, they would be left with big, bloody, significant pieces in their hands, and their covenant would mean something.[14]

The death and sacrifice of the goldfish are the foundation of the entire book, which to a large extent has a cyclical structure. After the fish dies,

Dolly looks at her dying dog and finally decides to give it a lethal injection. She has a similar reaction to the baby she finds in the dog undertaker's car, but she decides not to kill him, only because she is sure that the baby is so weak that he will die before the day is over. Even after Dolly begins to develop maternal instincts, she continues to ceaselessly endanger the baby's life, either through the scientific experiments she conducts on him or through her fear that she might throw him out of the window,[15] and she maintains a clear but twisted ideology. Dolly is simultaneously a mother and a doctor, who gives life and saves lives, but she is also a threat, a terminator, who is willing to sacrifice a child in the name of God, Country, or any other ideology. She tries to protect the tiny baby she finds in the garbage from the harmful world around it out of a desperate motherly care, and sacrifices herself daily, like characters in fairy tales, to ensure the baby's survival in a crazed city and a hostile world. But anxiety and aggression toward herself, the baby, and other family members, dead and alive, cause her to perform scientific experiments on him, cut him up to examine his internal organs, dissect him, give him medication for diseases he does not suffer from, and even scorch his skin and flesh here and there, for kicks. The son survives this torture, and at the end of the novel even saves his mother from attempted suicide and puts her in a retirement home, when she is forty-five.

Unlike many minor characters in the novel, who meet their demise as a result of Dolly's generous help, such as the caretaker who tortures the body of the dog he was supposed to bury, the locksmith thrown to the hungry Arabs on the bottom floors of a 400-story tower, the baby she gives birth to on the plane and the one she gives birth to in a women's prison, the daughter of the national airline employee who wants an abortion, the cancer-stricken woman in a cafe, and Macmillan, who tries to help Dolly find her son when he runs away, Dolly's son, Ben (literally son), grows up big and strong and enrolls in the Brutal Seamanship Military Academy. In the last scene of the novel, Dolly sees his picture in the paper as a suspect in a failed hijacking of the plane of a fictitious Israeli airline, B.OFF.

Dolly's motherhood is constructed on the representation of motherhood through Western culture, from Medea to Mary, and makes use of archetypes of the Big Mother from mythology to the present day.[16] However, above all, Dolly is an Israeli Jewish mother, who, according to Shiffman, "tends to paradoxically combine two contradictory aspects: on the one hand, the Mother is the familiar, well known Jewish mother, nurturing, caring, self-effacing and adoring: on the other hand, Israeli Jewish mothers are harnessed to the national effort."[17] As a Jewish mother, a version of the loving and overprotective "yiddisher mama," she glues her son to her back to keep him close to her. She vaccinates him against all diseases simultaneously, ceaselessly examines his heart and kidneys, and does not hesitate to perform open heart surgery on him, give him a kidney transplant, and even give him chemotherapy drugs for cancer. She does this repetitively, trying constantly to cure him, but in fact damaging him. But throughout his healing process, she also strives for Jewish justice. When Dolly discovers that her son is missing a kidney, she desperately searches for suitable prospective kidney donors:

> The decision to fly with the child to Düsseldorf, Germany, in order to obtain a kidney for him from a German baby, was made on purely *moral grounds*. At first I thought in practical terms. Where, I thought, could I kidnap a baby and remove his kidney without anyone giving a damn? [. . .] Then I thought: An Arab baby—they hate us; we hate them. [. . .] But then I frowned. Everybody knows that you can't mess with Arabs; even talking to them is dangerous and if you turn your back on them, you're dead. And then I sat and thought about the history of mankind. Of all the people ever lived, who were the most swinish—which of them had broken all the records? [. . .]
>
> It was no skin off my teeth—I wouldn't lose any sleep if I took some German baby from an orphanage in Düsseldorf and cut out his kidney and donated it to my son. On the contrary, *I felt a sense of vocation*.[18]

The thread of Dolly's thoughts is constructed causally as though her entire goal is to be moral, and that is why she seriously considers how to save her son while preserving justice in the world. Who should make the sacrifice? Who should be the target of revenge? How should justice be rendered to the Jewish people? She comes to the realization that taking a kidney from a German baby is the right moral act, and even feels a sense of calling. Nevertheless, Dolly's actions and her moral considerations do not occur in a moral vacuum, since in the anti-anti-Semitic quarter in the city of Dolly City, Holocaust survivors crucify a different non-Jew every day.

"All the trains in Dolly City hurtled to Dachau and back again,"[19] says Dolly, but then explains that they do not travel to *that* Dachau, the historic one, but to a place with a monument called Dachau. Dolly embodies the history of the Jewish people—"I wandered from field to field [. . .] like the Israelites wandering from place to place throughout the long years of exile."[20] Her world is committed to history. This commitment is part of Dolly the mother, and, grotesquely, it becomes part of her son's anatomy. In the scene that became the most famous passage from the novel, Dolly depicts a new covenant and the possible binding between her son and her twisted perception of Zionist ideology:

> The baby was still lying on his stomach. I put him to sleep, even though I still didn't know where I was going to cut. [. . .] I took a knife and began cutting here and there. I drew a map of the Land of Israel—as I remembered it from the biblical period—on his back, and marked in all those Philistine towns like Gath and Ashkelon, and with the blade of the knife I etched the Sea of Galilee and the Jordan River which empties out into the Dead Sea [. . .] drops of blood began [welling] up in the river beds cutting across the country. The sight of the map of the Land of Israel amateurishly sketched on my son's back gave me a frisson of delight [. . .] my baby screamed in pain but I stood firm [. . .] I contemplated the carved-up back: it was a map of the Land of Israel: nobody could mistake it.[21]

Dolly breaks "the boundary between private and public," to use Grumberg's phrasing.[22] Her body, and the body of her son, turn into an ideological construction. This instance of extreme violence may be the key to the ethical point the author is trying to make. By carving, Dolly replaces the *Brith* (circumcision) undergone by every Jewish male baby with another, explicit *Brith*—not between the boy and God, but between the boy and the map, between himself and national destiny.

In his essay on "Place and Men" in Hebrew literature, Schwartz examines the difference between the concept of the *akeda* in Amos Oz's and A. B. Yehoshua's stories from the 1960s and Castel-Bloom's from the 1990s. He argues that while Oz and Yehoshua created a parody of distorted reality, Castel-Bloom employs a postmodern comic fetish, to show how the kernel of the Zionist narrative is in fact a "dead story."[23] However, by showing that these narratives are no more than Zionist clichés, Castel-Bloom does not abandon the role of the author as critic. Rather, through the disparity between Dolly's position and that of the "implied author," the novel levels sharp ideological criticism. From Dolly's perspective, the act of carving corresponds to full identification with the idea that a Jewish mother should raise her son so that his body can serve national military aims, the first of which is the defense of the borders of Eretz Yisrael. Yet the narrative, through the implied author, does not endorse Dolly's views and highlights Dolly's twisted logic. Thus, carving the map of Eretz Yisrael in blood on the boy's back in its radicality constitutes an act of subversion on two levels: it presents the image of the map in its violent context, and it relates to the founding myth of the *akeda*.

In the political reality of Israel, a map is an authoritative way of establishing facts on the ground. The map supplies a direction, a description, and a presentation of the past, and aims to provide a blueprint for the future.[24] The map of Eretz Yisrael includes various borderlines, both past and present. It supplies a visual representation that is inherently removed from the actual geography and the people influenced by it. It is a model devoid of details or violence. Castel-Bloom, as Hannan Hever points out, refuses to "suppress the violence embedded in the occupation of the national space." In contrast to most Israeli writers, she exposes the violence by choosing to concentrate on the private body, rather than the collective territory. "The body itself," continues Hever, "reads as a text of violent acts, thus transgresses the national narratives and their concealment of collective violence."[25] By carving the map of Eretz Yisrael in the boy's flesh, Dolly explicitly expresses the human body's insertion within irredeemable national aspirations. This is just one (extreme) way to raise him as a soldier in the national army.

Dolly monitors her son's body, from the moment of his infancy, to be sure he is strong. She measures and weighs him and records the data on a growth chart;[26] even when he is very young she discusses his combat profile with her mother; when he is sick, she says he needs a "few days' sick leave" using the word *gimelim*,[27] the army terminology. Later when he joins the Academy of Brutal Seamanship she is proud of him when he sends "Polaroid snapshots of himself waving the Israeli flag on the open sea, or standing at attention during the morning parade on the floating school."[28] She keeps these photos, knowing that "maybe one day I'll stick them into an album for him,"[29] a phrase that can be interpreted as a memorial. In fact, Dolly's path as a mother of a child raised for the army is paved with bereavement in its horizon. There will always be someone who will remind Dolly that:

> You have to remember your child may die in battle. He may die in battle—you've got to get that into your head [. . .] you have to get it into your head that he may even die of cancer, but it's reasonable to assume that if he dies soon, it will be in battle [. . .] and then, if he does die in battle, you'll be a bereaved mother—just as if you die, he'll be an orphan.[30]

Castel-Bloom shows Dolly's radical internalization of the myth of national bereavement and its link to the *akeda*, but does so in a different way than A. B. Yehoshua. The founding myth of sacrifice is related to a religious context, as when she cuts up the fish in the first episode of the novel. But she is willing to go beyond this context. As discussed in the previous chapter, criticism of the founding myth of the *akeda* strengthened from the 1960s onward. For instance, the poet Yitzhak Laor called upon the biblical Isaac not to trust his father and reject the threat of being sacrificed for a cause that is not only unheroic, but also immoral. In one of his controversial poems, Laor turns to the Hebrew mother who is destined for bereavement. As he writes in the beginning of the poem:

> Show mercy on your son and do not trust the merciful. How alone
>   are you and your son
> in your teeth like a cub and the merciful does not even have advice
>   about what to do
> on the day your son will be of age to go to the army
>
> please, don't rely on the support of the wailers, because who else
>   but you
> knows your anonymous motherhood, before it wins
> cannibalistic fame over the open grave
>
> and while your son still lives, creep into his bed, quietly, tear
>   his flesh
> harm his eyes, break his thighbone anything so they won't want him
> forgive the mercies of the merciful poets [. . .][31]

Laor's poem is suggestive of Dolly's attitude toward her son; however, although Dolly tears her son's flesh, her rationale differs from the one Laor proposes. He tells a mother to harm a healthy body to prevent the son from going to war; the mother, in his poem, faces a cannibalistic tribe with an ideology that continuously demands human sacrifice. She can only prevent the death of her son by disfiguring his body. By contrast, Dolly, who carves the map of Eretz Yisrael on her son's back, creates an inverted ideological subversion by affiliating herself with a macabre cannibalistic circle. She wants to play a role in the ideological game. Like the image of the fish sacrifice at the beginning of the work, Dolly simplistically adopts the social code and attempts to replace the sacrificing father with the mother, who is willing to strengthen her son and prepare him, body and soul, to fulfill the purpose for which he was brought into the world. By this extreme adaptation of the myth, the text emphasizes its cruelty and absurdity.

The debate over the *akeda* is intertwined with intergenerational conflict, and specifically the divergence between the parents of the 1948 generation and their sons born in the statehood generation. The fathers preserved the Zionist ideology and institutional power, while the sons sought a different path. In her story, Castel-Bloom presents a new variant on this intergenerational relationship. Dolly's father died of cancer, and Dolly is haunted by this illness. Yet, absurdly, he continues to be a major focal point in her life and in the life of her child. Although she apparently lives by herself, soon after her son is adopted, she finds that her father is behind events affecting her son and his education. For example, after she undergoes a prolonged period of unconsciousness, she is surprised to discover that her child has had a *Brith* without her knowledge. When she tries to figure out who was responsible for the ceremony and the party afterward, including a photo album and a video, she calls the national airline, the B.OFF Company (a fictitious company), where her father worked for thirty-two years before he died.[32] Later she finds out that the B.OFF Company also arranged Ben's bar mitzvah "in the open air in the national park,"[33] and is about to pay for his psychoanalysis. B.OFF, the Israeli National Airline, provides financial support for Ben when he lives with her sister. Later, he joins the academy of Brutal Seamanship with the encouragement of the B.OFF Company. Finally, Dolly discovers that "my father had not left all his money to the society for War against Cancer, but had left some also for the naval training of my son, when he was born" and to "cover the expenses of the child's education."[34]

Dolly fights with the representatives of the B.OFF Company throughout the novel, because she feels that they control her life and the life of her son. Apparently, she wants to revolt against the institutional power of the father's generation, but in fact she adheres to their ideology completely.

She tries to raise her child as a Jew who is willing to strengthen his body and dedicate himself to the battle.

Her full acceptance and internalization is manifested in another episode in the novel. While her father is dying of cancer and she sits at his bedside, her father tells her: "Oh, Dolly, you have no *but* [goal, in French] in life. . . . Study something—study medicine—in Katmandu if you like, as long as you study."[35] Dolly does not understand that his reference to medicine is indirect, as is his reference to Katmandu, and she goes there to study medicine.

This exchange sheds light on Dolly's personality and can explain the ways she internalizes ideology. Throughout the entire novel, Dolly takes things at face value and does what is apparently expected of her. She lacks critical awareness and cannot understand indirect, suggestive, or allegorical speech. This is why she accepts the ethical viewpoints of her surroundings, and primarily the ideology of her father's generation, without hesitation. She follows the fantasy of avenging Nazis and their henchmen and views the killing of German babies as a calling; she accepts the picture of Jewish-national sacrifice and is willing to defend the whole of Eretz Yisrael with her son's blood. Thus, Dolly's deviation from her father's ideology does not take the form of being more critical (unlike many texts by A. B. Yehoshua), but rather the opposite. Not only does Dolly accept the concept of national sacrifice but in her variant it is more violent, cruel, and banal; she illustrates an absurd submission to ideology.

Dolly's seeming insanity may offer a certain excuse for her inverted interpretation. Many novels, throughout the history of literature, have depicted insane protagonists and created a disparity between the character's understanding of the world and the narrative voice (the implied author), as a way to formulate social criticism. However, in this text Dolly is only one example of an entire society that shares the same twisted ideological ideas.

Her sister, who takes her child and is supposed to save him, opens a shelter for children, but this shelter is financed by the B.OFF Company, so she "brings the kids up and the ones she recommends undergo aptitude tests to see if they're suitable to work at B.OFF."[36] When she takes in Dolly's child, she in fact is "confiscating him"[37] for a national cause. Again, the sister is not the only one who works in the industry of raising children for "national causes"; other mothers in the text are mirrors of Dolly. Dolly glues her child to her back, but this does not seem unusual, since there are a lot of mothers "with children stuck to their chests or backs."[38] She has a destructive and violent attitude toward her son, but when she visits the women's prison she discovers that "child murder in Dolly City is folklore."[39]

Illness

Dolly cannot separate herself from the ideological national Moloch, who demands child sacrifice; and the text takes a critical stance toward her. This is also expressed through the metaphor of illness. Illness often points to corruption. In Ben-Ner's *Delusion*, the smell emanating from Holly's body represents his immoral actions. Although he was not aware of it, it is a psychological and physical illness that cannot be cured. Grumberg argues that mental or physical illness is a central metaphor for alienation since it blurs the boundaries between "places of exclusion" and asylum and the normative world.[40] Dolly is both a doctor and a sick individual, but she is not the only one since the whole world seems to be sick, and Dolly the doctor wants to save it through her twisted logic. Dolly believes that the city suffers from cancer. She sees cancerous growths on faces, on the wheels of the buses, on the electricity poles. She sees growths on the trees and the newspapers. The streets are screaming and the terminal tumors are spreading.[41]

The source of the terrible sickness appears to be psychological: she "discovered a new type of phobia in Dolly City—Arabophobia, the fear of Arab."[42] She "had lots of those sufferers" as clients and she suggests they should "fuck Arabs if you're afraid of them. You fuck them and you see that they're not [such] monsters after all; they're just like everybody else."[43] Dolly also recognizes her (and others') mental illness and frames it in political terms:

> Madness is a predator. Its food is the soul. It takes over the soul as rapidly as our armies occupied Judea, Samaria and the Gaza Strip in 1967 . . . and if a state like the State of Israel can't control the Arabs in the territories, how can anybody expect me, a private individual, to control the occupied territory inside me?[44]

Anna Bernard argues that the link between Dolly and Israel is suggestive of the allegorical idea that Zionism is a collective pathology that can be "cured" (or "rehabilitated") by ending the occupation of the Palestinian territories.[45]

It is possible that this is the source of the illness, but while she might want to cure the epidemic, Dolly cannot overcome her madness and the phobia.

After several years during which her son is raised by her sister, Dolly meets him again and is amazed to find that the map of Eretz Yisrael on his back has "returned" to the 1967 borders:[46]

> The map was amazingly accurate and up-to-date; someone had gone over all the lines and expanded them according to the child's growth. I examined the map. One thing stood out—he had returned to the '67 borders. It was beyond belief!
>
> Yes. That's the generation gap for you, I reflected. My mother spits on the Arabs, I look them straight in the eye, and one day my son will lick their asses.[47]

Dolly is surprised at the change undergone by the map carved on her son's back. This change is tantamount to a rebellion by the son against his mother, who represents heritage and nation. Dolly is even alarmed by the "return" to the 1967 borders when her son joins a military academy: "He had returned to the '67 borders. And that's nothing to brag about in a military academy, because it endangers the security of the state."[48]

Dolly is both a patient and a doctor. She is sick and the world around her is sick. She knows Arabophobia has spread and that the Occupation is a predator that creates madness. She also knows that her entire life and the life of her son are controlled by her dead father and his generation, who "spits on the Arabs" and does not let them raise their heads. But she is also a "doctor," trying to cure the entire community, as well as the physical world around her, "the whole world was sick and the whole burden was on *my* shoulders."[49] She is in a state of limbo; she can feel the epidemic around her but she cannot cure herself or the people around her. As with her son's anatomy, the uncompromising repetition of the mending process is always unsuccessful and reeks of malaise. Thus, the novel shows that like a failed magic trick, something at the political, historical, and metaphysical level has gone irrevocably wrong.

From the Anatomy of the Body to the Anatomy of Death

Human Parts by Castel-Bloom marks the shifts from the First Intifada to the Second. It transforms *Dolly City*'s description of Ben's (Son's) scars into a sharp-tongued depiction, amidst the bursts of horror and laughter of the bodies of the dead and the physical and metaphorical scars they leave on others.

Castel-Bloom's *Human Parts* was described by Neri Livne as "the first Hebrew novel written during the time of and about the [Second] Intifada, with its objective reality updated to the level of army radio news flashes."[50] According to Todd Hasak-Lowy, this novel is considered a turning point in Castel-Bloom's writing style.[51] Yaron Peleg termed it "relative new realism."[52] This was her first novel written in the third person—narrated by an external narrator—which takes place in an undisguised Israel, and was her first work that included concrete events and plausible characters. Thus, she constructed a "historicization of the present," as Shiri Goren phrased it, while "creating a pseudo-historical or pseudo-anthropological account of contemporary Israeli life."[53]

The work describes a patchwork of human lives, all trying to survive in an impossible web of economic, military, and physical malaise. The main story line takes place in two locations in the heart of the country: an affluent, bourgeois, Ashkenazi neighborhood in northern Tel Aviv, and an impoverished neighborhood in the city of Lod in central Israel. Liat Dubnov, a resident of Amos Street in Tel Aviv, dies as a result of "Saudi flu," a lethal epidemic sweeping the country, which, according to some, is a product of biological weapons from Saudi Arabia. Her asthmatic brother, Adir Bergson, and his girlfriend, the Ethiopian model Tasaro, are left with the task of managing her assets and real estate. Iris Ventura is a recently divorced friend of the family who lives nearby, who is floundering under the strain of raising three children and even considers becoming Orthodox to qualify for religious charity handouts. She manages to buy a new washing machine and get dental treatment after she is hired by Adir to cook tasteless Jewish food for the guests at Liat's *shiv'ah*, and then arranges her possessions, which include a rare collection of Jewish calendars.

In Lod, the Beit-Halahmi family relationship is shattered after the mother, Kati, talks about the family's poverty on television and elicits the viewers' sympathy. Riding on the wave of the commercial success of her performance, she wants to make a new start in life, leaves the offices where she has worked for years as a cleaning lady, and embarks on a new career. After discovering that she is not entitled to any compensation or payment for her years of cleaning work, she sets a backup plan in motion, gets a large sum of money by extorting an important banker, and enrolls in a school for beauticians. Her husband, Boaz, an Ashkenazi from a small cooperative settlement, whose family disowned him after he married Kati, who is of Kurdish origin, sits at home, unemployed and bitter at the change he sees in his wife. He decides to visit a well-known fortune teller in Jerusalem, who reads coffee grounds, inputs the results into a computer, and encourages him to "pick himself up by his bootstraps." However, the fortune teller fails to foresee that Boaz will die shortly after the visit in an ambush on the road from Jerusalem to the town of Modi'in, on his way home. In macabre twist, the work ends on an optimistic note. The president of Israel, Tekoa, who was supposed to visit the family as an example of poverty but has had to postpone the visit because of the impossible task he has taken upon himself of visiting every funeral and condolence ceremony of every terror victim, can finally meet and console the family at the funeral of the father, Boaz. Now that the head of the family has lost his life in a terror attack, the twins of the Beit Halahmi family will be poor no longer: "at least they'll get Victims of Hostile Actions benefits now. Economically, they're all set."[54]

Human Parts incorporates actual political events including the peace process with the Palestinians, which "collapsed like one of the houses whose roof gave way under the weight of the snow,"[55] and the "death of entire families that went to have pizza" and were killed by a terrorist bombing. All these events are introduced through the television, Internet, and the news media, where all political debates seem hollow:[56]

> Many people said, at first hesitantly and then unabashedly that the government had no partner for dialogue [. . .] "we told you so," crowed those who had always expressed the opinion that there was never any point in talking to their Arab neighbors. "At least we tried," said those hovering in the center of the political map, where shock and disbelief were gradually giving way to disillusionment and somberness. And, for the far left of the political map, it was business as usual with the mantra of "End the Occupation."[57]

The Occupation, which in *Dolly City* was the source of madness, becomes yet another irrelevant slogan as clichéd as the others. This presentation of the political map appears throughout *Human Parts*, with simplistic extreme right-wing slogans such as "stick it to the Arabs good and proper and show them what's what,"[58] "Get it over already and kick the Arabs out of the country for good,"[59] and the opposing clichés of "understand them too"[60] and "admire Israel for its restraint."[61] These catchphrases reflect a culture that does not encourage discussion but only aspires to make headlines and ratings. The average Israeli (in the novel) does not have any opinion on the situation, as exemplified by the character of Adir Bergson, who does not have a solution to the conflict, but thinks that it will take many years until it is resolved: "maybe even thousands."[62]

The novel shows how the media simplify debates, and thus illustrates, as Grumberg suggests, a "fragmented and superficially politicized Israel."[63] While the narrator turns time and again to the news, opinion, and gossip sections of the daily papers to keep readers up-to-date with whatever is going on, the novel appears to depict a country that has chosen to be a slave to the media and escape from the reality of its representations.[64] These descriptions are highly characteristic of the media in contemporary Israel, which until the mid-1980s only operated one main television channel, and experienced a dramatic shift to multichannels and commercial channels that have diluted its themes but return full force to national unity whenever there is a political crisis.

However, although *Human Parts* describes the crazed reality of Israel, which has become a sort of Castel-Bloom-esque form of distorted reality, it is not a realistic work.[65] Shiffman's definition of Castel-Bloom's "sparkling realism"[66] works here as well: on the one hand, the novel has enough realistic components to enable the reader to identify events with Israeli reality, identify with characters who do their best to live in this reality, and see their helplessness. However, on the other hand, the work contains enough "air" to let readers float away to disengage from reality.

The tragedies in *Human Parts* take on apocalyptic proportions. As in *Dolly City*, the Israel of *Human Parts* encounters extreme weather. After seven years of drought, an extreme winter hits the region, with temperatures dropping to around 0 degrees Celsius, and snow even threatens to fall on the coastal cities. But "not only was the sky falling—the ground was trembling too."[67] Due to the unstable security situation and the collapse of the Oslo Accords, the Palestinians carry out daily shooting attacks and suicide bombings, which leave many dead and injured. All the news broadcasts lead with descriptions and pictures of human body parts scattered on the road after the daily attack, and with the accounts of the eyewitnesses, who always begin by saying "suddenly I heard a boom."[68]

Furthermore, the Israeli policy of restraint, as well as the weather, weaken citizens' immune systems and make it difficult to fight the "Saudi flu," which kills one out of every four. The hospitals are full of patients and terror victims, the undertakers are buckling under the workload, and the cemeteries begin to bury the dead in stacks, one on top of another. It is clear that Castel-Bloom's text relates to an actual situation but magnifies and accentuates it, and constructs Israel as a war zone and a natural disaster area, where catastrophe takes on metaphysical proportions. The use of the Hebrew calendar and the fact that many events take place in streets named after prophets (many of them prophets of doom) creates a link between the apocalypse and Jewish history. In this sense, the style of *Human Parts* is close to that of *Dolly City*.

The preoccupation with death replaces the preoccupation with the body in *Dolly City*, but continues to express the same critique of the banality of horror by depicting norms taken to the extreme. The long arm of death reaches out to every character in this work, but the death of one person is not equivalent to the death of another. When Iris Ventura goes to her friend's modest funeral, she sees a massive ceremonial funeral taking place at the other end of the cemetery. This is the funeral of Ziv, a seventeen-year-old from Alfei Menashe, who went missing for a week after taking his dog for a walk. Ziv was stoned to death by Palestinians.[69] Ziv is appropriated by the Zionist ideology, since his death is interpreted as what Harris termed "death for the nation,"[70] whereas the other deaths do not bask in this glory. The difference between the two funerals strikes Nir Bergson, who is grieving for his sister while wishing she had died in a terror attack and not from Saudi flu, because "now he won't be able to write anything dramatic in the obituary, such as May the Lord Avenge Her Blood."[71]

The pains of poverty, disease, and death are described with a touch of parody, which also departs from realism. The descriptions of death and dying are pathetic, despicable, and laden with clichés. For instance, Iris Ventura has an affair with Liat's brother Adir, but understands that their affair is doomed once Adir finds the Ethiopian model Tasaro and starts dating her. Tasaro obviously provides a "good story" "with a national, social and personal plot"[72] that includes her trek to Eretz Yisrael and a history of prostitution in Tel Aviv's Central Bus Station.

Kati Beit Halahmi from Lod also provides a "good story." She and her husband met for the first time in the ER; in the eyes of the media their relationship symbolizes the ingathering of the exiles since he is an Ashkenazi Jew and she is Sephardi. Her story garners even greater success when national components combine the personal and social. After her confession on TV, people respond by sending bags full of clothes and food for herself and her children. In the end, when Kati is presented in the media as a mixture of poverty and bereavement, she utters a ridiculous cliché to the entire nation: we "have to carry on and keep going. We have no other country."[73] Her words aim to create instant identification and an instant sense of belonging and patriotism. These examples confirm Bernard's comment that "If we allow for some distance between Castel-Bloom and her narrator, the nationalist clichés employed here read more like pastiche, bringing the novel into line with Castel-Bloom's previous work."[74]

From *Dolly City* to *Human Parts*

The shift from *Dolly City* to *Human Parts* cannot be described as a movement toward realism, just as it cannot be seen as the relinquishing of extreme poetics. In both novels Castel-Bloom continues to work with the body and to inscribe the political situation on the body. The violence and the blood, in both texts, are described in a bold way. In both texts, the characters who live in this nightmarish reality are somewhat flat and lack critical judgment. Dolly unequivocally accepts the social norms, and in her simplistic thinking even gives them an anatomical expression. The characters in *Human Parts* are comparable to Dolly: they are media-controlled robots who internalize the consensual framework of debate. However, this obliqueness and simple-mindedness constitute the major difference between the two works. Whereas in *Dolly City* the heroine's disorder leads her to try to fix what was broken, *Human Parts* is dominated by a gray and hopeless passivity since nobody wants to fix anything, and in fact, nobody has "a desire to live," but nobody has "any alternative either."[75]

In his essay entitled "Ha-mavet ke-derekh hayim" (Death as the Way of Life) David Grossman writes:

> The horrible thing that's happening to Israelis is that they're getting used to it. They're used to waking up in the morning and hearing about the terrorist attack that occurred at dawn. They're used to the sight of their injured and dead. Used to the stock phrases about the situation, to the formulaic photographs in the news. They've gotten so used to it

> that their emotions sometimes also seem like clichés. Like something that could be put into a computer, a blaring newspaper headline [. . .][76]

This is the situation of *Human Parts*. In *Dolly City*, Dolly tries to defend her son from a sick world, but constantly finds herself in a ceaseless process of repair: she hurts her son and tries to save him, then tries to strengthen him and simultaneously injures him. Although the novel is not realistic and the character is not reliable, it demonstrates the urge to repair, an awareness that something is wrong, recognition that there is a disease. The feeling of being in a world and a society that are terminally ill is also present in *Human Parts*, which is characterized by an apocalyptic image of omnipresent death and a feeling that we are part of history. Castel-Bloom herself said she "hopes that this is not the history of the last generation of the Jewish people living in the country."[77] But unlike *Dolly City*, in *Human Parts* no one tries to overcome or conquer history. There is not a single attempt, however desperate or ridiculous, to remedy or save. Each character tries to survive by adapting to the situation, taking refuge from a hailstorm, walking suspiciously down the street and avoiding any gathering that might prove fatal, quietly burying the dead and happily receiving the state's condolences and money if the death was a result of a terrorist attack.

Castel-Bloom's Moral Compass

From the start, Castel-Bloom, who is considered to have applied shock treatment to the most treasured myths of contemporary Israel, responded to a social and cultural need. In addition to her unwavering artistic honesty,[78] she succeeded, according to David Gurevitz, "to cure, through shock, a series of political and personal ills."[79] In an interview, Castel-Bloom commented on her writing as follows:

> In this world, which pulverizes and seemingly exhausts you, values must ceaselessly find new ways of expression [. . .] it's not my writing which is inhumane, it's the street, the office, the state of affairs [. . .] people are attacking my books, saying that I'm anti-Zionist, that my books strive to demolish what's already been gained, that I describe chaos, or even hell. Unfortunately, these people think that they've got the Jewish conscience by the horns. They think they have a monopoly on Hebrew, that their generation has long ago solved the identity problems of the new Israeli,

> and that there are some questions that should not be revisited [. . .] for me this is the artist's freedom, which comes with the strong faith that I have within me a moral clock, which is ticking away.[80]

Both *Dolly City* in 1992 and *Human Parts* in 2002 are obsessively preoccupied with the body and its organs, and with sickness and death as powerful elements in reversing the social system of values and norms. Through her grotesque metaphors of the nonindividual, living, dying, vacillating body, Castel-Bloom strived to formulate a critique of contemporary Israeli experience. It is clear that these novels mirror the periods in which they were written. Hasak-Lowy noted that in the First Intifada "nonlethal violence was the primary means of resistance to the Israeli occupation," while in the Second Intifada suicide bombers created fear among Israelis in major cities and caused the Israeli public to view "itself as the unfair target of unrelenting Palestinian intransigence and violence."[81] This situation led, according to Peleg, to a state of melancholy.[82] The previous chapter discussed the shift in the writings of A. B. Yehoshua in response to the disarray in the ranks of the Left at the time of the Second Intifada; Castel-Bloom wrote in a different style to show the same pattern. While she is highly critical in both novels, she reveals the changes in national temperament. Hence it is clear why *Dolly City* expressed much stronger condemnation and activism, whereas *Human Parts* emphasized confusion and passivity.

Both texts express, as she phrases it, a "moral clock." Both show the failure of Israeli society to cope with the political situation, but in different ways. The first focuses on the deleterious consequences of the ideological Moloch and demands a cure for the illness (the Occupation), knowing that no cure is in fact possible; the second describes passivity and despair. In *Dolly City,* Castel-Bloom voices uncompromising criticism of the Occupation and the issue of borders, and takes a blunt, provocative, and active approach through the character of Dolly. In *Human Parts,* written ten years later, during a time of economic recession and political crisis, bereavement and terror, she presents a more passive picture that describes the oppressive sensation of Israeliness that moves from moral decay to great fear, passivity, and submission. Instead of reacting to corruption or longing for a different political reality, the characters submit themselves to the current situation while focusing on their personal struggles, and prefer to look at the world through the eyes of the media and let their fear turn them into puppets on the historical and political stage.

CHAPTER 6

Terrorism and the Face of the Dead Other

In 2015, Zeruya Shalev, a well-known Hebrew author, published a novel entitled *Ke'ev* (Pain). The novel is about Iris, a school principal, who lives with her husband and two children in Jerusalem, and meets her past love by chance. This new encounter upends her entire world and forces her to reinterpret her past and present. The title of the book relates to a terrorist attack that took place ten years previously, in which Iris was injured. Since then, Iris has suffered from terrible pain that no one can cure. In despair she decides to go to the most highly respected specialist in the field, only later to discover that he was her high school boyfriend. Although Shalev's novel was not written within the timeline of this book and will not be discussed in detail, it expresses the dramatic effects of terrorism that became part of everyday life in Israel. Although the novel is not engaged with political issues, and the main story revolves around love and choices people make in their lives, terrorism and its trauma permeate the book.

Terror attacks and scenes of bombings form the core of the two novels discussed in this chapter. Shifra Horn's novel *Himnon la-simha* (Ode to Joy) and A. B. Yehoshua's novel *Shlihuto shel ha-memune al mash'abei enosh* (A Woman in Jerusalem), both published in 2004 during the al Aqsa Intifada, engage with the traumatic consequences of a terror attack in the heart of Jerusalem. The routine lives of the protagonists in both novels are disrupted by the bombing, and they are jettisoned into a personal journey when they encounter one of the anonymous victims, a casualty who is a total stranger.

Horn's and Yehoshua's novels relate to the Intifada and the Israeli political situation, yet they seem to focus on incidents tangential to the conflict. Their depiction of the impact of the conflict on Israeli civilians provides an opportunity to discuss the ways in which it affects daily life. Unlike works that examine the relationships between the home front and the battlefront through discussions of parents and their children, who are soldiers or supposed to be soldiers, in these texts the soldiers are strikingly absent, and rather than dealing with the military, politics, and ideology, they examine the situation in a new way. These works offer an ethical view focused on the relationship between two people through the image of the face. To better understand the implications of this approach, this chapter suggests a reading of Horn's and Yehoshua's novels based on Emmanuel Levinas's concept of face-to-face relationships with the Other. It deals with the notion of ethical responsibility, and the question of responsibility toward the dead Other in these novels. I show how these themes are intertwined with spatial context, specifically by the act of leaving a known space and entering unknown territories to understand and develop responsibility for the Other. These ethical explorations, hence, provide a new take on the context of the Intifada.

On Levinas and Otherness

In 1948, in his early essay entitled "Reality and Its Shadow," French philosopher Emmanuel Levinas articulated his approach to art. Like Plato's criticism of representational art in the *Republic*, Levinas condemns art as "the very event of obscuring, a descent of the night, an invasion of shadow."[1] He rejects ontological claims that art is something that can provide knowledge: "art does not belong to the order of revelation. Nor does it belong to that of creation"; it "moves in just the opposite direction."[2] He states that art creates images that should not be trusted, that "impose themselves on us without our assuming them"[3] without our consent. It produces illusions, which act like a sleight-of-hand; they are distorted and deceiving by nature.

Levinas's ethical project is a criticism of Western philosophy, which he condemns in *Totality and Infinity* as the "imperialism of the same."[4] The subject's search for coherent structures of meaning leads to subordinating the particular to the general and reducing the unknown to the framework of "sameness."[5] This reduction also occurs in relationships between two people, when one person approaches the other and tries to know and comprehend him/her. In Levinas's thinking, ethical relations are based on a face-to-face encounter with another person. They do not depend on knowledge or understanding, but instead involve a welcoming of the unknown and the incomprehensible.

In "Reality and Its Shadow" Levinas argues that the power of art to recruit the imagination in ways that involve deep emotional engagement with the artwork neutralizes real relationships (the actual world) and invokes blindness and passivity, which thus may impede the possibility of ethical relationships between the self and the other.[6] However, this objection is only one layer of Levinas's attitude toward art. His writings on literature are ambivalent as to whether literature fosters or undermines ethical thought.[7] Nevertheless, despite all his reservations regarding the problematic power of art and literature, books were an important part of Levinas's childhood. Pushkin, Gogol, Dostoevsky, and Tolstoy were part of his basic education, and literature influenced his philosophy. In *Time and the Other*, written in 1947, he admits that "it sometimes seems to me that the whole of philosophy is only a meditation on Shakespeare."[8] Levinas wrote several essays on literary texts that appear in the collection *Proper Names* (originally published in 1975). Unlike his comments regarding the misleading nature of artwork, in this collection he shows that literature indeed "cast us up upon a shore where no thought can land."[9]

In Levinas's essay on S. Y. Agnon, "Poetry and Resurrection," published in 1973, he suggests that the essence of art can be found "between the lines—in the intervals of time, between times—like a footprint that would precede the step, or an echo preceding the sound of a voice."[10] He focuses on Agnon's short story "The Sign," which combines the memories of Holocaust victims with a dreamlike episode in an abandoned synagogue where he meets the eleventh-century Andalusian Hebrew poet Ibn Gabirol, but forgets his poem. Levinas sees the power of Agnon's text to go beyond "the anecdotal or social curiosities, the narrative or fictive element which it is sought,"[11] to a place "older than Saying, by which the non-sense of death is put in question, by which the resurrection begins in death itself."[12] Levinas reads literature between the lines and "between times," focusing not only on the possibility of encountering the Other, but also as a way "to call us back to error,"[13] confront death, and reveal the "tragic affirmation in face of the horror of being."[14]

Yael, the protagonist and narrator of Horn's *Ode to Joy*, is a married mother and a doctoral candidate in anthropology, investigating the mourning customs of the Ultra-Orthodox community in Jerusalem. Her life changes when she finds herself in the midst of a terrorist bombing. A few minutes before the explosion, she is in her car, waiting for the bus ahead of her to leave the bus station. While waiting, she plays peekaboo with a little blonde girl who waves to her from the rear window of the bus. As she bends down to hide during the game, she hears an explosion and then sees its deadly consequences. Crouching down in fact saves Yael's life, but the trauma leaves its mark and Yael continues to see the face of the little girl and obsessively tries to find out more about her.

Yehoshua's protagonist, who is not named and is simply called "the human resources manager," works in a well-known bakery in Jerusalem. One evening he is asked by the bakery owner to handle the affairs of a non-Jewish immigrant named Yulia Ragayev, who was badly injured in a suicide bombing and died alone in the hospital. While trying to identify her in the hospital, a pay stub from the bakery was found in her belongings. A scandal-sheet journalist plans to reveal how she was "abandoned" in an article entitled the "Inhumanity behind our Daily Bread." Just before he releases the article for publication, he asks the bakery owner for his comments. The human resources manager finds himself on a journey through Jerusalem: he goes to Yulia's apartment to collect documentation, visits the hospital morgue in the middle of the night, and then travels with her coffin to Eastern Europe to arrange her funeral. Although he has absolutely no recollection of even interviewing her for a job, the human resources manager gradually attempts to discover who she was.

Both Horn's and Yehoshua's protagonists encounter a stranger, who strays fleetingly across the trajectory of their lives and elicits their attention and responsibility. The novels illustrate their encounter with the Other and examine the protagonists' mental and spatial journey toward taking responsibility for individuals who became significant to them only after their deaths.

The Encounter

"Since the upheaval I went through on that Sunday morning, the 20th of January, 2002, my life hasn't been the same and the new one dictated to me has never returned to normal,"[15] admits Yael, Horn's protagonist, on the first page of the novel. Saturday, the day before the encounter, was "a thousand years earlier" for her.[16] The incident with the little girl intertwines with the bombing scene, which is powerfully portrayed in the novel. It is preceded by a frightening prophecy by her friend Louisa, who predicts that "tomorrow there's going to be a horrendous storm, the end of the world."[17] In the morning, as Yael is driving to work "lightning flashed and thunder rolled and like a thousand drums warning of impending danger the fat raindrops drummed on the window."[18] Along with the sound of the rain and the thunderstorm, she listens to *Ode to Joy* (Beethoven's Ninth Symphony) that is being played on the radio. The rain and the sound of the music allow the girl and Yael to play a silent game of gestures. She sees the child smile as she bends down under the wheel before popping up again.

> "Peekaboo! Peekaboo!" and my call was answered by a dull drum roll followed by a blinding flash of lightning and all hell was let loose, and my car was rocked from side to side, "And the people saw the sound and the lightning and the mountain smoking." With difficulty I straightened up and the steering wheel hit the back of my neck and the sweet little head that had peeped out in front of me disappeared, the daylight turned into darkness [. . .] In the terrible silence that suddenly fell after the noise, I heard the "Ode to Joy" enthusiastically sung by the choir on my car radio.[19]

This cosmic explosion is followed immediately afterward by a terrible silence. For Yael, it was "a second in life when everything fell apart,"[20] "a trauma" as her psychologist friend Nechama insists on calling it, "an accident" according to her mother, "a disaster," as her friend Louisa sees it. Yet, it was also a moment of miracle: although the bus burst into flames, she was found and pulled out of her wrecked car with almost no injuries, saved by the game. This miracle/trauma/accident/disaster is crystallized in the unforgettable image of the face of the little girl that disappears a minute later: "Ever since that little girl had vanished in smoke and flame, before my eyes, my life had been radically changed."[21]

The face of the Other is a major component of Levinas's work, which is based on the concept of an alterity that cannot be conceptualized. He inquires into our commitment and responsibility to the Other as a total stranger, someone who "exceeds the bounds of my knowledge" but "demands acknowledgment."[22] Most people see all realities as elements of "the same," creating a unified self by "shaping the encounter with world as part of the domestic and the familiar";[23] however, Levinas stresses the moment when the Other invades their life. The appearance of the Other shatters subjectivity, destroys their monism and their universe, and does not permit a restoration of any previous order.

In Levinas's "The Trace of the Other" he articulates the first appearance of the Other. The Other's "presence consists in coming unto us, *making an entry*."[24] "A face enters our world from an absolute alien sphere—that is, precisely out of absoluteness, which in fact is the name for fundamental strangeness."[25] This appearance is, in Adriaan Peperzak's words, an earthquake, composed of "infinite surprises, shocks, overwhelms";[26] "the Other comes to the fore and surprises me, disrupts my world, accuses, and refuses my egoism."[27]

Horn's text describes the encounter with the Other as a powerful cosmic-traumatic experience, which is also a miracle. It is a moment when space changes its shape and become unknown, as in a moment of immediate displacement, a deterritorialization when all clear routines and the systems of thought and categorization are shattered. By contrast, in A. B. Yehoshua's text, the first encounter with the Other is not articulated in such dramatic terms. Clearly the circumstances that brought the dead woman into the protagonist's life were terrible, in that she was injured by a terrorist bombing in the Jerusalem open-air market, had fought for her life in the hospital for a few days with no one at her bedside, and even after her death lay the hospital morgue abandoned and unidentified. Nevertheless, Yehoshua suggests that it was not "really such a shocking exposé"[28] since it was the time "when pedestrians were routinely exploding in the streets."[29] However, the human resource manager cannot refuse to take on the mission, and though it is evening and he is about to go home, he accepts the elderly owner's urgency and understands that there is *no choice.*

> And those determined and simple words, "no choice," first announced by the owner would echo within him like a comforting mantra—and not just on that first long, meandering night, by the end of which he was conjuring the dead. No, in the strange days following, too—on the funeral expedition that same weekend to the steppes of a far country—in the hardest moment of indecision, the worst junctures of crisis and uncertainty—he would rally his companions with the same phrase. It

> was like a banner in battle, the beacon from a lighthouse, flickering in the dark to give them courage and direction.[30]

In this passage, the human resources manager sees the mission solely as a troublesome duty that has to be done for the sake of his relationship with the owner of the bakery. Yet, at this moment, which operates as a foreshadowing, the author hints that the mission has a power over the protagonist that will develop throughout the novel.

Yehoshua describes the encounter with the Other differently from Horn: not as a powerful thunderstorm but as a routine, albeit somewhat urgent request from the bakery owner. However, in both texts this encounter with a person who only appears in their lives in the context of death is accompanied by an inevitable call that cannot be dismissed. Like Yael, who did not initiate her encounter with the face of the little girl, the human resources manager did not seek this mission. Nor did he find it interesting or appealing. Nevertheless, even if not from the start, it gradually becomes clear that he had "no choice" but to go on the journey, to actively move out of his safe zone and dedicate himself to a total stranger.

In *Totality and Infinity* Levinas states that "the alterity of the Other does not depend on any quality that would distinguish him from me [. . .] the Other remains infinity transcendent, infinity foreign,"[31] but although the Other cannot be caught within the individual's agonistic framework, his face "imposed on me without my being able to be deaf to its appeal nor to forget it."[32]

Horn's protagonist, Yael, is driven to discover the identity of the little girl. Yehoshua's protagonist tries to collect information on Yulia Ragayev. For both the horror of the terror attack created a rupture in their lives, a kind of deterritorialization that came in the form of "radical discontinuity," to use a term coined by Lee Jarvis.[33]

Yael's research project on the "Burial and Mourning Customs in the Jerusalem Ultra-Orthodox Community" entails spending weeks "in the kingdom of the dead [. . .] I met twenty corpses face-to-face, took part in twenty-nine funerals, visited eleven homes in mourning,"[34] yet the encounter with the little girl shows how self-oriented she was in her research, in that she was dealing with the bereavement of people whom she did not really see or acknowledge.

The human resources manager is in charge of all the employees of the bakery, interviews new workers, and handles their social benefits. As his secretary recalls, "if you didn't notice her when you hired her, that's because you live inside yourself like a snail,"[35] thus suggesting that he is extremely self-centered. Yehoshua gives a name to the dead woman, while all the other characters in the novel are only identified by their professional monikers. Thus, he poses the dead woman as the only defined human being in the text. This clearly invites an allegorical reading, which according to Kartun-Blum recalls morality plays such as *Everyman*, where the characters represent different facets of suffering and redemption.[36] Viewing the text as a modern allegory may thus provide a stronger justification for an ethical reading.

The Face of the Other

"A sweet face of a little girl"[37] is the image that haunts Yael.

> I lay on my back with my eyes closed and saw the little girl whose name I didn't know with her nose pressed against the window and her breath surrounding her face like the halo of a saint in a Christian icon.[38]

This image prompts her to return to the scene of the explosion to attempt to collect some evidence and come to grips with the twists of fate. She has the feeling that "although the little girl was a stranger to me, her death was all mine and I had to know her name and age, discover her parents, and find out where she lived."[39] She goes through the newspapers, searching for indications, reading the names of the victims and their ages, but does not find the little girl. She examines "the photographs of the dead whose names had been released"[40] but does not recognize her. The face, which appears only after death, captivated her but remains unreachable.

Looking and identifying the face involves a mental, but also a physical journey in which Yael leaves her home and goes to unfamiliar spaces to see the Other. This happens when she accompanies her husband when he pays his respects at the *shiv'ah* (seven days of mourning after the death of a family member) of the Wasserstein family, an Ultra-Orthodox family, who lost a mother and child in the explosion. Her husband, a dentist, was asked to identify the dead child whose corpse was severely damaged in the bombing by examining his dental X-rays: "his face had been totally mutilated."[41] Yael goes with her husband to the home of the Wassersteins and is enchanted by their warm greetings and dignity. A few days later, she decides to return to the house of mourning alone. Then the father shows her the picture of his wife and child:

> I saw a happy family, father, mother and son, dressed to the nines, upside down. I turned the photograph over and it suddenly became heavy and I almost dropped it; the eyes of the little girl were looking at me from the silver frame. [. . .] "It's her," I wept, and immediately corrected myself, "It's him." I saw him just a second before it happened. He was sitting in the back seat. I thought he was a girl. [. . .] He was playing with me.[42]

The girl she was looking for was an Ultra-Orthodox boy, Davidl, whose parents, according to Jewish custom, were planning to have his hair cut for the first time in a ceremony on Mt. Meron at the age of three.

The face and its secrets haunts Yehoshua's protagonist as well, and leads to his journey.

> Although there was no need to linger over the snapshot of this forty-eight-year-old woman, her open face and light eyes gave him pause. An exotic arch, northern European or Asiatic, ran from each eyelid to the nose. The neck, exposed in all its perfection, was long and rounded. For a moment he forgot that she was no longer a living being, that nothing was left of her but a bureaucratic indifference to her fate.[43]

Yulia Ragayev's face is also revealed through a journey. Yehuda Shenhav points out that this unique face is given an Oriental depiction,[44] yet escapes any context or categorization.

The power of the face and the moment when the protagonists confront the face, the picture, or the memory of the face, are central to both works. According to Levinas, it is the face that calls for my responsibility, targets me exclusively, without any ability to refuse,[45] without a replacement, and "without waiting for reciprocity."[46] The face is defenseless and vulnerable, "forbids us to kill,"[47] and dictates the primordial imperative "you shall not commit murder."[48] Given his Platonic distrust of visual images, it may seem surprising that Levinas articulates the responsibility for the Other through the concept of the image of the face.[49] Yet, unlike an artificial image, the concept of the face in Levinas is not "reducible to a plastic image, surface, or mask" since it is "always on the move [. . .] confronting the self with its expression, speaking a primordial speech."[50] Ironically, in both novels, these faces are silent evidence of the violation of the imperative that forbids killing a human being.

The faces in Horn's and Yehoshua's novels present the concrete face of an unknown person, imagined through memory and photographs. Although the faces do not make any gestures and are not able to express feeling or distress like the face of a living person, they are not frozen images. Yael sees the face of the little girl/boy at different times and shapes. In her memory, the face of the little girl merges with the face in the picture she found in her own father's secret drawer, a picture of a child he lost in the Holocaust—a child she was not able to replace when she was born: "A yellowish photograph. A lovely little girl of about three wearing a sailor suit smiles at me, her face freckled like mine."[51] The lost face also resonates in the image of her son, who is the same age as Davidl:

> And the child smiled at me and called "peekaboo," and her features suddenly blurred, dissolved and changed, until I found myself looking at Yoavi's face. And my son waved his chubby hands through the rear window of the bus.[52]

In Yehoshua's novel the face is not a still image either. Although the human resources manager has her picture and continues to look at it from time to time, he deliberately avoids opening the coffin or looking at her face and tries to reconstruct it from memory. Thus, in the morgue he refuses "to look at the dead woman, even though her beauty was considered special by all who saw her picture."[53] Later, he thinks about opening the coffin: "Perhaps a close-up view would tell him if the Tatar eyes were real or imagined,"[54] but later feels that he had a "clear notion of what the cleaning woman must have looked like."[55] During the ceremony in her mother's village, he decides not to walk up to the open coffin like everyone: "I didn't look at anything, sir. Nor do I intend to. There's no need. That woman is inside me by now. I even dream about her."[56] By knowing her face without looking at her, the protagonist acknowledges Yulia's absolute alterity.

In both novels the images of the face do not play a figurative role, but rather become the sources of an inner command and journey. The face of the Other calls for a fundamental obligation to open ourselves to the need (and especially the suffering) of another person. Levinas uses the Hebrew word *hineni* ("here am I")—the phrase Abraham and Moses used to answer God when he called them—to express the ultimate responsibility to the Other.[57] Using biblical vocabulary is no accident here. Relating to the concept that humans were created in the image of God, Levinas suggests that God "is not the model of which the face would be an image. To be in the image of God does not mean to be an icon of God, but to find oneself in his trace."[58] According to Levinas the "face is of itself a visitation and transcendence."[59] "The Other is not the incarnation of God, but precisely by his face, in which he is disincarnate, is the manifestation of the height in which God is revealed."[60] The face-to-face relationships with the Other and the ultimate devotion to another person fashion the trace of transcendence, the trace of God. Interestingly, this trace is clearly manifested in the two novels, which confers a divine meaning on the occurrences.

Jerusalem, the holy city, is the location of both Horn's and Yehoshua's novels. Both texts describe the city as a spiritual place, where holiness and prophecy exist alongside political conflicts and terrorist threats. The spatial background weaves a complex web between the known and unknown spaces that serve as a condition to find the Other, since the Other can only be perceived in a state of displacement but is related to the movement of time, memory, history and myth. The first encounter with the face in Horn's text is described as a divine moment of revelation as depicted in Louisa's prophecy, the rain and thunderstorm, the dramatic swell of Beethoven's music, and the sound of the explosion. The chapters of the book are titled according to the story of the creation in Genesis. The first chapter is called "In the beginning" (Genesis I,1), the second, "And there was evening and there was morning, the second day" (Genesis I,8:30), and so forth. The explosion appears at the moment of creation, a moment of radical change, where all the raw material takes shape. It marks the instant of acknowledgment, which is both very intimate and personal, but at the same time has transcendent meaning. It is also symbolic, since the instant of the terrible bombing eventually also fosters the ethical relationships between one person and another.

Yehoshua also endows his story with transcendent meaning. The eighty-seven-year-old owner of the bakery is driven by religious fervor not only to apologize for the loss, but to redeem himself.[61] In his appearance and his dominance over the protagonist, the bakery owner points back to other characters in Yehoshua's works who play "God," like Mr. Kannaout in his short story "Masa Ha-erev shel yatir" (The Yatir Evening Express, 1959).[62] In this early story by Yehoshua, the lives of citizens of the remote village of Yatir revolve around the railroad station, where once a day the express train passes without stopping. When a conspiracy develops to stop the express train from traveling this stretch of track, the supervisor-general, Mr. Kannaout, goes to the village. He is the only one to visit the village from the outside, and he arrives in a flurry of dust and wind, suggesting that he is all-powerful, "nothing escaped his sharp eye," and he "rules with a firm hand."[63] In *A Woman in Jerusalem*, the owner of the bakery is mysterious, awake and asleep at strange hours, is admired by people, and imposes imperatives no one can escape from. Since none of the characters aside from Yulia have names, the novel suggests a kind of allegorical (Christian) reading. The owner is "God," and the journalist is called "the snake" ("nahash" in Hebrew), like the "nahash" in the garden in Eden that seduced Eve to taste the fruit of the tree of knowledge (in the English translation of the novel he is called "the weasel"). As a snake, he appears without warning in different places and "once he sinks his teeth into someone, he won't let go."[64] His intention, in his materialization as a reporter, is to publish a scandalous article about the inhumanity of the bakery who left a worker to die alone. This makes him like the snake in the Garden of Eden, who pretends to be the agent of the differentiation of good from evil.

The journey to Eastern Europe is phrased in Christian terminology. The subtitle in the Hebrew original of the book is "A Passion in Three Parts," and the second part of the book is called "The Mission." The novel's Christian symbolic space and its necrophilic tendencies raise issues of blame and responsibility, and the place of a possible atonement, where Jerusalem plays a role in the text's Judeo-Christian dialogue.[65] Nitza Ben-Dov points out that the route taken by the coffin out of Jerusalem and then back to the city is analogous to the journey of the Jewish people who carried the Ark of the Covenant in Samuel I. It may also refer to Chyngyz Aitmatov's *The Day Lasts More Than a Hundred Years*, which also describes a journey with a coffin through Eastern Europe in search of a burial site.[66] In an interview, Yehoshua related to the Christian structure of the book: "I felt that there is a Passion here, of the suffering of this foreign employee. A Passion of the suffering of all of us. [. . .] I am not a religious person. [. . .] But in this novel a certain religious energy erupted."[67]

The tendency in both novels to stress the divine and the spiritual articulates the notion that the encounter with the face of the Other and the protagonists' engagement is not only a personal or earthly experience, but rather has a transcendental quality.

The Responsibility to the Other Who Is Dead

> "The dignity of the dead?" The weasel sounded truly startled. "Do you really think that's what I'm fighting for? You'll have to excuse me, mister, but you're missing the point. [. . .] The dead are dead. [. . .] I'd think that a personnel director like you would understand that if I feel pain or sorrow, it's for the anonymous living, not the undignified dead."[68]

The face of the Other calls for ultimate responsibility. Yet in what sense can we talk about responsibility toward the face of the dead? When Levinas developed his face-to-face concept, he did not directly consider encounters with the dead. However, entertaining such a possibility is not totally alien to Levinasian thought. "'You shall not commit murder' is the nudity of the face," according to Levinas.[69] Death violates the commandment, but since this violation occurs in my proximity, "Is the nearness of the neighbor not my responsibility for his death?"[70]

> This question—the question of death—is unto itself its own response: it is my responsibility for the death of the other. [. . .] the relationship with the Infinite is the responsibility of the mortal being for a mortal being.[71]

The face calls for responsibility, yet confronting the face of the Other who is dead does not lead to immediate dialogue since the dead have no voice. Levinas uses two different terms to articulate human interactions: the Saying and the Said. The Saying brings about absolute irreducibility and incomprehensibility.[72] The Saying is unthematizable and impossible to delimit, "it is the meaning of language, before language scatters into words, into themes equal to the words and dissimulating in the said."[73] At the moment the Saying is phrased, the Said appears, organized by concrete language, and becomes thematized and limited.[74] The nude face of the dead is the Saying, and it has the potential to create a rare opportunity to extend the moment when the Saying is exposed, the instant before it is translated into the Said and loses its nudity.[75]

The face of the Other who is dead preserves the moment before language takes control and becomes concrete. It also constitutes the ultimate alterity. As Simon Critchley put it: "the first experience of an alterity that cannot be reduced to the self occurs in the relation to death, to the ungraspable facticity of dying."[76] Since the I cannot perceive his own death, the death of the Other forms an extreme situation of alterity. Moreover, the individual cannot expect any gratitude or reward from the Other who is dead;[77] thus his/her responsibility will always be "without response."[78] In Levinas's essays on Agnon, he hints at the ethical obligations that death imposes on the self:

> If everything were comprehensible in death, as a reasonable enterprise, it would fit into the limits of life. It would lose the surplus with which it exalts life. Life, sustaining its allegiances to the confines of death, thus goes beyond its being, its limits reaching beyond those limits; and, beyond being, it tastes the taste of the Resurrection.[79]

Death is indeed incomprehensible; it is an instance of extreme Otherness that transcends life. Yet it poses an ethical challenge by creating a new foundation of responsibility for the Other and even a source of resurrection. Can this be said about the Horn and Yehoshua novels? The face of the girl Yael saw just a second before the explosion haunts her through the entire novel. When Davidl's family realizes she was probably the last person to see their son alive, they accept her warmly. Avshalom, the father, cries with her as though she was part of their bereaved family, and Yael begins to identify with his (dead) wife.

> And although I had not conceived him, and it had not been my blood that flowed when he was born, Davidl was mine too, I had a part in him, even though for only a few minutes.[80]

The blood from the scene of the terror attack that Yael witnessed is intermingled with the blood of birth. Yael appropriates Davidl's death, making it part of her life, as though she herself had lost a child. This very extreme reaction casts doubt on her capacity to act ethically. Previously, when working on her research, Yael looked down at the Ultra-Orthodox community. She claimed to understand them, but in fact she was examining them in terms of their similarities and differences to her own way of life. She then becomes overly emotionally involved with Davidl's family and begins to identify with them, as though she is one of them. Yael is torn between two extremes, both of which are problematic in Levinasian terms, since they are based on a self who projects herself, with her thoughts, feelings, and beliefs, onto the Other without acknowledging his alterity.

Levinas articulates the death of the Other in the context of the Holocaust. He argues that "one can feel oneself to be already a responsible survivor."[81] Yael feels guilty for the lost child who died instead of her three-year-old child. When she was pregnant and took part in a political demonstration with the "Women in Black" against the Occupation, an anonymous woman wearing red cursed her, saying that her unborn child would be killed in a terrorist attack. Like the reference to the *akeda* story, she feels responsible for her child, who may be at risk because of her. Throughout the novel this prophecy haunts her and when she become acquainted with the family, Yael believes that she can save her child if he replaces Davidl, wondering "whether the curse was edging towards me, whether it was now my Yoavi's turn" or had the curse "harmed another child, Davidl,"[82] just like she replaced the daughter her father lost in the Holocaust.

She goes to see Davidl's and Batsheva's new graves, feeling they are part of her body and soul. Then suddenly "I found myself asking Batsheva's permission. Permission to love her husband."[83] She breaks off her relationship with her husband, which for years had been cold and unsatisfactory, and attempts to exchange her old family for a new one:

> I wanted to tell him that there was no random chance here, that Batsheva's and Davidl's lives had been sacrifices to that we could be together. [. . .] Take me, take me instead of Batsheva, and I'll give you my Yoavi for a son, and we'll raise him together.[84]

Yael's fantasy of creating a new family and substituting Avshalom's lost wife and child distances her from the ethical journey of reaching the Other. She returns to an egotistical and twisted perception of preserving her life and the life of her child and is blind to the alterity of others. Yael's ethical lapse evolves throughout the narrative, but the text's emotional nature might suggest another reason for this flaw. Levinas was suspicious of art's deceptive role,[85] since this deceptive quality may lead to an emotional absorption that involves empathetic identification, a state in which a person "partakes of" the mental states of another person, and can "look into" the

Other's mind and share that Other's experience. Empathetic identification, whether in the context of real people or fictional characters, is based on the tendency to assume that people share universal feelings and experiences.[86] However, this type of identification is a denial of the other person's uniqueness, and thus does not enable ethical relations with the Other as an unthematized stranger. Horn's text is highly stirring and emotional. Hence both the reader and Yael are drawn into this traumatic-fascinating literary plot and may also be left in an emotional-egotistical-passive state, which is ethically inappropriate, according to Levinas.

Yehoshua's novel differs radically in this respect. Unlike the emotional style of Horn's text, Yehoshua's narrative is restrained and distanced. Although the reader may have a naïve expectation of reading a steamy, sensuous plot about either the manager or the dead woman, nothing of the sort occurs, as though the author decided to deliberately block emotional immersion. Such writing may protect the reader from entering a delusive-emotional state, and thus preserve the dignity of the Other as a stranger for whom we are responsible.

The weasel in Yehoshua's text claims that dignity is not possible for the dead but for the "anonymous living."[87] Levinas states that "we are answerable not only for the death of the Other but for his life as well."[88] In other words, death is not separate from the life that preceded it. This is the path Yehoshua's protagonist choses. Yulia Ragayev is a stranger without an aura (unlike Horn's little child), and what he discovered about her is not stirring. However, from a Levinasian perspective, the ethical relationship begins with the responsibility of the self and responsiveness toward the stranger, who does not invite an empathetic identification. Yehoshua's novel succeeds in creating such a character.

The protagonist's journey, which is also the journey of becoming ethically responsible for the face of the dead woman, unfolds in three main stages. In the first part, "the manager," the protagonist is given his mission and starts searching for her in Jerusalem; in the second part, "the mission," he takes her body back to her country; in the third part, "the journey," he travels to her mother's village. At the end of the novel, another voyage is implied—the journey of bringing her back to Jerusalem—the city she chose to live in. Throughout the novel, the protagonist experiences ethical progress during which he reexamines his roles and duties.

At the beginning of his inquiry he looks at her intimate belongings, feels tired, and considers taking a nap in her bed, "But I am who I am.

I'm not a lover, or in love, or a beloved. I'll just fold the blanket neatly and move on."[89] His unclear status is emphasized by the voice of the chorus in the novel, a group of people who view the event from the outside, presenting their thoughts in the plural, which are written in a different font in the novel:

> *Naturally, we wondered about him. Was he a relative? A friend? A neighbor? Perhaps a lover?* [. . .] *To our surprise, the man had not even known the deceased. He was the personnel manager of the Jerusalem bakery in which the victim* [. . .] *had found work as a cleaning woman.*[90]

The human resources manager's actions puzzle the outsiders. They are surprised to see that this individual, who seems to be involved in her life, scarcely knew her and is acting in his capacity as a manager in the bakery she used to work in. His thorough investigation does not stem from any emotional involvement, but from duty. He is an emissary, as the bakery owner states.[91] While escorting her abroad in the Eastern European winter, "He considered packing his old overcoat in the valise with the woman's belongings, but decided against blurring the line between the living and the dead."[92] Whereas in Horn's text Yael appropriates the dead child and makes him part of her life, in Yehoshua's text the protagonist preserves the distance between the two. In the passage where he introduces himself to her (coffin) he uses formal definitions:

> I'm the manager of the bakery's personnel department, better known as its human resource division, and you, Yulia Ragayev, having worked as a cleaning woman there, have all the rights of a terror victim as defined by National Insurance.[93]

The human resources manager tries to figure out the nature of his relationship with this woman. By phrasing the relationships between them in this way, the manager chooses to emphasize her rights, and positions himself as a person who is obligated to fulfill these rights. This is not only a practical attitude but an ethical one, since it poses the Other as person who demands responsibility. This attitude, along with the conviction of his duty, is also evidenced when he meets her ex-husband and son, who are furious. The husband is angry at her for going to Jerusalem and returning in a coffin, leaving their child behind. The son is confused and refuses to bury his mother and sends them to his grandmother: "She had sent his mother to Jerusalem—now let her answer for her blood."[94] The manager decides to continue the journey, rents a car, and drives for days in terrible weather on rough roads to her mother's small village; the mother is now traveling with a Christian missionary group. He acknowledges that "A foreign woman ten years older than myself, whom I can't even remember, has become my sole responsibility."[95]

Driving a converted army-surplus truck with huge steel plated wheels,[96] he finally gets to a reconverted Soviet military bunker, and a kind of subterranean hostel and hospital where he suffers from terrible food poisoning that almost kills him. This surrealistic episode metaphorically cleanses his soul: "He was purged not only of the poisonous stew from the market but also of many older, forgotten toxins too, going back to his school years and the army."[97] The journey over the lands of this collapsing state in one of the Asian republics that was part of the Soviet Union in the army-surplus truck, the former Soviet military bunker, the strange episodes and people, is suggestive of Hades. During the journey the protagonist learns to see Yulia Ragayev as an equal, who cannot be classified into any system of hierarchies but demands responsibility. A grotesque carnival episode brings this realization to its peak, strips everyone of their status, and reveals their uniqueness that cannot be expressed.[98] This process of dismantling hierarchies that culminates in the ex-Soviet military bunker paves the way for taking ultimate ethical responsibility for the Other.

When he reaches the mother's village he addresses the people by presenting himself not as a courier "who comes and goes" but as a "human resources manager whose duty is to remain with you until the last clod of earth has fallen on this woman's grave."[99] When Yulia's mother asks him to take the coffin back to Jerusalem, to the city where Yulia actually chose to immigrate—"the city that had taken her life"[100]—he decides to bring her back to Jerusalem and thus go on another journey with "two new residents, an old woman and a handsome young man,"[101] and he is willing to do this even at his own expense.

The journey of the human resources manager is indeed a mental journey of a person who was, as the secretary noted, a snail, who led an egocentric life, who could not even have a family life, who is dealing with human resources but was not able to see the people behind the paperwork. Unlike Horn's protagonist, the human resources manager does not fall in love with the dead and her family, nor does he experience an emotional involvement. He does not fully understand the woman, and clearly does not identify with her mother and child. Does he become responsible for the Other who is dead?

The protagonist is a practical person who is obligated to the owner of the bakery, who sent him on the mission. As long as he follows the owner's instructions it is difficult to ascribe an ethical quality to his acts. Yet during the journey, he changes and gradually learns to think for himself, first when he decides to continue to the mother's hamlet, only asking the bakery owner's permission afterward, and then at the end of the novel, when he decides to bring her back to Jerusalem, this time presenting this act as an undisputed given. He turns, as Shenhav says, "from emissary to a (religious) leader."[102] The human resources manager indeed undergoes a process in which he changes his perspective, as he gradually internalizes his responsibility for another person.

In "Adieu," dedicated to Levinas after his death, Derrida asks "what happens when a great thinker becomes silent, one whom we knew living, whom we read and reread, and also heard, one from whom we were still awaiting a response?"[103] In his very personal response, he suggests that "I will never stop beginning or beginning anew to think with them [Levinas' thoughts and ideas] [. . .] and I will begin again and again to rediscover them."[104] Likewise, our responsibility to the Other who is dead involves constant affordances, continuous beginnings to discover and rediscover the Other and what he has left behind.[105] We can search for the projection of the dead over the living and can start knowing the dead or even relate our life-path to them, even if we did not know them during their lifetimes. In the case of Levinas, as a philosopher, his projection is widely accessible through his writings. Thus, his legacy enables the reading and rereading of his writings and allows the philosophical dialogue to continue.

In the case of Yulia Ragayev, her story can be told by her husband and child, her mother and her birthplace. Throughout the journey of resurrection, the protagonist discovers and rediscovers Yulia. This discovery has no end and is always incomplete since we cannot fully understand or know her. Hence each discovery leads to a new journey. In the last episode in the novel, the protagonist independently decides to bring her back to Jerusalem, determined not to listen to the people around him, but to the people around her, and to internalize what she may have wanted in her life.

In his article "Facing Images," Hagi Kenaan explores the linguistic aspect of the word "face," in Hebrew *panim*.[106] *Panim* is a unique Hebrew word. It is plural and appears in the language as both feminine and masculine. It is derived from the verb *pana,* which means to turn to the Other in a movement of changing orientation and to face him. Another word derived from the same root is *peniyya,* which means both to address someone and to move in the other direction. Kenaan uses the concept of *peniyya* to formulate his argument about the image of the face. One way to broaden this concept is to consider the relationship between *panim* and its derivatives as a movement between the I and the Other; namely, the I that not only sees the Face, the *panim*, but *poneh* (moves) toward him, changing orientation and direction. These linguistic features are important in the case of Yehoshua's novel, since they serve to articulate the protagonist's ethical behavior. Space and ethics work together here, since the human resources manager needs to respond to Yulia's life and her suffering while listening, discovering, and rediscovering who she was, in a continuous *peniyya*—a continuous change of direction, as he follows her. Thus, he shows his devotion to her in his willingness to follow in her footsteps and even change the trajectory of his life. This is a spatial movement that is also ethical. By doing this, he achieves what Levinas articulates in the context of Agnon: a resurrection "that begins in death itself."[107]

A Call for a Different Ethics

Horn and Yehoshua wrote their novels in the midst of the Second Intifada, in a period of tense political upheaval. These novels are realistic and describe terror and political insecurity, but they do not make the Israeli-Palestinian conflict their main topic, and do not criticize the situation or offer political alternatives. They focus on face-to-face relationships between two strangers. Though the novels do not seem strictly political, they have political relevance, but in a different way.

Despite the fact that the texts do not focus directly on the conflict between the Israelis and the Palestinians, certain elements in the novels contain a political agenda, which is generally aligned with the political Left. Horn's novel illustrates political oppositions: Yael's father is a Holocaust survivor who believes that the Jews will be safer with wide territorial borders. He hangs a map of greater Israel on the wall and tries to inculcate right-wing concepts in his daughter. Yael, his daughter, moves left: at first, she takes part in a *Shalom Akhshav* (Peace Now) demonstration, but later, with the encouragement of a friend, she becomes a radical leftist, joining

Bnot Shalom (Peace Daughters) and *Nashim be-shahor* (Women in Black). After she is cursed by the woman in red, she stops taking part in political activities. At the end of the novel she leaves Israel to study and work in England with her child, protecting herself and him from the threat of terrorism. Avshalom, Davidl's father, has a charged political past. He was raised in in a secular kibbutz and later, as a fighter pilot, he was involved in controversial acts of bombing innocent children across the border. He became strictly religious to atone for the role he played in the military, but still believes that the loss of his wife and child is divine punishment for his past sins.

Yehoshua's text also has political elements. The history of the Israeli-Palestinian conflict left its mark on the history of the bakery.[108] The owner asks the human resources manager to resolve Yulia's case, since he "won't let my or my ancestors' reputation be tarnished."[109] The founder of the bakery, it seems, came to Jerusalem at the beginning of the twentieth century during the Zionist waves of immigration. In the hard days of the Intifada, the owner admits that his business actually benefited from the situation: "I never thought I'd be as wealthy as I've become, especially since the start of this terror, which makes the whole world want bread and cake."[110] His success is due to security issues since "the destruction by the army of several small Palestinian bakeries suspected of harboring bomb makers had only added to the shortage."[111] The fact that the bakery flourished specifically at these times makes the owner feel that he needs to atone "not only for keeping flawed records but for the bomb attack too."[112]

The human resources manager was an officer in the military, while other people who worked at the bakery had military experience as well, and military norms affect their work. In the Soviet military bunker the manager experiences a purification process that makes it possible for him to leave the traces of his "toxic" military past behind him.[113] Eventually his decision to bring back the coffin in the company of Yulia Ragayev's mother and the son, who are Christians, hints at a new political concept of Jerusalem as the city of all religions.

Such references to Israeli politics are evidenced in these novels, but the political importance of the texts lies beyond them. Yehoshua lost a close friend in a terror attack in Jerusalem in 2002 and dedicated the book to her. In an interview with Maya Jaggi, he expressed his sorrow for all the victims of the terror attack—Jews, Arabs, or others. In the same year, in a terror attack at a popular seashore restaurant in Haifa, two Arab writers he knew well lost their lives: they "were killed in a terrible bombing, with a whole [Jewish] family."

> We're used to soldiers dying, but the problem is how to mourn civilians dying in the city streets—Israelis, Arabs, foreign workers. What's the meaning of someone drinking coffee who's killed in a café, or a housekeeper on a bus? We have to give meaning to this absurd death, instead of trying to repress it.[114]

Yehoshua does not wish to repress this bereavement, but rather to ask questions about it. This is why he chose to deal with "the most anonymous, most marginal death." Ariana Melamed argues that in his book, Yehoshua dares to do something that has never been done before, to "force us to look at reality in the opposite way than we are used to."[115] This is also the main path Horn takes in her novel.

In the preface to *Totality and Infinity*, Levinas introduces his ethics as an answer to war, politics, and history. He states that the face of the Other "that shows itself in war is fixed in the concept of totality, which dominates Western philosophy," so "individuals are reduced to being bearers of forces that command them unknown to themselves."[116] The fallacy of Western philosophy lies in the fact that even when trying to replace war with peace, "the peace of empires issued from war rests on war."[117] Levinas suggests a return to a prepolitical stage that does not involve power relationships between nations and political controversies—a return to the "primordial and original relation with being."[118] For Levinas "peace is inherent to the originary relationship of unique individuals."[119] Thus, he calls for the replacement of any engagement in politics and wars that does not see the individual but trains him to play a role that eventually alienates people from each other, with a primordial relationship between two human beings facing each other. Levinas's insight in his preface suggests a link between ethics and politics, since it demands a change of perspective. Thus, rather than thinking about politics in terms of nations and leaders, representation and wars, Levinas directs us to see individuals.

This is the trajectory in Horn's and Yehoshua's novels, though it is accomplished with differing degrees of success. While in Horn's text the narcissistic nature of the protagonist and the way in which the reader is carried away by its stirring content undermine the ethical overture, Yehoshua's novel explores this alternative and dares to engage in a journey toward the Other. Yehoshua claims that "as a writer, my ethical duty is to use my pen to pierce the black plastic shroud, to open the heart towards death, with love and pity."[120] This mission is of course ethical, but it also has spatial and political implications. The texts show that only a process of displacement and deterritorialization can lead us to see the Other, and thus the protagonists face an event that makes them leave their safety zone and go on a journey to the unknown. Only there, by looking at a stranger they would never have met, examining their ethical behavior, and taking responsibility, can literary works make it possible for the reader to move beyond the Israeli, the Ultra-Orthodox, the foreign worker, the Christian, the Leftist, and the Holocaust survivors, and see a human being as he or she is. The opportunity to remove all the tags and masks from the individual and to foster an encounter between two strangers suggests an ethical mission, whose resolution in the Levinasian spirit can bring about peace.

CHAPTER 7

Dismantling Borders: A Female Perspective

In an article written in 2006, Michal Govrin reflects on the construction of "The Wall," which has altered the landscape of Jerusalem. She writes:

> The armed conflict of the Second Intifada broke out in the fall of 2000. For long months Jerusalem has been under siege, with dozens of terrorist attacks and suicide bombers leaving hundreds of dead and wounded. The Frontier Patrol shack was turned into an armored post, and on the road coming up from Jabel Muchabr a checkpoint was installed. [. . .] One day I was amazed to discover bulldozers on its slope. A few months later the stunningly beautiful new Promenade, designed by Laurence Halpern, was ready, as if an echo to *Snapshots*. The Promenade has not been officially inaugurated, because of the danger. Yet, in summer afternoons its paths are visited by Arab children and mothers from Jabel Muchabr, some courageous joggers, and a few strollers.
>
> Once again, these very days, Jerusalem's space is radically changing. Facing the hilltop on the slopes of the Mount of Olives, the construction of the Separation Barrier, known as "The Wall," advances like a snail, crossing Abu-Dis, reaching southwards. It painfully changes lives. It radically changes the city, the region's space. It cuts Jerusalem from Bethlehem, from Hebron and from the natural space

> of the Judean Mountains. It creates a barrier between Arab villages. It condemns to isolation or dismantling Jewish settlements. It separates de facto Israel from Palestine.
>
> [. . .] I climb the hill, watching this complex space changing, [. . .] I stand on the hilltop in the midst of an oppressive present moment. I watch this intense space imprinted with history like an Archive of the layered story of Western civilization, with its heights of belief, love, and poetry and its abysses of stupidity, fanaticism, jealousy, and cruelty.[1]

Michal Govrin's description of the construction of the wall stresses its dramatic visual existence that has radically changed the landscape. Govrin's decription juxtaposes the physicality of the wall with the Green Line, which appears on maps but does not have an actual concrete existence. The wall creates a dramatic massive boundary but does not follow the demarcation of the Green Line. Govrin gazes at Jerusalem's heights with love and compassion, but at the same time with deep disappointment. She wrote this text after she finished *Snapshots* (2002), which focuses on the same geographic space. In her book she presents a feminist poetic alternative that subverts the concept of borders altogether by formulating a radical spatial critique of national territory and its sovereignty.

This chapter analyzes two novels, Ronit Matalon's *Sarah, Sarah* (Bliss, 2000) and Michal Govrin's *Hevzekim* (Snapshots, 2002), and shows how these works present, both thematically and poetically, a different and radical concept of space and borders that lead to a new reflection on the political and ideological situation.[2] Both novels depict female protagonists who are not involved in the military. Through these protagonists and the literary structure, the authors dismantle the borders and create deterritorialization through a severing of social and political relations with the national territory. They do so not only in the context of the liminal space of the Occupied Territories, but also in terms of the entire national space and sovereignty itself. In both works, the narrative trajectory converts the linear narrative into a rhizomatic reality (as defined by Deleuze and Guattari)[3] that branches out multidimensionally, unfettered by direction or hierarchy. Thus, they open possibilities for another form of spatial thought that can constitute different social and cultural identities. The female protagonists wander within spaces, creating a mode of nomadic existence in their journeys, their love lives, and their art. Thus, these works incorporate new ideas about the perception of the sovereignty of territory and its significance.

The Rhizomatic Space

According to Deleuze and Guattari, biologically a rhizome is a branched root-like stem that connects rootless plants, such as grasses and weeds, to the earth by means of horizontal (not vertical) networks: "The rhizome itself assumes very diverse forms, from a ramified surface extension in all directions to concretion into bulbs and tubers. [. . . A] rhizome has no beginning or end," and can expand and contract.[4] The rhizome is very different from a tree, which often acts as a metaphor for a stable mechanism, a genealogical hierarchy, movement in a single spatial as well as temporal direction from the roots up, and from past to future, in a binary axis, such as inner/outer, male/female, mind/body, and so on. Unlike a tree, the rhizome's trajectory is not subject to causality.[5] Because the rhizomatic knot provides a different model of thinking detached from historical thought, it can eliminate categorizing and hierarchical borders.[6] Rhizomatic thought thus may lead the narrative toward deterritorialization, because the rhizome rules out the idea of holding on to anything, whether land, a genetic code, a household, through a principled definition of what belongs and what is Other.[7]

Ronit Matalon (1957–2017) was a major player in contemporary Hebrew literature, who lent a new voice to women and Mizrahi minorities. Matalon was born to Egyptian Jewish immigrants. The nine books she authored constitute an alternative to the canon of Hebrew and Israeli literature and won several prizes. She worked as a journalist in Gaza during the First Intifada and was a social activist and a senior lecturer of Hebrew and Comparative Literature at Haifa University.

Matalon's novel, *Bliss*, describes the story of the long-term friendship between Sarah and Ofri that enters into a state of crisis just as Ofri is about to leave for France. The conversation between the two women takes place at the airport, where Sarah grasps the full implications of her misery and Ofri musters her resilience. From the neutral space of the airport, the narrative develops in four main spatial and temporal locations. The first takes place in the early 1980s and describes how the women met. It is set against the ethnic and economic differences between Ashkenazi Sarah and Mizrahi Ofri. The second takes place in the late 1980s during the First

Intifada, when Sarah—then a photographer in the Occupied Territories—marries Udi. The third covers the first half of the 1990s and narrates the birth of Sarah's son, Mims (Emanuel), her relationship with Marwan, and how she then abandons him, followed by her divorce from Udi. The fourth and final phase describes Ofri's stay in Le Plessis-Belleville, France, until the news of Yitzhak Rabin's assassination ends the narrative, both structurally and chronologically.

Michal Govrin was born in 1950 in Tel Aviv. Her father was an Israeli pioneer and her mother was a Holocaust survivor. She published poetry and fiction including two major novels. Govrin received her PhD from the University of Paris in theater and directed award-winning performances in theaters in Israel. She also published numerous academic, nonfiction, and personal essays. Govrin is a full professor and the academic chair of the Theater Department of Emunah College.

Her novel *Snapshots* is set in a similar period as *Bliss*. Ilana Tsuriel, known as Lana, is killed in a road accident on the Strasbourg-Munich autobahn, on her way to lecture about the peace monument that she plans to construct in Jerusalem. Among the possessions she leaves behind is a notebook of "snapshots," which is handed over to Tirtsa, her childhood friend from Haifa. Typographically, the notes are printed as distinct sections, in different styles and fonts, and they interweave various stories, times, and spaces that reveal Lana Tsuriel's relationships with the three men in her life. The first underlying relationship is with her father, Aaron Tsuriel, whose life story mirrors the history of Zionism, immigration to pre-statehood Israel, and the nation-building project; the snapshots are addressed to her father and were written during the year after his death. The two other men in Lana's life are her husband, Alain Greenberg, a French Jew with anti-Zionist opinions, a Holocaust survivor whose life is devoted to archival endeavors directed at unearthing material about the Second World War; and her lover, Sayyid Ashabi, an actor and director in the Palestinian Theater in East Jerusalem, whose story reveals the Palestinian narrative. The novel is set in the early 1990s against the backdrop of the First Intifada and the First Gulf War. During these events, Lana and her two sons—David and Jonathan—travel between New York, Paris, and Jerusalem.[8]

Both *Bliss* and *Snapshots* present nonlinear narratives in which space is a pivotal protagonist. Matalon's narrative begins at the airport, a neutral space that is detached from place and time, a kind of Foucauldian heterotopia.[9] This space creates an equivalence between Israeli and French territory, since it is expropriated from both of them.

The spatial tracks refer to different time periods of efflorescence and decline; the relationships between Sarah and Ofri, Sarah and Udi, and Sarah and Marwan, lack chronology and hierarchy. In many cases, this adversely affects causality and creates an intentional ambiguity. For example, Marwan's apparent violent reaction to Sarah remains unclear due to the dismantled chronological and causal sequence. The reader only deduces toward the end that what sparked the violence was Sarah's decision to have an abortion. But this assumption may be erroneous because Sarah avoids meeting Marwan after the abortion and phones the police when he attempts to approach her house or call her. David Jacobson, who has studied several stories by women authors describing intimate relations between a Jewish woman protagonist and a Palestinian man, including works by Savyon Librecht, Emuna Elon, and Michal Peleg, suggests that there are several features these relationships have in common. The Israeli and Palestinian characters in these texts encounter each other in the context of work. The female characters have less prejudiced views of Palestinians, thus making intimacy a possibility. This intimacy develops but is not sustained, and the Palestinian men decide to retreat from the relationship, usually because they feel slighted. While the Jacobson account may be accurate regarding the authors he chose to read, his conclusion cannot be inclusive. Matalon's and Govrin's texts depict different alternatives and explore much more complex relationships between Israelis and Palestinians.[10]

Matalon's narrative does not adhere to the laws of linearity or hierarchy, and its structure is rhizomatic. When Ofri reconstructs the act of narration, she cites Sarah's words, "You're my biographer, Ofri," but adds, "I take revenge, devouring whatever I can lay my hands on. [. . .] Once in a while I [Ofri] require her [Sarah's] assistance, but she infects me with her vagueness."[11] Ofri's "choice" builds an ahistorical narrative, "a rhizome-book, not a dichotomous, pivotal, or fascicular book."[12] A narrative of this kind provides us with a different perspective of the political arena by constructing what Nitza Keren termed a patchwork quilt.[13] In this mosaic, the relationships between the major and minor characters are fractured, and the act of narration is transparent and undermines principles of hegemony.

Hannan Hever notes that the novel alternates between the personal and the political. Ostensibly, the novel is structured in the familiar form of a personal plot and a political one, with reciprocal parallels. While the Parisian plot seems to be related to the family plot, the Tel Aviv plot seems to depict an Israeli political story. However, the two function in tandem.[14] The Parisian story is crammed with references to Israeli politics that emerge in ideological discussions; it also concludes with the statement: "They've murdered your Rabin."[15] Matalon herself states that she rejects "the separation between the personal and political," and rather than a "reduction of the personal," she aims to broaden it.[16] According to Hever, the mixture of the personal and political creates "a narrative language with which one can provide grounds for, and describe, the complex and often mysterious transitions between private suffering and the violence of the general Israeli condition."[17]

The categories of the personal and political are not the only ones to be combined in this work. Ethnic, national, and gendered facets are transformed from a linear, binary, and hierarchical structure into a rhizomatic one. For example, Sarah violates the dichotomy between home and the public sphere, and in so doing, annuls ethnic and national differences. Sarah flips between the Ashkenazi family represented by her parents, who want her to be part of the family business and often support her financially, and Udi's family with its patriotism: "his father was a retired colonel and his mother owned a lingerie store in the Neveh Avivim center."[18] Sarah has always yearned to be part of Ofri's family: "She used to linger in my mother's kitchen for days, picking up everything with the speed of light and never forgetting. All I despised about the kitchen Sarah embraced enthusiastically."[19] She longs to meet Marwan's family: "I'm going with him to Shfaram at some point, to visit his family. We may go next week."[20] She gets involved in the Palestinian family, who shelter her when she is caught up in riots that break out during her work, and where she spends the night: "At eight-thirty the family got ready for bed. They offered her a separate mattress, but she refused. She sat on the couch all night with her legs folded beneath her."[21] She is also involved with the family of Busaina, the little girl killed by IDF gunfire: "During the last few months of 1989 she wove her own version of Busaina's story, squeezing the entire Intifada into the tiny portrait of the girl standing between her four brothers that stood on the coffee table in her parent's house in Khan Younis."[22]

Although Sarah has a home and family, her behavior blurs the distinction between home and what is external to it. She lives like a homeless woman. Matalon writes:

> She did not think that each person has to know his place [. . .]—she denied the place. The map of her place was a sort of city with tunnels—soft, rounded, passageways leading from one place to the next, without traffic lights, flowing incessantly, and changing formation, with multiple options, from site to site.[23]

The conflation of the internal with the external is clearly one of Sarah's defining traits, but it also constitutes a central theme in the description of other characters, particularly those who represent minority groups. Ofri, who in many ways can be considered the heroine of the work, also switches residences (moving from her Levantine childhood home to Sarah's home). Similarly, the character of Marwan embodies attempts to cross borders and wander from home to home, as depicted in his abandonment of his childhood home and enrollment at Tel Aviv University.

Sarah and other characters in the book undermine the categorical structures between home and what is external to it, between the personal and political, as well as between sexual and gendered dichotomies. Matalon shatters these binary dichotomies by replacing a conjugal relationship (man/woman) with triangular structures. Ofri is one pole of the love triangle with Sarah and Udi. She replaces Sarah in motherhood roles, and grows more intimate with Udi. Hints of a lesbian relationship emerge in Ofri's context but do not materialize. Michel, the cousin, who dies of AIDS, is portrayed as having relationships with men, who are in relationships with women. His wish to plan his own burial is another example of crossing boundaries—he wants a religious ceremony and then to have his body cremated, an unacceptable procedure for the religious Jewish establishment. Sarah, her husband Udi, and her lover Marwan form another triangle. Here too Udi moves closer to Marwan; he openly encourages the relationship, invites Marwan to their home, takes lessons in Arabic from him, and repeatedly tells Sarah she's in love with him: "'You're in love,' he grates at Sarah. 'You're afraid of the fact that you're in love. Why shouldn't you be in love? He's a lovely young man.'"[24]

Mims, who is everyone's son, personifies the triangular relationship. He becomes the focus and the apparent offspring of love in each triangle. When Michel visits Israel, he turns out to be a skilled father to Mims; Ofri shows maternal responsibility when Sarah is unable to take care of him; even Marwan serves as a kind of a father to Mims by demanding that the divorce arrangements will entitle him to time with Mims, one afternoon a week.[25]

In an interview, Matalon admitted her affection for triangles:

> I have quite a few triangles. I seem to love this configuration, the triangle; it has multiple options and imaginations, with many entrances and exits. Apparently in the world of my story there is not much intimacy between partners, the wife and the husband. Something must burst in—the third person, who is your other identity, your other sexuality. There are hardly any simple encounters: you're a man, I'm a woman. Every encounter is immediately expropriated by the public. In the triangle there is a certain level of publicness.[26]

Matalon's triangles not only shatter the dichotomies between the private and public, but also negate binary categories and enable lines of flight from systems of power of all types (Oedipal, binary, or genealogical)[27] and in this context from ethnicity, Israeliness, Jewishness, heterosexuality, and the stereotypical place of women and the female narrative.

Michal Govrin also constructs triangles in her writing, which, in turn, also constitute a rhizomatic narrative. The geographical triangle consists of Lina's movements between New York, Paris, and Jerusalem. Railway stations and bus stations, observations of passengers, views from the window, and the anonymity of an individual roaming through space are the basis for Lana's written snapshots addressed to her father. Her notes are packed with descriptions of nature and human landscapes, scenes of forests, huge billboards, people waiting at stations—each distinctive in terms of its color and language—airports and cafés, and the hotels where she meets her lovers. Like Matalon's characters, Lana's starting point is not a specific space, but rather the heterotopic antispace of transition sites between cities and countries.

To some extent, as Shlomith Rimmon-Kenan suggests, Govrin's text relates to Michel de Certeau's basic distinction between the concepts of place and space: "the distinction emerges not as a binary opposition but as a relationship of potentiality and realization [. . .] while place is 'objectively there,' the constructed cultural given, space is what the subject makes of place in order to inhabit it."[28] Place is static, whereas space is created by the subject in a changing context and is always dynamic. Place can be observed from the outside, but space is experienced from within. In Certeau's words, "in relation to place, space is like a word when it is spoken."[29] The distinction between place and space is analogous to that between a map and an itinerary or trajectory, where space is a specific realization of place. While the map shows lines and borders, by wandering through space and crossing borders, the subject may transform borders into bridges and thresholds, and thus generate deterritorialization.

In her movements through space, Lana removes borders, builds new bridges, and creates lines of flight from the territorial system. She transforms striated spaces, which according to Deleuze and Guattari are arranged, divided, classifiable spaces, spaces of supervision, and territorial borders[30] into smooth spaces, without demarcations, perspectives, or distinguishing marks. These are rhizomatic centerless spaces, which consist of lines of flight and an unstable dynamism, offering a sort of "flat multiplicity" without any hierarchy.[31] Since the different spaces do not contrast and can intermingle, the movement between them defines their "state."[32] This, in fact, is what Govrin's protagonist does: Lana does not progress from one point to the next, navigating toward some kind of objective or goal; rather, she moves along a free, dynamic course with no center, no home. Yoram Meltzer terms the spatial movement in the novel a "quantal way," as a way to reveal the different narratives enveloping Israeli existence.

> All the narratives unfold in a transparent aquarium, hurtling around in their universe like skittering electrons in a world of Heisenbergian uncertainty. [. . .] The representatives of those narratives, as well as many of their sub-characters, are in constant movement from place to place. The focus on a defined point [. . .] whether a geographic point or a temporal-ideological point, is liable to extract something of their substance from them and diminish their vitality and self-perception.[33]

Lana leaves Israel after graduating in a reaction to her father's generation of pioneers, whose dream of settlement took them on a journey toward Israel. However, to use Gurevitz and Aranne's terminology, Lana cedes on the Zionist dream of "place" as a home and choses to replace it with nomadic journeys.[34] Hannah Naveh argues that an individual only leaves home when a change occurs, "in his inner space or his outer shell that interfaces with his environment, or in his individual place in the home. Journeys of migration begin when some imperfection comes to light in the primary home, an imperfection that can be some form of diminution, either material or mental."[35] Lana's abandonment of Israel is nurtured by ideological (left-wing) motives, prompted by a sense of disappointment with the

Israeli state. However, when she explains it to herself, she paradoxically perceives herself as continuing her father's wandering. Perhaps his tales of emigration and wandering have infiltrated his daughter's persona. She cannot be satisfied with a ready-made home and prefers to reconstruct his trajectories. As she herself says "everything just to get as far away as possible from your story, Father. To live on the other side of the century, the story of our own wanderings."[36] Elsewhere she says:

> Father, how to tell you that what you bequeathed me, in a genetic mutation of generations—beyond the Zionist interim, beyond the thin layer of connecting to the Land of Israel—is that passion for wandering. [. . .] The curse of wandering. [. . .] That madness to escape, to uproot. Cain can't hide, is vomited up again and again.[37]

Lana divides her time between New Jersey and Paris, crisscrossing the world to give lectures in New York, Amsterdam, and Copenhagen. In Paris, she lives with Alain, her husband, but spends very little time there: he too is away from home most of the time. Alain—"this professional wandering Jew"[38]—believes that only wandering can ensure the continued existence of the Jewish people, and personifies anti-Zionist attitudes:

> The Zionist lunacy of gathering all the Jews in one place, preparing the conditions for an easy final extermination! What blindness! That madness of destroying the Diaspora. That's the only reason the Jews survived, because they could move, find temporary shelter in another place every time.[39]

Alain was born in Czernowitz and was four when the Second World War broke out. He hid in the woods for six years, until he was found and taken to a Christian shelter. He devotes his life to searching for testimonies of the war in archives: "his double life in that international group of historians, attorneys, prosecutors—mostly Jews, taciturn, survivors like him, always on the move, tracking down aging war criminals with fake identities, budding neo-Nazi organizations. [. . .] They gather evidence, catalogue."[40]

Palestinian Sayyid, the third party in the romantic triangle, reincarnates the journey Lana's father took the Promised Land and Alain's search for archival. He constantly competes with Alain and the figure of Lana's father by trying to reconstruct old maps of Palestine.

> Understand, whenever I sit on the bus to Tel Aviv, in my head there's a map that's erased. I pass Lod, Ramle, Beit Lid, and my heart is cut with pain. I hear my father describing the aunt who'd bring lemons from the tree. The yard, the chickens . . .
>
> And at some point through the words Alain's voice started echoing from when we first met, when I teased him in front of the maps hanging in his study [. . .] "It's not exactly a map of future plans . . ." with a slow look, he checked whether he could talk candidly with me. "You know, I deal with the architecture of the past. Places buried in fields, forests. Here [. . .]." He moved his hand from one point to another, poking names that had previously been in the fog of names of rabbis or yeshivas for me.[41]

This excerpt shows the ties between the striated Zionist space and the striated European space. In both spaces, the process of disciplining the space erases signs and installs new lines in their place. Against the backdrop of Zionist territorial discipline, Sayyid—who was born in Silwan in Jerusalem—feels foreign in his birthplace, and wanders through Amsterdam, Paris, New York, Beirut, Tunis, and Jerusalem. Sayyid stages a play about the Nakba and the 1948 expulsion, about a generation of uprooted people that may parallel, but also contrasts with the generation of Lana's father. Lana is surrounded by Holocaust survivors, Palestinians, and the refugees to whom she devotes her architectural work.[42] Lana and Sayyid meet in places that are inevitably transient, such as a hotel, a car, and they form ties in neutral changing territories in Jerusalem and outside of Israel: "The hallucinatory driving from one side of Jerusalem to the other. The night before we leave. Outlining a secret map with the turns of the steering wheel, in a last attempt to explain something to Sayyid."[43]

Besides the three men—the Oedipal father, whom she always betrays, and her husband and lover—the text introduces another lover, Claude, who is neither a Jew nor a Palestinian. Lana's encounters with him are also transient and occur when their paths cross: "Meeting with Claude. Betrayal of betrayal. Of Alain with Sayyid, of both of them with Claude. Though in fact, if there is a betrayal here, it's only of you, Father. Forever, with everyone. Or maybe fidelity to your sperm, an eternal flame destroying me."[44]

By contrast to these journeys between lovers and between spaces, the novel depicts Jerusalem as a closed space when Lana and her children live there during the Gulf War. Lana does not shape her itinerary to comply with borders on a map, or with any political event, and so she decides to visit Jerusalem as the Gulf War approaches. She decides not to cancel her scheduled visit during which she intends to promote her architectural project (which ultimately never materializes) and to visit her father's grave, a year after his death. Alain flies to consult archives in Russia, while she goes to Jerusalem and spends the months of the Gulf War there. Her travels are replaced by a closed, suffocating room, though she remains in touch with the world through television and by phone. She also forms ties with the neighbors, the people in the architect's office, and new characters who provide access to other spaces: she becomes closer to the Moroccan family that helps take care of her sons; Gil, a young Mizrahi architect who is traumatized by his memories of the Intifada and is willing to listen to her ideas; and develops a relationship with the older neighbors and a family of emigrants from the Soviet Union. Her time in Jerusalem, though spent in an apparently closed space, allows her to break down the borders of ethnicity, origin, and religion. Accordingly, although she is spatially restricted, her deterritorialization persists.

Her stay in Israel is cut short, and though Lana is not able to carry out her plans, she does not try to extend her stay. "The return to Paris on a fixed date seems natural now, too. The place can be dropped. To take on the roads a place that has no place in the world. Jerusalem is open like a thicket to the stars, the sky."[45] She returns because the sand in the hourglass of wandering has resumed its trickle, and she sets out for the airport with her sons David and Jonathan. "[*Once again, open suitcases. How many times this year?*] [. . .] looking at David's immigrant's pack [. . .] smiling to myself at the little wanderer I had raised, Father. A second generation, a third? A tenth."[46] Lana returns to Paris, to another family reunion, in a home she does not acknowledge as her own. "Home?" she asks herself, as she surveys "the unrecognizably neat apartment."[47]

At the end of the novel, Lana's relationships with the three men in her life merge into the embryo she carries in her womb. Lana has no idea who the father is. The unknown identity of the embryo's father manifests, it seems, the conflation of the three male figures: "[. . .] then I recalled how, for the first time, Alain and Sayyid changed in me, got mixed up in one another within the voice of Sayyid lying next to me in the Scottish Hospice, his feet twined between my legs."[48] Yet it is her father who demands the crown;[49] he is present at every intimate moment, resonating in *Don Giovanni*, the opera that Lana loves listening to:[50]

> Standing at the bed in the room overlooking the dark bend in the river [. . .] lying down next to me [. . .] Body along body. Enormous excitement;[51] [. . .] And meanwhile, until the genetic test, fantasizing that you're the father of the child. That your seed has impregnated the hut of my womb.[52]

The entire work can perhaps be seen as revolving around Lana's desire to find lines of flight from the Law of the (Zionist) castrating Father, implying that the deterritorialization may be directed chiefly against him, the addressee of her snapshots. At times she appears to have found a line of flight and retreats from his immense power: Lana seems to represent another way to cope with the Law of the Father, not by fleeing, but by clearly and unequivocally making him part of her sexual relationships. She thus takes a hyper-Oedipal position, which violates the father's place by concretizing the Oedipal, as Deleuze and Guattari suggest in their discussion of Kafka:

> Oedipal incest corresponds to the paranoiac transcendental law that prohibits it, and it works to transgress this law, directly if it can bear to do so, symbolically. [. . .] Schizo-incest corresponds, in contrast, to the immanent schizo-law and forms a line of escape instead of a circular reproduction, a progression instead of a transgression.[53]

Lana's yearning for her father is blended with "a sweet thickness of a layer of seed poured on the tongue, filling the gullet."[54] Her father's seed is absorbed in a variant on incest: it appropriates his position as the father-figure, and makes him an equal partner in creating her embryo. This in turn provides her with a line of flight (by crossing the cultural border of incest) from his castrating power. At the end of the work, Lana is killed while traveling, away from any form of home: the identity of the embryo's father is not disclosed, as though his anonymity makes possible every permutation and inference.

Nomadic Art

> *Where there is close vision, space is not visual, or rather the eye itself has a haptic, nonoptical function: no line separates earth from sky, which are of the same substance; there is neither horizon nor background nor perspective nor limit nor outline or form nor center; there is no intermediary distance, or all distance is intermediary.*
>
> —Gilles Deleuze and Félix Guattari[55]

Sarah and Lana choose not to belong, like the "wandering Jew" or nomads. Sarit Shapira argues that the term "wandering" entails the forfeit of belonging to a "home"—a place where movement ceases, becomes fixed, and accepts stable borders. In this sense, "home" refers to any fixed structure, whether mental, conceptual, linguistic, ethical, or physical. Instead, while wandering, every station is a temporary halt in territory that occurs in a borderline situation and serves as an observation point for what lies beyond it.[56] Sarah stops at interim points but without striking roots. She adopts different sorts of national and ethnic homes but never sees herself as part of them. She is not part of the occupying mechanism, but neither does she feel at home in a Palestinian residence, where she spends a night. She refuses to belong, and thus sees the conflict from the outside: "The Israelis are just beating the crap out of them, and they're trying to construct a national myth."[57] Lana also prefers not to belong to any territory, moving hectically between different zones, trying to discover her own wandering identity.

As Naveh notes, the nomad, as someone who does not belong, undermines the consensus and values of permanent residents:

> The touch of the nomad on a settlement-based culture always has a problematic aspect [. . .] because the nomad lives beyond the consensus and social structures that their owners consider universal. Because he has no aspiration for territorialization, the nomad does not function in the universal roles deriving from those structures: the roles and duties of family and home, social functions and obligations, and the institutions of the nation-state as defined and structured in Western society that has constructed itself a home attached to a piece of land.[58]

The nomadic gaze is therefore a subversive gaze from the outside that brings deterritorialization with it, and may relate to what Deleuze and Guattari defined as "nomadic art." It exchanges long-distance vision, in which one cannot see details but can identify objects, with close-range vision, in which shapes and colors have no meaning. This creates a haptic, tactile space lacking boundaries or categories.[59] Matalon's and Govrin's nomad protagonists develop the concept of nomadic art and its political implications through Sarah's photography and Lana's architecture.

Sarah works as a photographer and enters the Occupied Territories at the height of the Intifada.

> Back then she was making two or three trips there a month, with or without the reporter. She would come home as if she was ill, staying in bed a whole day, swigging down bottles of mineral water, leafing through the glossy pages of *Elle* and *Vogue*, staring at the large damp spot on the wall, sleeping for hours. When she regained her strength a little, she would shuffle around in her slippers and spend hours stirring granola into a container of yogurt, looking at the mail and the bills, cooking, sorting her photos.[60]

Sarah returns home distressed by what she saw, but this does not stop her from going back. On the contrary, she finds herself attracted to the Territories: "she had been working almost around the clock for the last week"[61] and "she took whoever agreed to be taken: friends, fellow activists, distant acquaintances, strangers, Udi, even Maman."[62] Sarah is a professional photojournalist, but also takes pictures "for herself"; that is, she engages in photography as a profession but also as an art. These photos are not placed in an envelope or sent to the person who commissioned them. The photos she takes for herself are mainly of people, including adults, children, Palestinians, and Israelis, in a state of sleep: "people in Gaza asleep in different positions, different spaces, inside or outside houses; men, women, soldiers, old people, hospital patients, children; together and alone."[63] Udi, her husband, fails to understand these photos: "They weren't important at all. Just ordinary pictures of people sleeping."[64]

Sarah's photographs have a crucial significance, which correspond to the notion of nomadic thought and deterritorialization. Her photos are distilled expressions of nomadic art that depict rhizomatic processes and movements and have no predetermined goal. In contrast to the commissioned photographs, sorted into envelopes, these photographs have no addressees.

> She divided them into two groups: commissioned and noncommissioned. The commissioned photos, the ones for the paper, roamed the house in brown envelopes that were transferred from the kitchen table to the phone stand in the hallway, from the bookshelf to the pile of phone and utility bills, from among the scattered newspapers to the

> couch and under the clothing removed from the laundry lines. She never showed the other ones, the noncommissioned photos; those she arranged in exemplary order in a specially purchased filing cabinet.[65]

The noncommissioned photographs have no specific purpose, no direction or center. At the airport, when Ofri asks her what she did with the photos, Sarah replies, "Nothing. They're in a drawer somewhere. Sleeping."[66]

Tamar Libes and Anat First discuss pictorial images from the Intifada and their political power. They focus on the example of Muhammad Dura's picture and argue that the picture represents "the need for effective, minimalism, touching, visual footage," which in turn "brings about the selection of dramatic images, transmitting emotional, empathy-arousing images that can be simultaneously absorbed everywhere."[67] Sarah's pictures of sleeping people subvert this tendency of the media to offer dramatic images.

In his study on practices of professional photography of the Occupation, Regev Nathansohn presents three forms of photography: banal photography that replicates the existing social order by fixating identities, power structures, and intensifying control mechanisms; aesthetic photography, which camouflages the banal aspect by figurative sophistication and references to the observers and their sensibilities; and transgressive photography, which dismantles the accepted patterns of the banal and aesthetic representations and ruptures their boundaries.[68]

The banal mode of representation creates a figure that does not reveal anything new. It arranges reality and renders it understandable. Banal photography is shot from a panoptic position that sees everything, serves the government's logic, and enables control and supervision as well as displaying clear categories of identity, space, and time. The identity of the people photographed ("what is photographed") is unequivocal; the national marking of the space ("where the picture was taken" and "what preceded it") is clear. Often, as Nathansohn claims, this photography also presents binary axes of here/there, soldiers/Palestinians, and so on. By contrast, the transgressive mode of photography provides a gaze that is

> disturbing, unfamiliar, likely to lead to fresh thinking, as well as criticism. Observing photos of this kind leaves us, the spectators, confused and discontented: the imaging unravels its conventional

> understanding, the categories we are familiar with rule out any possibility for decoding what is presented to us, and what was taken for granted until that moment is subverted.[69]

This photography captures areas hidden from the eye; it abandons the panoptic perspective and power relations, and is characterized by creating private archives, in contrast to a catalogued, organized archive that functions as a supervision mechanism. In such photographs, the identity of the photographed subjects is not always clear; sometimes they are not doing what is expected of them, there is no clear location or binary contrast, or causality. Photographs of this kind generate deterritorialization for the institutionalized gaze.[70]

These distinctions regarding transgressive photography coincide with the notion of rhizomatic and nomadic art, which does not permit categorizing and therefore lacks a center. Sarah's photographs reflect this form of art, since she exchanges the catalogued and sorted archive for an unclassifiable collection. Sarah seeks another mode of photographing. She disdains the notion of

> capturing subjects during their momentary suspension of consciousness during which the photographer captures someone who is not watching. She belittled the opposite effect as well: cooperation between photographer and subject, when the subject would turn himself into a third entity, material.[71]

However, there is another aspect to these pictures. Taking pictures of sleeping people can be a primal violation of anyone's rights, since the sleeping subjects did not give their permission and the photos were taken in a "momentary suspension of consciousness." This is the reason Sarah does not share them.

Snapshots presents another form of nomadic art that examines the territorial dispute and the Occupation. For Lana, the twentieth century is defined by refugeedom and she decides to dedicate herself professionally to the problem.[72] Her dissertation for her architecture degree in Israel is entitled "Refugee Settlement in Early Statehood." Later she chooses to construct residential complexes for refugees in Europe. At the same time, Lana is planning an antimonument to peace in Jerusalem, to be built around the Jewish concepts of *shmitta* (literally "release"—the Sabbatical year of releasing the land, when the land is left fallow) and *sukkot* (temporary huts open to the sky built and slept in during the seven days of the Sukkot holiday). Her professional decisions, both for housing refugees and for constructing the antimonument, spark tensions between building a home and possessing the land, and releasing it.

Elizabeth Grosz argues that architecture is the evolution of primordial art and forms a shape and a frame:

> The frame is what establishes territory out of the chaos that is the earth. The frame is thus the first construction, the corners, of the plane of composition. With no frame or boundary, there can be no territory. [. . .] Architecture is the most elementary binding or containment of forces, the conditions under which qualities can live their own life through the constitution of territory.[73]

Architecture creates shape, imposes borders on space, and is directly related to territory. However, in Govrin's text, Lana shows that deterritorization can occur in an architectural framework as well. The choice to build complexes to house refugees incorporates the inherent opposition between the refugee with no territory and the concept of a home. In the context of the political conflict and while the Intifada is raging, Lana pores over her antimonument to peace, which embodies a utopian position concerning the land. The antimonument is the antithesis to monuments that have a physical presence, are attached to the land, and are supposed to remind us of the past. Instead, Lana tries to create an antimonument with an unstable physical presence. This antimonument would be located in a liminal region, which faces the future, as its primary message projects the notion of *shmitta*. In a one-on-one interview with Claude, conducted between the sheets, Lana unfolds her vision:

> In fact it all started four years ago with the project of the yeshiva in Strasbourg. I agreed to work on a religious project when I learned that more than fifty percent of the yeshiva students were refugees from the Soviet Union. I decided I couldn't discriminate against refugees just because they're Jews who insist on studying Torah. Refugees are refugees are refugees [. . .] there for all places [. . .] I found a stunning model of thought about building, and completely different notion of

> place, of dwelling [. . .] an architecture of nomads. [. . .] Look at the Talmudic discussion of Sabbatical year and the laws of Sukkah. Here you can find the most radical definition of the relationship between nation and land—an unnatural relationship. [. . .] As it says in the wonderful chapter of Leviticus 'for the land is mine'. Mine—God—not man's. The land doesn't belong to anybody! It was given as a promise to the nation that came to it from far away, and the promise is 'on condition'. It will be kept only if the nation is at an ethical level that will justify it. Otherwise the nation will be send into exile. And how do you stay conscious of that condition? By the law of the Sabbatical Year! Every seven years, in the year of Sabbatical, the fences around the property have to be destroyed, everybody has to given food from its produce [. . .] to let go of ownership. [. . .] Think about a place that can't be owned! Especially in the Land of Israel, Jerusalem, the place everybody wants to conquer, to own! Jerusalem, the longed-for city, the woman, the place of yearning . . . to let go of her . . .[74]

Lana proposes an antimonument consisting of temporary huts. Instead of looking at the monument, people are asked to build a hut and live in it for a short time. She plans to build a kitchen, library, and meeting rooms designed as spaces midway between the temporary and the permanent, with roofs open to the sky. It will be made of a colony of huts, with a restricted life cycle; it will be built on the edge of the desert, with a moat around it.

Through her antimonument, Lana expropriates the power from the architectural project and creates a art for the people, temporary art, that frees the territory instead of clinging to it and allows every guest to construct his/her own hut on foundations, which based on a nomadic ideal, without sovereignty. As Rosi Braidotti notes, "the nomad has a sharpened sense of territory but no possessiveness about it."[75]

Lana chooses the Hill of Evil Counsel as the location for her antimonument, a place that is both border and threshold, as the author herself attests:

> Ilana's fictional project is located in a real place: on the highest hilltop of Jerusalem, The Hill of Evil Counsel. [. . .] just outside downtown; yet it remains a foreign "enclave," belonging to another space and time. [. . .]

> A space intensely layered—topographically, ethnically, politically and textually. The hilltop's name, The Hill of Evil Counsel, is a quote from the New Testament, and looking northwards it faces the Holy Sepulcher with Jesus' grave. To this hilltop Abraham and Isaac, with the young men and the donkey who accompanied them, arrived after three days walk, and watched "from afar" Mount Moriah. And from here Celestial Jerusalem was shown to Ezekiel by the Angel. Beyond the Old City walls, constructed by Suleiman the Magnificent, stands the golden dome of The Mosque of Omar, where Mohammed leaped on horseback to heaven.[76]

Rimmon-Kenan argues that Lana's antimonument creates bridges between religious, ethnic, and national territorial frameworks, and removes their boundaries. Its location is liminal, and the notion of the Sabbatical Year and the huts underscores the deterritorialization and the annulling of sovereignty over land. By the same token, Lana's life of wandering and love affairs is equally associated with that notion and provides a concretization for the transformation of boundaries to thresholds.[77] Lana thinks of Jerusalem as a woman: "Jerusalem the woman. Loyal, unfaithful, saint and whore, the city of God's lust, the city that maddens all those who yearn to own her, to demand an exclusive claim to her."[78] For this very reason, she wants the city to be a state that will belong to no one: "untouched. Not the homeland of any tribe." In an interview with Dalia Karpel, Govrin remarked that "It's impossible to understand the conflict or anti-Semitism without addressing the erotic-perverse aspect of this city."[79] In fact, the *shmitta*/release in the work takes on a sexual significance: like a woman's body, the released territory cannot be violated or controlled. Moreover, Lana as a woman intends to examine this ideal herself, with her own sexuality, to see whether she can withstand the release of "loving without violating, without claiming ownership."[80]

Lana and Sarah propose another way to manage space. As nomads who engage in nomadic art, they aim to smooth the striated spaces and to convert the national, ethnic, religious, and gendered categories into a rhizomatic reality that would make it possible to construct a network of lines of flight from the violating territorial discourse. Can the aesthetic and ethical path they suggest come into being?

Deterritorialization and Femaleness

> *As a woman I have no country, as a woman I want no country, as a woman my country is the whole world.*
>
> —Virginia Woolf[81]

Hever states that Matalon's text describes an incessant, undefined process of identity-formation, which because of its instability, paradoxically enables a new space of moral responsibility:

> This notion of personal and moral identity in the novel [. . .] is inevitably a notion of a flexible, unstable identity that shifts and connects to other identities, but chiefly an identity that must be constituted recurrently, a never-ending effort at self-definition, again and again. Because definition is elusive, the identity must constantly be redefined.[82]

In their writing on nomadism and rhizomatic thought, Deleuze and Guattari ascribe a pivotal place to *becoming* as a way of escaping the territorial system of power (Oedipal, binary, genealogical). By replacing the aspiration for a stable, unchanging identity, becoming is associated with an identity that develops ad infinitum. Braidotti explores nomadism from a feminist point of view, and links nomadism to the notion of identity: "This figuration [becoming] expresses the desire for an identity made of transitions, successive shifts, and coordinated changes, without and against an essential unity."[83] This perception abandons aspirations for unity, and instead stimulates the desire for a process of infinite becoming that results from the rhizomatic outlook where there is no center or boundary, and lines extend everywhere. Nomadic movement is also connected to the notion that things are subject to a process-based continuing context, with no place for fixation. The absence of the fixation of the home, and the temporality of borders, generate an unending process of becoming.[84]

Becoming is only possible in the context of a minority; "there is no becoming majoritarian; majority is never becoming. All becoming is minoritarian."[85] For Deleuze and Guattari, "all becomings begin with and pass through becoming-woman. It is the key to all other becomings."[86] In Matalon's and Govrin's texts, the processes of becoming that project deterritorization are evident in Sarah's and Lana's lives as women but are also present in other characters in the novels who may be defined as members of a minority, such as Ofri, Michel, and Marwan in Matalon's book and Alain and Sayyid in Govrin's.

The connection between nomadism and the endless becoming of the subject's identity, the links between them and the notion of *becoming-woman* (as a minority) forms the crux of feminist criticism of Deleuze and Guattari. Specifically, although Deleuze and Guattari describe becoming as becoming-woman, they follow the philosophical tradition in which Woman is the philosopher's Other. Luce Irigaray, for instance, identifies this as a male implication, again based on a metaphysical axis of difference between masculinity and femininity, because only those who maintain the stable position of a subject (i.e., white males) can suggest conceding it. She argues that "The metaphor of becoming-woman is a male appropriation and recuperation of the positions and struggles of woman. As such, it risks depoliticizing, possibly even aestheticizing, struggles and political challenges crucial to the survival and self-definition of women."[87] It is worth recalling that while becoming is intended toward a specific stable essence, in the Deleuzian model the project of becoming is infinite and without direction. Braidotti and Grosz view rhizomatic thought as an immensely powerful tool, a vital resource that can be used for the feminist struggle.[88] In Matalon's and Govrin's texts, these ties between nomadic lives and art and constantly form identities as femininity take on further ethical and political significance.

The female protagonists' choice to abandon the concept of home in favor of nomadism appears as a choice made by women, characterized by their contrast with the prevalent image of women as located in the home; that is, as subjects who are supervised by boundaries. For women in general, and for the women characters in the two novels, the home—which can symbolize intimacy and security—is a locus that is ruled, supervised and restricted. It is a political space, which fashions a binary division and does not permit the boundaries to be crossed. The nomads confront this space. Though they are subject to uncertainty and hazards, they are also able to cross borders, thus breaking through the subject's fixated identity, allowing her to replace binary, genealogical relations with rhizomatic, temporary, and multishaded contexts.

The two female protagonists, Sarah and Lana, act and behave as an antithesis to the prevailing stereotype linking women to the home and locating the men outside the home; a figure in which the women wait while the men go to war. When women leave their homes and access the war zone, which is considered a male region, they can provide a different gaze. Daniela Mansbach interviewed women who were part of the *Machsom Watch*; she argues that the female gaze undermines prevailing social perceptions: "it is not fettered to traditional militarist perceptions, but represents criticism that does not fall silent when confronted with security issues."[89] Sarah produces an image that corresponds to what Tamsin Lorraine defines as the "becoming-imperceptible model": a situation that refuses the determinism of the self and signifies openness to the surrounding territories.[90]

However, Sarah's professional choice is only one facet of the whole. Her private life also reflects the theme of nomadism, as does her unstable identity as a female subject. Sarah chooses to leave home and its restricted space, and to roam between spaces and other homes. She has relationships with Udi and Marwan, as well as with Ofri. In fact, she chooses the nomadic track, without anticipating a stable coherent existence. Thus, in her intimate life she embodies an anti-sovereignty perspective. And yet, as a part of a minority, Sarah cannot enforce her perspective on those around her. The strongest expression of her choice and its failure is embodied in her abortion. All the characters consider Mims, her biological son, to be the center: everyone wants him to be theirs, everyone wants to share him. For this reason, she decides not to bring another child into the world. Avner Holzman writes that everyone around Mims "clings to him and demands a place in his life."[91] However, unlike Holzman's interpretation of these feelings as a yearning for a kind of innocence, clinging to Mims can reflect a different orientation. Mims violates the nomadic principle since he creates a focus of attention. Like a land whose ownership is unclear, Mims is also positioned as the focus of the struggle over sovereignty. In order to avoid creating another such focus, and to implement the nomadic principle (and perhaps to some extent, in the spirit of Govrin's work to follow the idea of *shmitta)*, Sarah has an abortion. Those around her cannot forgive this act, which in fact shatters the life that Sarah created, and the relationships that had previously worked in equilibrium and equivalence.

Lana, in Govrin's work, undergoes a similar process. She also finds herself pregnant at the end of the book but dies without the father's identity being revealed. Like Matalon, for Govrin, the connection between territory and female intimate space reflects the failure of the option of release, of conceding sovereignty. Sarah and Lana's embryos may represent the fulfillment of the concept of an open place without sovereignty. This idea undermines both the conservative perception of woman as home,[92] woman as territory, woman as stability, and the political perception that territory is contingent on borders and possession.

Thus, the place of the unborn child within the conflict and between the men in the lives of both Sarah and Lana demonstrate women's power of fertility and the strong national implication of motherhood. Unlike Castel-Bloom's Dolly, who adopts a boy and takes the national mission upon herself, these protagonists decide not to play into this role. However, their decision threatens their environment and leads to violence. In Matalon's novel Marwan becomes violent, while in Govrin's text the violence is both private and public. Lana sees war as an act of male violence and compares war to rape: "Disgust wafts from the exhausted body. A woman with two children who were raped again,"[93] and male power in battle as sexual power: "waving phallic weapons, by ejaculating shots from rifle barrels, cannons, the devastating erection of missiles and soaring of planes into the night."[94]

Lana's experience during the first Gulf War, and particularly in the context of being a single mother of two small children in Jerusalem, emphasizes the destructive nature of war, which works against the female force that is prepared to release the land. Lana's idealistic female interpretation of abandoning the idea of sovereignty cannot be accepted by battle-hungry male society. This perspective generates deterritorialization of male conceptions of female sexuality: while the woman represents the earth, territory is presented as a masculine matter.[95] Lana tries to explain to her husband, to Sayyid, and to the left-wing activists who want to include her in their struggle that release/*shmitta* offers the solution:

> I tried to explain to Sayyid that it's not us or you. It's beyond ownership. Robbery, argument about who was here first, who expelled whom [. . .] If there's any meaning at all to the return of the Jews to their land [. . .] it's to make a new revolution in the concept of nationalism, reformulate the connection between nation and land, give up the passion to conquer, to own.[96]

However, she soon understands that she is alone:

> I feel quite alone with those thoughts. Far from the ideologies of the right, far from my friends on the left, far from the dream of the Zionist founders, like my father, and also far from Sayyid's dream of

> independence, which doesn't even begin to deal with the multilayered uniqueness of the land of Israel, and remain in the original definition of ownership, *tsumus*, a jihad liberating the Muslim holy lands.[97]

Whereas Lana dreams of taking down the borders and redeeming territory from any form of ownership, she discovers that everyone who seemed to support her is trying to create reterritorialization. In other words, for them, removing the borders is only one chapter in the chronicles of building new borders and declaring a different sovereignty over the disputed territory. Yochai Oppenheimer notes that the work reflects a "contradiction between the utopian idea and excessive refusal to concede the motherland or to share it with others."[98]

Both Matalon and Govrin present an unusual aesthetic: an ethical, and female approach to the issues of territory and sovereignty. Amir Eshel argues that Govrin's text creates "a set of metaphors about land possession and the possibility of land sharing that allowed Israelis and Palestinians to [. . .] consider relating differently to their disputed land."[99] In choosing the rhizomatic model, in which nomads create open spaces, span bridges over borders, and enable flexibility in the subject's never-ending becoming, both authors suggest a revolutionary angle on representations of Israeli society, the Occupation, and the Intifada in Israeli literature. Because of the revolutionary nature of their gaze, and its implications that threaten the core of political and gendered power, this alternative is doomed to fail. Hence alongside the radical choice, these works also propose a realistic view that portrays how the female and ethical perspective is crushed and threatened with violence. Ultimately, the abandonment of sovereignty and possession cannot succeed in a place where men thirst for war, a place where weapons continue to assault Jerusalem over and over again.

Epilogue

> *We have nothing that can be used to bridge the gap. Literature could, of course, be such a bridge, because it helps you to see that other people are human like us.*
>
> —Dorit Rabinyan[1]

In December 2015, Israeli literature was the hottest topic on prime-time Israeli media. Education Minister Naftali Bennett had just confirmed that Dorit Rabinyan's book *Gader haya* ("Border Life"; in the English translation the title is *All the Rivers*, 2014) would not be on the official reading list for Hebrew high school literature classes, since it depicts a relationship between a Jewish woman and a Palestinian man favorably and portrays the Israeli soldier in a highly negative light.[2]

Liat, the protagonist of *All the Rivers*, moves to New York for a year and meets Hilmi, a painter who was born in Hebron, then moves to Ramallah and subsequently to New York. Liat and Hilmi fall in love, but she hides their relationship from both her Israeli friends in New York and her family in Israel. The relationship ends when Liat returns to Tel Aviv.

Dalia Fenig, an Education Ministry official, admitted that teachers had asked for the book to be included on the recommended curriculum. However, a ministerial committee decided that the book "could do more harm than good,"[3] and argued that relationships between Jews and Palestinians are detrimental to Jewish identity. Although several canonic books on the school literature curriculum, such as A. B. Yehoshua's *The Lover*, describe intimate relationships between Jews and Arabs, the ministry officials stated that the educational system in Israel cannot appear to be in favor of relationships that may encourage Jews to assimilate or marry non-Jews.

Israeli authors, teachers of literature, as well as center and left-wing politicians criticized this decision, and the book immediately became a bestseller. The book became available in bookstores and libraries, and people were eager to read what high school students were prohibited from studying at school for political reasons. However, they soon discovered that this love story was doomed to fail from the start and that the author considered this relationship impossible. Liat and Hilmi can fall in love in the neutral territory of New York City, but they cannot preserve their relationship in the reality of Israel and the Second Intifada. Thus, the return to Israel/the Palestinian territories can only spell tragedy.[4]

All the Rivers is beyond the timeline of this book, which explores literature within the period from 1987 to 2007. Clearly, while the book concentrates on the twenty years from the beginning of the First Intifada to the aftermath of the Second Intifada, the issues discussed continue to be relevant in literature published in the next decade. *All the Rivers* illustrates a certain literary trend that is slowly gaining momentum in the Israeli literary milieu. Neither the Occupation nor the Intifada is the main topic of the novel, which is more of a universalized Romeo and Juliet story. Most of the narrative is located outside Israel and the reality in the Territories, and there are only a few minor descriptions of soldiers. However, the conflict permeates the narrative in different modes and places. This text, like many others that have been written in the last decade, shows that Hebrew literature continues to intensively discuss issues of borders, territories, and ethics. Whether engaging in a realistic description of places, like in Zeruya Shalev's *Ke'ev* (Pain, 2015) or a dystopian-distorted version of Israel as in Ilana Bernstein's *Ha-ir ha-mizrahit* (The East City, 2013); whether the spatial setting are the hills of the West Bank as in Assaf Gavron's *Ha-giv'a* (The Hilltop, 2013), which tells the story of Ma'aleh Hermesh C, a fictional unauthorized settlement in the West Bank, or in foreign remote space as in Ilai Rowner's *Arik* (Deserter, 2015), whose protagonist is tormented by his military trauma and flees to Paris but still cannot find peace, the impact of the Occupation cannot be ignored. Rabinyan's novel, as well as others, not only emphasizes the relevance of these issues but demonstrates the depth of emotions sparked in both readers and politicians when the conflict and its spatial context are expressed in a literary mode.

Questions of borders, territory, and ethics haunted Israeli society in the past, continue to haunt it today, and unfortunately will continue to haunt it in the future. David Grossman's book of essays *Ha-zman ha-tsahov* (The Yellow Wind) was published in 1987, just before the first Intifada broke out, and is based on a series of columns that originally appeared in the weekly *Koteret Rashit.* In its title, as well as in the first edition of the book, Grossman refers to the time that elapsed since the Occupation started: "I belong to the generation that celebrated its Bar-Mitzvah during the Six Day war,"[5] and since then "everything happened, and it is as if nothing happens."[6] Grossman spend seven weeks traveling in the West Bank, interviewing Palestinian and Israelis, Arabs and Jews, to understand the Occupation twenty years after. His purpose was to remove the "'block' in our soul," stating that as long as we accept the Occupation, "little by little we learn to make detours, to distance ourselves from that same closed area. Our access to it is blocked. Without our noticing, it ceases to be ours."[7]

In 2016, almost thirty years later, writer Nir Baram outlines a similar trip in his book *Ha-arets she-me'ever la-harim* (A Land Without Borders: My Journey around East Jerusalem and the West Bank), collecting interviews from people in the West Bank, Gaza, and East Jerusalem. Baram grew up in the 1980s, the period that Grossman describes in his book. In many ways Baram was raised in a different setting and reality characterized by the political upheaval and the rise of the Likud Party, and the First Lebanon war. However, not everything has changed—the Occupation is still here, the borders are still blurred, and the rift between the Zionist liberal legacy and the control of millions of Palestinians is still clear. Beyond scrutinizing the past, Baram is concerned about the future, and asks: "what will our future look like? What sort of country will be here? [. . .] I realized that what has evolved in Israel over the past few years is a collective repression of the future."[8]

Grossam and Baram abandoned their fictional writing to write these volumes and embarked on a quest to better understand what is happening to Israeli society and its core values. They have been brave enough to criticize not only the small groups of hawkish Palestinians and right-wing activists and settlers, but also society as a whole, which by remaining silent and focusing on personal lives and personal prosperity denies spatial instability and avoids ethical concerns.

Israeli literature, which has adhered to the Zionist enterprise from its beginnings, is an integral part of today's artistic and poetic soul-searching in Israeli society. This book offered an exploration of this contemporary writing through a new perspective on the multifaceted relations between space and ethics. From the development of the concept of deterritorialization and the relevance of *moral luck*, to questions of the representation of the Other, the myth of national sacrifice, and the vision of Levinas's philosophy, this book attempted to formulate a set of theoretical tools to grasp the role of spatial and ethical considerations in contemporary Hebrew literature. Each of the seven chapters analyzed issues such as militarism and humanism, soldiers' duties to the state and to themselves as moral individuals, and the nature of Zionist education, as well as questions regarding the role of national myths and bereavement, and the possibility of ethical acknowledgment of the Other. The overall picture reveals how these literary works voice critical expressions and implement effective and surprising poetic strategies that shed light on many of the dark sides of the Occupation.

Many contemporary writers of the past decade such as Rabinyan, Bernstein, Gavron, and Rowner were not discussed in this book, but core questions concerning the nature of the State of Israel will continue to function as the source of literary creation. "We have lived for twenty years in a false and artificial situation," Grossman told us in 1987, a situation that is "based on illusions, on a teetering canter of gravity between hate and fear, in a desert void of emotion and consciousness, and the passing time turns slowly into a separate, forbidden entity hanging above us like a suffocating layer of yellow dust."[9] People can close their eyes and hearts, but literature continues to find new ways to disperse this yellow dust. It is my hope that this study will provide new insights into contemporary Israeli literature and a key to a new, future contemplation and actions in these critical moments of Israel's existence.

Notes

Introduction

1. Grossman, *Writing in the Dark*, 108. Translated by Jessica Cohen.
2. In Taub, "Mehapsim safa aheret" (Looking for Another Language). Translated by Tamar Gerstenhaber.
3. Kemp, "Ha-gvul ki-fnei Janus" (The Border as Janus's Face), 16. See also Peled, *Ha-ribon ha-israeli* (The Israeli Sovereign), 2.
4. Gurevitz and Aranne, "Al ha-makom" (On the Place).
5. Kemp, "Ha-gvul ki-fnei Janus" (The Border as Janus's Face), 16.
6. I do not focus on the specific issue of East Jerusalem, which requires a separate analysis. I also do not deal with the Sinai or the Golan Heights, since my main concern is literature dealing with Israeli rule over the Palestinian population.
7. Feige, *Shtei mapot la-gada* (One Space, Two Places), 30.
8. Lustick, *Unsettled States*, 353.
9. Feige, *Shtei mapot la-gada* (One Space, Two Places), 30
10. Ibid., 31.
11. Ibid., 12–13.
12. Weizman, *Hollow Land*, 4.
13. See: Kimmerling, *The Israeli State and Society*.
14. See: Goldshmid, "Ha-gvul shel ha-sifrut" (The Border of Literature).
15. Grumberg, *Place and Ideology*, 131–2.
16. Ophir and Azoulay, *Mishtar ze she-eino ehad* (This Regime Which Is Not One).

17. Note that full democracy and equality have been curtailed within Israeli borders as well. Palestinians who are also Israeli citizens were subject to martial law from 1948 to 1966, when emergency regulations were enforced.
18. Agamben, *State of Exception.* See also: Humphreys, "Legalizing Lawlessness."
19. See also: Abujidi, "The Palestinian State of Exception," Shenhav, "Halalei ribonut" (Casualties of Sovereignty), and Peled, *Ha-ribon ha-israeli* (The Israeli Sovereign), 5–11.
20. Hever, "Tnu lo badranim" (Give Him Entertainers).
21. Peleg, *Israeli Culture*, 33.
22. Levy, "Nation, Village, Cave."
23. See, for example, Hever, "We Have Not Arrived" and *Producing Modern Hebrew Canon.*
24. See also Oppenheimer's article "The Arab in the Mirror."
25. Other scholars, who are part of this "spatial turn," have explored literature in different contexts. Schwartz's research offers a reading of Hebrew literature from the mid-nineteenth-century Hebrew writer Avraman Mapu to contemporary Israeli writers such as Amos Oz, and identifies what he terms the "vector of passion" for "the place" and the unbridgeable tension between this dreamlike place and the gray manifestation of the everyday space. See: Schwartz, "Human Engineering," *Ma she-ro'im mi-kan* (What We See from Here), *Ha-yadata et ha-arets* (Did You Know the Land). In Mann's *Space and Place in Jewish Studies*, spatial gaze challenges the idea of the Jewish home, through an investigation of concepts of space and place, diaspora and homeland, home, street and garden, and the notion of sovereignty. Mann examines locations various texts and through major categories of Jewish thought, phases in the history of the Jewish people, and concrete realizations in the Land of Israel, thus articulating the symbolic role of places. Two books have been written on specific cities: Mann's early book *A Place in History: Modernism, Tel Aviv and the Creation of Jewish Urban Space* discusses Tel-Aviv and Gold's work *Haifa: City of Steps* focuses on the specific location of Haifa and discusses the city's cultural significance by examining its unique history, geography, port and heterogeneous population.
26. Hever, *Producing Modern Hebrew Canon.*
27. Deleuze and Guattari, *A Thousand Plateaus*, 10. See also: Deleuze and Guattari, *Kafka*.
28. Foucault, Preface, xiii.

29. Deleuze and Guattari, *A Thousand Plateaus*, 4–5.
30. Patton, "Deterritorialization and Politics," 73–4.
31. Svirsky, *Arab-Jewish Activism*, 28.
32. Murdoch, "Against Dryness," 20.
33. For an introduction to ethical criticism see Mendelson-Maoz, "Ethics and Literature: Introduction."
34. Hever, "Mapa shel hol" (Map of Sand), 168.
35. Hazaz, "Ha-sifrut ha-ivrit ba-zman ha-ze" (Hebrew Literature in This Era), cited in Oppenheimer, *Me'ever la-gader* (Barriers), 169.
36. Oppenheimer, "Aliyato u-nefilato" (The Rise and Fall), 282. See also: Oppenheimer, *Me'ever la-gader* (Barriers).
37. Abramson, "Oh, My Land, My Birthplace," 225.
38. Peled's book offers a good example for this inclination. *Peled, Ha-ribon ha-israeli* (The Israeli Sovereign).
39. Urian, "Cinema and Stage," 298.

Part 1

1. In the story, Keret imitates the Arab speakers' pronunciation of the sound "p" as "b."
2. Keret, *Ga'aguay le-kissinger* (Missing Kissinger), 64–5. Translated by Miriam Shlesinger and Sondra Silverston.
3. Ibid., 66.
4. Ibid., 66–7.
5. Ibid., 68.
6. Ben-Eliezer, *Old Conflict, New War*, 9. See also: Ben-Eliezer and Feinstein, "The Battle over Our Homes."
7. Ibid., 10.
8. Goren, *The Home Front*, 47.

Chapter 1

1. Yizhar, "Hirbet Hiz'a" (Khirbet Khizeh), 88–9. All quotations from the story were taken from the English translation by Nicholas de Lange and Yaacob Dweck.
2. Ibid., 12.
3. Ibid.
4. Ibid., 11.

5. Anita Shapira discusses the acceptance of the story throughout the years and focuses on its role in shaping the collective memory of the war. See: Shapira, "Hirbet Hizah."
6. Grumberg, *Place and Ideology*, 36.
7. Patton, *Deleuzian Concepts*, 43.
8. Levy-Barzilai, "Yefei ha-nefesh, nim'astem" (Sensitive Souls, Enough).
9. Ball, *Prosecuting War Crimes*, 220; Holmes, *Acts of War*, 276.
10. Grossman, *On Killing*, 96, 160.
11. Ibid., 107.
12. Ibid., 119.
13. Ibid.
14. Ibid., 137.
15. Hersh, "Torture at Abu Ghraib."
16. Ben Ari, "Hayalim be-masekhot" (Soldiers in Masks), 110.
17. Holmes, *Acts of War*, 32–6.
18. Lieblich and Perlow, "Transition to Adulthood."
19. Meisels, "Likrat giyus" (Before Recruitment).
20. Holmes, *Acts of War*, 56, 93–4.
21. Breines, Connell, and Eide (eds.), *Male Roles*.
22. Grossman, *On Killing*, 95.
23. Yizhar, "Hirbet Hiz'a" (Khirbet Khizeh), 51.
24. Ibid., 25.
25. Ibid., 60.
26. Ibid., 46.
27. Ibid., 53.
28. Ibid., 64.
29. Ibid., 37.
30. Holmes, *Acts of War*, 57.
31. Yizhar, "Hirbet Hiz'a" (Khirbet Khizeh), 80.
32. Kochavi, "Degel shahor e'had gadol" (One Large Black Flag), 144.
33. Lubin, *Isha koret isha* (A Woman Reads Woman), 226–9.
34. Kravitz, *Ani Mustafa Rabinovitch* (I, Mustafa Rabinovitch), 9. All quotations from the novel were translated by Tamar Gerstenhaber.
35. Ibid., 21.
36. Munk, *Golim be-gvulam* (Exiled in Their Borders), 41–8.
37. Foucault, *Discipline and Punish*, 200–9.
38. Valentain, *Shahid*, 6. All quotations from the novel were translated by Tamar Gerstenhaber.

39. Usher, "Children of Palestine," 12. See also: Nassar, "Stories from under Occupation."
40. Kravitz, *Ani Mustafa Rabinovitch* (I, Mustafa Rabinovitch), 10.
41. Ibid., 36–7.
42. Ibid., 38.
43. Ibid., 41.
44. Ibid., 245.
45. Burman, "Innocents Abroad," 240.
46. In these cases, there is no trial or court hearing. This is a variant on the Israeli army's doctrine of *hisul memukad* (targeted elimination), which has been widely discussed and often criticized in military and political circles.
47. Yehoshua, *Esh yedidutit* (Friendly Fire), 288. Translated by Stuart Schoffman.
48. Iczkovits, *Dofek* (Pulse), 251. All quotations from the novel were translated by Tamar Gerstenhaber.
49. Ibid., 197.
50. Kravitz, *Ani Mustafa Rabinovitch* (I, Mustafa Rabinovitch), 49–50.
51. Oppenheimer, "Aliyato u-nefilato" (The Rise and Fall), 290.
52. Nevo, *Mish'ala ahat yemina* (World Cup Wishes), 152. The following quotes were translated by Tamar Gerstenhaber from the original Hebrew version (in the published English version translated by Sondra Silverston, this episode appears on pages 152–9).
53. Ibid., 153.
54. Ibid., 155.
55. Ibid., 157–8. In the English, 159.
56. Lahav, *Lekh le-aza* (Go to Gaza), 6–7. All quotations from the novel were translated by Tamar Gerstenhaber.
57. Neumann, *Hayal tov* (Good Soldier), 170. All quotations from the novel were translated by Tamar Gerstenhaber.
58. Ibid., 170–2.
59. In: Evron, *Mar'eh makom* (Reference), 22. All quotations from the story were translated by Tamar Gerstenhaber.
60. Ibid., 31.
61. Amireh, "Between Complicity and Subversion," 750.
62. Ibid., 751.
63. From the "Rape Song" in *Mammy* by Hillel Mittelpunkt, translated by Tamar Gerstenhaber. The full text of the song can be found on the Shironet

site: https://shironet.mako.co.il/artist?type=lyrics&lang=1&prfid=1256&wrkid=3810

64. Lahav, *Lekh le-aza* (Go to Gaza), 136.
65. The English translation is from the site "Poets from Palestine," http://www.barghouti.com/poets/darwish/bitaqa.asp
66. Kravitz, *Ani Mustafa Rabinovitch* (I, Mustafa Rabinovitch), 35–6.
67. Nevo, *Mish'ala ahat yemina* (World Cup Wishes), 156 (in the Hebrew version), 157 (in English).
68. Gilad, "Matai hit'halnu" (When Have We Started).
69. Lahav, *Lekh le-aza* (Go to Gaza), 63.
70. Ibid., 71.
71. Kristallnacht took place on November 9–10, 1938, when hundreds of synagogues and Jewish businesses were vandalized or destroyed by the Nazis.
72. Lahav, *Lekh le-aza* (Go to Gaza), 130–1.
73. Ibid., 218.
74. Evron, *Mar'eh makom* (Reference), 26.
75. Ibid., 33.
76. Ibid., 37.
77. Lahav, *Lekh le-aza* (Go to Gaza), 6.

Chapter 2

1. Žižek, "A Soft Focus on War."
2. Hochberg, *Visual Occupations*, 145.
3. Libes and Blum-Kulka, "Yorim u-vokhim?" (Shooting and Crying?).
4. See: Levy, *Mi sholet al ha-tsava?* (Who Governs the Military?).
5. Greenbaum and Elitzur, "Ha-hashlakhot ha-psychologiot ve-ha-musariot" (The Psychological and Moral Implications), 321.
6. Deleuze and Guattari, *A Thousand Plateaus*, 55, 133.
7. Shapira (ed.), *Si'ah lohamim* (Fighters' Discourse).
8. On the censorship of material in this book see: Laor, "Mahshavot al tsenzura" (Thoughts on Censorship), and Izikovitch, "Si'ah lohamim" (Fighters' Discourse).
9. Zartal, "Al si'ah lohamim" (On Fighters' Discourse), 5–6.
10. Shapira (ed.), *Si'ah lohamim* (Fighters' Discourse), 7. A brutally ironic gaze at this phrase appeared in *Sliha she-nitsahnu* (We Apologize for Our Victory), which was published in 1967 and contains a collection of

texts by political commentator and humorist Ephraim Kishon and Dosh's (Kariel Gordosh) caricatures originally published in *Ma'ariv*. The book was reprinted in 2017, marking fifty years after the war.

11. The publication in *Ha-olam ha-ze* dates back to 1976; however, the first publication of the column may date to 1973 when it appeared in the "Pi ha-aton" section, thus making the publication in *Ha-olam ha-ze* the second printed version. In 1981, journalist Nahum Barnea entitled a volume of his collected articles published in the Davar newspaper *Shooting and Crying*.
12. Many artists, singers, and songwriters protested the ban, including Gidi Gov, Shlomo Artzi, Corinne Allal, Ehud Manor, and Shalom Hanoch. When she came to Israel on tour in 1998, Joan Baez performed the song in Hebrew with Palestinian singer Amal Marcus. See: Morgenstern, "Yorim u-vokhim" (Shooting and Crying); Harsonsky, "Ovrim le-reshet gimel" (Moving to Gimel Radio Station); Avisar, "Mefaked galey tsahal" (The Commander of IDF Radio Station). The full text of the song can be found on the Israeli site Shironet: https://shironet.mako.co.il/artist?type=lyrics&lang=1&prfid=753&wrkid=12506. Joan Baez's performance of the song can be found on YouTube: https://www.youtube.com/watch?v=XOCMtY-_acU.
13. See also: Ne'eman, "Aliyatam ve-nefilatam" (The Rise and Fall).
14. Peleg, *Israeli Culture*, 58.
15. Rozen and Hammerman, *Meshorerim lo ikhtevu shirim* (Poets Will Not Write Poetry), 152.
16. http://www.breakingthesilence.org.il/
17. Grassiani, "The Phenomenon of 'Breaking the Silence,'" 256.
18. Arens, "Shovrim shtika she-eina kayemet" (Breaking the Silence That Does Not Exist), and Lior, "Breaking the Silence."
19. Grassiani, "The Phenomenon of 'Breaking the Silence,'" 251. See also: Menuchin, "Ha-hayal ha-tov" (The Good Soldier), 29–30.
20. Yosef, *The Politics of Loss*, 143.
21. See Nagel, *Mortal Questions*, 26. Nagel's book was translated into Hebrew in 2010. *Moral luck* is a controversial term and has been extensively discussed. See for instance: Andre, "Nagel, Williams, and Moral Luck"; Browne, "A Solution to the Problem of Moral Luck"; Enoch and Marmor, "The Case against Moral Luck"; Hannah, "Morality 'De Re'"; Jensen, "Morality and Luck"; Norvin, "Luck and Desert"; Rescher, "Luck"; Rondel, "Equality, Luck and Pragmatism"; Rosebury, "Moral Responsibility and 'Moral Luck'"; Stanovsky, "Stealing Guilt"; Sverdlik, "Crime

and Moral Luck"; Williams, *Moral Luck*, "Postscript"; Zimmerman, "Luck and Moral Responsibility," "Taking Luck Seriously." See also: Mendelson-Maoz, "Hurled into the Heart of Darkness."

I focus on Nagel's investigation of the term, since his categorization of different types of *moral luck* is detailed and helpful to my analysis. In using the philosophical term in the context of literature, I follow Nussbaum in *The Fragility of Goodness.*

22. Nagel, *Mortal Questions*, 26.
23. Ibid., chapter 3.
24. Ibid., 33.
25. Ibid., 34.
26. Tamar, "Hazon Yeshayahu" (Yeshayahu's Prophecy).
27. I will not go into the question of how normative people are able to commit atrocities in extreme situations of war and specifically how this could have happened in the context of the Nazi regime. From Milgram's experiments to Hannah Arendt's work, it is widely acknowledged today that in certain circumstances and under specific conditions, even normative people can be transformed into killers. See for example: Arendt, *Eichmann in Jerusalem.*
28. Zimmerman, "Luck and Moral Responsibility," 379.
29. Statman (ed.), Introduction; italics in the original.
30. Ben-Ner, *Ta'atuon* (Delusion), 80. All quotations from the novel were translated by Tamar Gerstenhaber.
31. Ibid., 53–4.
32. Levy, "I Punched an Arab."
33. Mendelson-Maoz, "Checkpoint Syndrome," 224.
34. Ron Furer, *Tismonet ha-mahsom* (Checkpoint Syndrome), 94. All quotations from the book were translated by Tamar Gerstenhaber. The internet site of *If America Knew* holds a translation of Ron Furer's text to English: http://ifamericaknew.org/download/checkpoint_syndrome.pdf
35. Ibid., 62.
36. Polity, *Arnavonei gagot* (Roof Rabbits), 274–5. All quotations from the novel were translated by Tamar Gerstenhaber.
37. To further explore Opher's argument concerning the body, see Rawls's argument on utilitarianism. Rawls, *Theory of Justice*, 22–4.
38. Polity, *Arnavonei gagot* (Roof Rabbits), 205.
39. Ibid., 264.
40. Malach-Pines, "Et mi shoheket ha-intifada?" (Who Suffers Burnout from the Intifada?), 55.

41. Walker, "Moral Luck and the Virtues of Impure Agency," 245–7.
42. Ron Furer, *Tismonet ha-mahsom* (Checkpoint Syndrome), 3–4.
43. Deleuze and Guattari, *A Thousand Plateaus*, 204.
44. As Axinn states in *A Moral Military*, 2: "the fact that the act in question was carried out under an order of a superior authority [. . .] does not constitute a defense in the trial of an accused individual." See also: Denton, *Limits of Loyalty*; Schafer, "The Buck Stops Here." In the Israeli context, see: Parush, "Bikoret mivhan 'ha-degel ha-shahor'" (A Critique of the "Black Flag" Test); Schiff, "Bizkhut mivhan 'ha-degel ha-shahor'" (In Support of the "Black Flag" Test).
45. See the following websites:
http://www.yeshgvul.org/index_e.asp
http://www.seruv.org.il/english/default.asp
46. See: Linn, "Soldiers with Conscience Never Die."
47. Nagel, *Mortal Questions*, 28, 32. Enoch and Marmor reject this type of *moral luck*, stating that people's inclinations and temperaments must be acknowledged, but that people are expected to control their inclinations and better themselves. Enoch and Marmor, "The Case against Moral Luck."
48. Mayer, *Gender Ironies of Nationalism*, 15.
49. Shapira, *Yehudim hadashim* (New Jews), 184, see also: Almog, *The Sabra.*
50. See: Meisels, "Likrat giyus" (Before Recruitment); Sion, *Dimuyei gavriyut etsel lohamim* (Images of Masculinity among Combat Soldiers).
51. See: Lieblich and Perlow, "Transition to Adulthood," and Lieblich, *Transition to Adulthood.*
52. Libes and Blum-Kulka, "Yorim u-vokhim?" (Shooting and Crying?), 86. See also: Klein, "Our Best Boys."
53. Kravitz, *Ani Mustafa Rabinovitch* (I, Mustafa Rabinovitch), 148.

Chapter 3

1. Levy, *Otiyot ha-shemesh* (Letters of the Sun), 161. All quotations from the novel were translated by Tamar Gerstenhaber.
2. Ibid., 163.
3. Ben Ezer (ed.), *Be-moledet ha-ga'aguim ha-menugadim* (Sleepwalkers and Other Stories); Domb, *The Arab in Hebrew Prose*; Feldman, "The Other Within"; Levy, "Shvuim be-bid'yon" (Prisoners of Imagination); Morahg, "New Images of Arabs"; Oppenheimer, *Me'ever la-gader*

(Barriers), "The Arab in the Mirror"; Perry, "The Israeli-Palestinian Conflict"; Ramras-Rauch, *The Arab in Israeli Literature*; Shaked, "The Arab in Israeli Fiction."

4. Parr (ed.), *The Deleuze Dictionary*, 71.
5. Mackie, *Ethics*, 83.
6. Carroll, "The Wheel of Virtue."
7. These three novels are not the only texts narrated by Palestinian protagonists. I will also comment on two short stories published in *Ha-aretz* in 1989. Two other interesting texts written by women should be mentioned here: Ilana Bernstein's short story, "Ma'atsar" (Imprisonment) in *Iyim shel sheket* (Islands of Calm, 1999) presents a realistic monologue of a Palestinian woman whose husband is arrested by the Israeli military. The narrative is constructed in such a way that it does not expose the Palestinian identity of the woman or her husband at the outset. Thus, the reader is sensitized to the woman's fear for her husband's well-being and her difficulties in caring for her family alone, independently of the political setting. The text only later reveals the life and the choices of her husband through her monologue. Ayelet Shamir-Tulipman's novella "Ha'im ata ro'e et ma she-ani shome'a" (Can You See What I Hear, 2002), which is based on the true story of a Palestinian who was arrested and tortured. She turned his story into a challenging, fragmented, and very blunt text, in which a Palestinian in jail, who cannot see a thing, testifies to the violence of the torches directed at him. The point of view of Palestinians also appears in Michael's novel *Yonim be-trafalgar* (Pigeons in Tragalgar Square, 2005).
8. Maoz, "D'yokano shel Na'im" (A Portrait of Na'im).
9. Ibid., 520–3.
10. Oppenheimer, "The Arab in the Mirror," 214–15.
11. Fanon, *Black Skin*, 2–3.
12. Hall, "Cultural Identity and Diaspora"; "Ethnicity: Identity and Difference"; Bhabha, "Arrivals and Departures"; "DissemiNation," in *Nation and Narration*, 291–322; *Location of Culture*, 88–9.
13. Oppenheimer, "The Arab in the Mirror," 217.
14. Ibid.
15. Brenner, *Inextricably Bonded*, 89, 108. The term "present absentee" is an Israeli phrase that designates Palestinians who fled or were forced away from their homes during the 1948 war, but remained within what became Israel, and thus lost their villages, houses, lands, and property to the State's Custodian of Absentee Property. The term can also serve as a metaphor

for the lost identity of the Palestinians who are Israeli citizens, as in the title of Grossman's book, *Nokhehim nifkadim* (Present Absentees, 1992).

16. Shammas's novel portrays a literary dialogue between Paco, a Palestinian writer, and Yehoshua Bar-On, an Israeli-Jewish writer, producing a different poetic frame for the question of the Israeli-Palestinian voice in Hebrew literature. Shammas's novel not only depicts Bar-On as an ill-disguised A. B. Yehoshua, but also refers to Bialik's poetry. The debate between Yehoshua and Shammas was widely commented on (by Silberstein for example), Michael Gluzman shows how Shammas used Bialik's text "Habrekha" (The Pool) to criticize Yehoshua, and specifically his protagonist Na'im. The narrator of *Arabeskot* uses Bialik's lines when describing the lake he and Bar-on visit in Iowa. Paco claims this reminds him of the homeland and quotes Bialik's wonderful lines describing the lake, but then deliberately throws an empty can into the water, littering not only the lake but also the image of Bialik. See Silberstein, *The Postzionism Debate*, 139–43, and Gluzman, "The Politics of Intertextuality," 327.
17. Horn, *Facing the Fire*, 74.
18. Lockard, "Somewhere between Arab and Jew," 52.
19. Morahg, "New Images of Arabs," 160.
20. Grover, *Zionism*.
21. Grossman in an interview with Runo Isaksen. In: Isaksen, *Literature and War*, 42.
22. Gertz, "Imprisoning the National Identity," 196.
23. Brenner, *Inextricably Bonded*, 253–4.
24. See: Morahg, "New Images of Arabs," 155–6.
25. Green, *Agadot ha-intifada* (The Intifada Tales), 79. All quotations from the novel were translated by Tamar Gerstenhaber.
26. Levy, *Otiyot ha-shemesh* (Letters of the Sun), 98.
27. Ibid., 124.
28. Ibid., 164.
29. Ibid., 120.
30. Spivak, "Can the Subaltern Speak?"
31. Alcoff, "The Problem of Speaking for Others," 6.
32. Ibid., 13.
33. Ibid., 20.
34. Said, *Orientalism*, 49.
35. Ibid., 38–9.
36. See: Metres, "Vexing Resistance."

37. Raz-Krakotzkin, "Be-hipus ahar ha-anima" (In Search of the Anima).
38. Levy, "Avak shel bustanim" (Dust of Orchards).
39. Shats, "Te'enim" (Figs).
40. Raz-Krakotzkin, "Be-hipus ahar ha-anima" (In Search of the Anima).
41. Green in: Aginsky, "Le-Ali ha-katan" (Little Ali).
42. Oppenheimer, *Me'ever la-gader* (Barriers), 340.
43. Masalha, "Hutspa israelit" (Israeli "Hutspa").
44. Ibid.
45. On the new style in Hebrew literature, see for instance: Hever, *Sifrut she-nikhtevet mi-kan* (Literature Written from Here), 142–70; Balaban, *Gal aher* (A Different Wave), 48–59.
46. See: Peleg, *Israeli Culture*; Grumberg, *Place and Ideology*, 65–6, 72–3.
47. Oppenheimer, *Me'ever la-gader* (Barriers), 341–2.
48. This information is based on both Green's and Masalha's websites.
49. Kashua, "Welcome to the Israeli Arab Ghetto."
50. Grumberg, *Place and Ideology*, 147.
51. Levy, *Otiyot ha-shemesh* (Letters of the Sun), 6–7.
52. Agamben, *Means without End*, 38.
53. See also: Humphreys, "Legalizing Lawlessness," and Abujidi, "The Palestinian State of Exception."
54. Shenhav, "Halalei ribonut" (Casualties of Sovereignty), 206.
55. Agamben, *Means without End*, 42–3.
56. Ibid., 40.
57. Majumdar, *Migrant Form*, 101.
58. Kayser, *The Grotesque in Art.*
59. Cohen Shabot, "Towards a Grotesque Phenomenology," 64.
60. Bakhtin, *Rabelais and His World.*
61. Ibid., 26.
62. Ibid., 317.
63. Ibid., 322.
64. Harpham, *On the Grotesque*, 8.
65. Tsur, "Tsafnat pa'ane'ah" (Solving Riddles), and Thomson, *The Grotesque.*
66. Bhabha, "The Other Question," 80.
67. Majumdar, *Migrant Form*, 103.
68. Gluzman, "The Politics of Intertextuality," 329.
69. Harpham, *On the Grotesque*, 8.
70. Majumdar, *Migrant Form*, 103.

71. Grosz, *Volatile Bodies*, 23.
72. Grossman, *Hiyukh ha-gdi* (The Smile of the Lamb), 66. All quotations from the story were taken from the English translation by Betsy Rosenberg.
73. Levy, "Nation, Village, Cave," 12.
74. Ibid., 17.
75. Grossman, *Hiyukh ha-gdi* (The Smile of the Lamb), 67.
76. Ibid., 71.
77. Ibid., 74.
78. Ibid., 112.
79. Ibid., 63.
80. Frykman and Lofgren, *Culture Builders*, 177.
81. Douglas, *Purity and Danger*, 35.
82. Kristeva, *Power of Horror*, 4.
83. Ibid., 93.
84. Grossman, *Hiyukh ha-gdi* (The Smile of the Lamb), 236.
85. Ibid., 234.
86. Compare with Mahmoud Darwish's poem "Identity Card," where he mocks the soldier who asks him to produce the card, and instead refers to his natural connection to the land and his reproductive ability; as cited in chapter 1 of this book.
87. Green, *Agadot ha-intifada* (The Intifada Tales), 41.
88. Bakhtin, *Rabelais and His World*, 196, 303–67.
89. Green, *Agadot ha-intifada* (The Intifada Tales), 36–7.
90. Ibid., 55–6.
91. Bakhtin, *Rabelais and His World*, 322.
92. Chapter 4 elaborates on the myth of the *akeda* and the national sacrifices.
93. Green, *Agadot ha-intifada* (The Intifada Tales), 94.
94. Ibid., 95.
95. See: Bakhtin's *Rabelais and His World*, which discusses the grotesque in the context of the carnival in the folk culture of the Middle Ages and the Renaissance.
96. Levy, *Otiyot ha-shemesh* (Letters of the Sun), 5.
97. Bakhtin, *Rabelais and His World*, 10.
98. Levy, *Otiyot ha-shemesh* (Letters of the Sun), 8–9.
99. Ibid., 56.
100. Ibid., 100.

101. "The majority is never becoming. All becoming is minoritarian," Deleuze and Guattari, *A Thousand Plateaus*, 106.
102. Levy, *Otiyot ha-shemesh* (Letters of the Sun), 12.
103. Ibid., 54.
104. Ibid., 55.
105. Ibid., 79.
106. Thomson, *The Grotesque*, 2–3, 7.
107. Levy, *Otiyot ha-shemesh* (Letters of the Sun), 44.
108. Ibid., 136.
109. Ibid., 48.
110. Ibid.
111. Ibid., 50.
112. Ibid., 9.
113. Ibid., 89.
114. Thomson, *The Grotesque,* 2–3.
115. Tsur, "Tsafnat pa'ane'ah" (Solving Riddles), 147.
116. Green, *Agadot ha-intifada* (The Intifada Tales), 124.
117. Ibid.
118. Amireh, "Between Complicity and Subversion," 751.
119. Said, "Permission to Narrate."
120. Grossman, *Ha-zman ha-tsahov* (The Yellow Wind), 6. All quotations from the book were taken from the English translation by Haim Watzman.
121. Ibid.
122. Ibid., 21.
123. Ibid., 12.
124. Oppenheimer, "The Arab in the Mirror," 224.
125. Green, *Agadot ha-intifada* (The Intifada Tales), 11.
126. Ibid., 12.
127. Levy, *Otiyot ha-shemesh* (Letters of the Sun), 23.
128. Ibid., 76.
129. Ibid., 122.

Part 2

1. Grossman, *Writing in the Dark*, 96–7. The quotation was taken from the English translation by Jessica Cohen.
2. See: Sinai, "Ke-shlish me-ha-israelim" (A Third of All Israelis).
3. Peleg, *Israeli Culture*, 121.

Chapter 4

1. Yehoshua in Cargas, "Zionist as a Writer," 139; my italics.
2. Hever, "Tnu lo badranim" (Give Him Entertainers).
3. See: Yehoshua, *Ha-kala ha-meshahreret* (The Liberated Bride); Hever, "Tnu lo badranim" (Give Him Entertainers); Laor, "A. B. Yehoshua ve-ha-sin'a ha-mizrahit" (A. B. Yehoshua and the Mizrahis' Hatred); "Ha-roman shel shuliyat ha-kosem" (The Novel of the Sorcerer's Apprentice), "Motar ha-mizrahan" (The Orientalist is Preferable); Goldshmid, "Ha-gvul shel ha-sifrut" (The Border of Literature); Yaar-Edelbaum, "Normali ze hakhi" (Normal Is the Best); Morahg, "Simanim mukdamin" (Early Indications); Omer-Sherman, "Guests and Hosts," and "On the Verge of a Long-Craved Intimacy." Given the intensive scholarly writings on this novel, this text is not discussed here.
4. Yehoshua, "Hatima" (Sealing), 396–7.
5. Nancy Berg views Hebrew literature, as a whole, as a father-son literature that responds to the dynamics of the changing generations in the evolving Zionist culture. See: Berg, "The Politics of Paternity."
6. See: Shaked, *Gal hadash* (A New Wave).
7. Harris, *An Ideological Death*, 70.
8. Schwartz phrases it with a pun referring to the Hebrew word "Ha-makom" that means both "place" (and land) and "God." Schwartz, *Ma she-ro'im mi-kan* (What We See from Here), 45.
9. In: Maoz, *Pulhanei medina* (Rituals of State), 111; my italics.
10. Poets such as Natan Alterman, Uri Zvi Grinberg, Avraham Shlonsky, and Haim Gouri, as well as songwriters like Haim Hefer and Natan Yonatan and authors such as Yigal Mosenzon and Moshe Shamir include aesthetic interpretations of this myth in their writings. Examples of this myth in Hebrew poetry include Alterman, "Magash ha-kesef" (The Silver Platter); Gouri, "Ha-reut," in *Mishpahat ha-palmah* (The *Palmah* Family), 233, and "Hine mutalot gufotenu," in *Pirhei ha-esh* (Flowers of Fire), 65; Shlonsky, *Shirim* (Poems); Yonatan, *Shvilei afar* (Dust Roads). In Hebrew prose: Mosenzon, *Be-arvot ha-negev* (In the Negev Desert); Shamir, *Bemo yadav* (In His Own Hands), and *Hu halakh ba-sadot* (He Walked through the Fields).

    Among the many studies in this field, see in particular: Miron, *Mul ha-ah ha-shotek* (In Front of the Silent Brother), and Gluzman, *Ha-guf ha-zioni* (The Zionist Body). Almog also refers to this myth in his book *The Sabra.*

Many literary specialists have written about the *akeda* in the context of Israeli culture and literature, including Ofrat (ed.), *Akedat Yits'hak ba-omanut ha-israelit* (Isaac's Binding in Israeli Art); Ben-Gurion (ed.), *Al tishlah yadkha* (Do Not Lay Your Hand); Feldman, *Glory and Agony*, "Shel mi ha-korban haze" (Whose Sacrifice is it?), and "Yits'hak o Oedipus" (Isaac or Oedipus); Abramson, "The Reinterpretation of the Akeda"; Kartun-Blum, "Me'ayin ha-etsim ha-ele be-yadi" (Where Do These Trees Come From); Weiss, "He'arot livhinat akedat Yits'hak" (Comments on Isaac's Binding).

11. Feldman, "Shel mi ha-korban haze" (Whose Sacrifice Is It?), 127; Sagi, "The Meaning of the *Akedah*," 46.
12. Yizhar, *Yemei tsiklag* (Days of Tsiklag), 804.
13. Gouri, "Yerusha," in *Shoshanat ruhot* (Compass Rose), 28.
14. See: Gilboa, "Yitzhak," in *Shirim ba-boker ba-boker* (Poems in the Morning Morning); Amichai, "Akeda," in *Me'ahorei kol ze* (Behind All This), "Kah et binkha et yehidkha," in *Patu'ah sagur patu'ah* (Open Closed Open), and "Hagibor ha-amiti shel ha-akeda," in *Sh'at ha-hesed* (The Hour of Grace); Levin, "Avi ha-yakar" and "Akeda," from "Malkat ha-ambatya," in *Ma ikhpat la-tsipor* (What Does the Bird Care?); Laor, "Ha-metumtam haze Yitzhak," in *Rak ha-guf zokher* (Only the Body Remembers), and "Ha-metumtam hazeh Yitzhak" (later version), *Laila be-malon zar* (Night in a Foreign Hotel).
15. On the changing forms of the *akeda* in his work, see also: Shalev, "Hotam ha-akeda" (The Signs of the Binding). Shalev's article explores the trope of the *akeda* in several texts but does not suggest an explanatory developmental framework.
16. Yehoshua, *Ha-me'ahev* (The Lover), 3. All quotations from the novel were taken from the English translation by Philip Simpson.
17. Ibid., 296.
18. Ibid., 283.
19. Ibid., 298.
20. Yehoshua, *Mar Mani* (Mr. Mani), 166. All quotations from the novel were taken from the English translation by Hillel Halkin.
21. Ibid., 318.
22. In this chapter, I do not address the psychological-Oedipal aspect of this crisis. For a discussion of the *akeda* myth in this context, see: Feldman, "Yits'hak o Oedipus" (Isaac or Oedipus), and "Shel mi ha-korban haze" (Whose Sacrifice Is It?).

23. Yehoshua, "Hatima" (Sealing), 395.
24. Yehoshua, *Be-t'hilat kayits—1970* (Early in the Summer of 1970), 34. All quotations from the story were taken from the English translation by Miriam Arad.
25. Ibid., 37–8.
26. Ibid., 42.
27. Ibid., 33.
28. Ibid., 17.
29. Ibid., 64.
30. Ibid., 68.
31. Ibid., 55.
32. Ibid., 16.
33. Ibid., 22–3.
34. Ibid., 23.
35. Ibid., 25.
36. Ibid., 32.
37. Ibid., 62.
38. Ibid., 38.
39. Yehoshua, "Hatima" (Sealing), 397.
40. Gantz, "Ha-herut lelaket zradim" (The Freedom to Collect Twigs), 293.
41. See: Fledman, *Glory and Agony*, 240–2.
42. *Ruhot* in Hebrew, meaning both "winds" and "ghosts."
43. Yehoshua, *Esh yedidutit* (Friendly Fire), 77. All quotations from the novel were taken from the English translation by Stuart Schoffman.
44. Some critics have identified Canaanite references in Yehoshua's book regarding the concept of history. See, for example: Oren, "Hasifrut ha-israelit" (Hebrew Literature), and "Pitputon mishpahti" (Family Chatter).
45. Yehoshua, *Esh yedidutit* (Friendly Fire), 279.
46. Ibid., 275.
47. Ibid., 57.
48. Ibid., 192.
49. Ibid., 24.
50. Ibid., 134.
51. Ibid., 74.
52. Ibid., 147.
53. Ibid., 170.
54. Ibid., 210.
55. Ibid., 269.

56. Ibid., 256–7.
57. On ghosts, see: Shamir, "Bein sof le-vein saf" (Between an End and a Threshold).
58. Yehoshua, *Esh yedidutit* (Friendly Fire), 332.
59. Ibid., 37.
60. Ibid., 288.
61. Ibid., 329.
62. Hever, "Tnu lo badranim" (Give Him Entertainers), 197.
63. On the "worlds of shadows" see: Ben-Dov, *Ve-Hi Tehilatekha* (Studies of Agnon, Yehoshua, and Oz).
64. According to the Meretz website: https://meretz.org.il/tag/%D7%90-%D7%91-%D7%99%D7%94%D7%95%D7%A9%D7%A2/
65. Ophir (ed.), *Zman emet* (Time for Truth), 16.
66. Algazi, "Me'ahorei ha-homa" (Behind the Wall), 241.
67. Yehoshua in Weitz and Mishani, "Esh yedidutit" (Friendly Fire).
68. Ibid.
69. Oz's novel has been extensively criticized, notably by Golan and Shapira. Whereas Avirama Golan criticizes Oz for accepting the Zionist narrative, and even claims that this was done in a manipulative manner, Anita Shapira praises him for responding to post-Zionism. Golan, "Ha'im ha-sipur shelo hu ha-sipur shelanu" (Is His Story Our Story?); Shapira, "'Ha-siper ha-zioni' shel Amos Oz" (Amos Oz's "Zionist Narrative").
70. Oz in Shavit, "Ha-yehudi ha-sored" (The Surviving Jew).
71. Oz, *Sipur al ahavah ve-hoshekh* (A Tale of Love and Darkness), 345. The quotation was taken from the English translation by Nicholas de Lange.
72. See also: Mendelson-Maoz, "Amos Oz's 'A Tale of Love and Darkness.'"
73. Grossman, *Isha borahat mi-bsora* (To the End of the Land). There are numerous critiques of this book. See in particular: Glassner, "Isha borachat mi-bsora" (To the End of the Land); Melamed, "Mehir ha-shtika" (The Price of Silence); Gluzman, "Im lo tihi'ye Yerushalaim" (If There Would Be No Jerusalem); Binyaminov, "Ha-akeda ha-leumit" (The National Binding); Benziman, "Disket gibui la-hayim" (Backup for Life).

Chapter 5

1. Grosz, *Volatile Bodies*, 23.
2. Ibid.

3. Along with other writers, such as Etgar Keret, Gadi Taub, Uzi Weil, and Gafi Amir.
4. Mendelson-Maoz, "On 'Human Parts.'"
5. Castel-Bloom, *Dolly City*, 128. All quotations from the novel were taken from the English translation by Dalya Bilu.
6. Ibid., 45.
7. Shiffman, "Orly Castel-Bloom and Yoel Hoffmann," 216.
8. See: Mendelson-Maoz, "Situatsiot kitsoniyot" (Extreme Situations).
9. See: Bachur, "Olam shel hitroknut" (A World of Emptying Out).
10. Blich, "Dolly City Me'or ha-dor" (Dolly City, the Generation's Light).
11. Ben-Yosef Ginur, "Ha-distopia ha-tsiyonit" (The Zionist Dystopia), 356.
12. Ophir, "Al ktiva postmodernit" (On Post-Modern Writing). See also: Eaglestone, *Ethical Criticism*, 104–5.
13. Grumberg, "Female Grotesque," 145.
14. Castel-Bloom, *Dolly City*, 11.
15. Ibid., 38–9: "There was a moment when I almost flung the baby down. Ten times over, I checked that I was still holding him."
16. Melamed, "Ha-epos ha-eimtani shel ha-imahut" (The Formidable Epos of Motherhood), 30.
17. Shiffman, "Motherhood under Zionism," 139.
18. Castel-Bloom, *Dolly City*, 50–1; my italics.
19. Ibid., 57.
20. Ibid., 109.
21. Ibid., 44.
22. Grumberg, "Female Grotesque," 157.
23. Schwartz, "Mi-'makon aher'" (From "Different Place").
24. In this sense, "the territory no longer preceded the map, nor survives it. Henceforth, it is the map that precedes the territory" (Baudrillard, "The Map Precedes the Territory," 76). See also: Anderson, *Imagined Communities*, 163–85.
25. Hever, "Mapa shel hol" (Map of Sand), 187.
26. Castel-Bloom, *Dolly City*, 24.
27. Ibid., 84, 56 in the Hebrew version.
28. Ibid., 146.
29. Ibid.
30. Ibid., 170.
31. Laor, *Shirim 1974–1992* (Poems 1974–1992), 121. My translation.
32. Castel-Bloom, *Dolly City*, 34.

33. Ibid., 135.
34. Ibid., 167.
35. Ibid., 95.
36. Ibid., 136.
37. Ibid., 127.
38. Ibid., 125.
39. Ibid., 154.
40. Grumberg, *Place and Ideology*, 87–93.
41. Castel-Bloom, *Dolly City*, 72–3.
42. Ibid., 70.
43. Ibid.
44. Ibid., 110.
45. Bernard, *Rhetorics of Belonging*, 117–18.
46. The reference is to the borders of Israel before 1967. At the time, Judea, Samaria, and the Gaza Strip, as well as East Jerusalem, were not part of Israel.
47. Castel-Bloom, *Dolly City*, 132.
48. Ibid., 171.
49. Ibid., 72–3.
50. Livne, "Ha-intifada ha-pratit sheli" (My Private Intifada), 28.
51. Hasak-Lowy, "Postzionism and Its Aftermath," 97–8, and Bernard, *Rhetorics of Belonging*, 123.
52. Peleg, *Israeli Culture*, 125.
53. Goren, *The Home Front*, 177.
54. Castel-Bloom, *Halakim enoshiyim* (Human Parts), 240. All quotations from the novel were taken from the English translation by Dalya Bilu.
55. Ibid., 5.
56. As Goren notes, "The media, especially electronic-visual media (television and internet), play an especially critical role in framing and amplifying the effects of terrorism, and scholars pay special attention to its impact on psychological responses to terrorism" (*The Home Front*, 52).
57. Castel-Bloom, *Halakim enoshiyim* (Human Parts), 5–6.
58. Ibid., 101.
59. Ibid., 112.
60. Ibid., 72.
61. Ibid., 112.
62. Ibid., 37.
63. Grumberg, *Place and Ideology*, 87.

64. See: Meltzer, "Ha-metsi'ut hi uvda" (Reality Is a Fact), and "Sfarim lema'an ha-rega" (Books for the Instant).
65. Like Castel Bloom, in *Tanin pigu'a* (Croc Attack), published in 2006, Assaf Gavron describes terrorism in a plastic way, and deviates from realist writing toward a kind of carnivalistic representation.
66. Shiffman, "Re'alizm mugaz" (Carbonated Realism).
67. Castel-Bloom, *Halakim enoshiyim* (Human Parts), 6.
68. Ibid., 7.
69. Ibid., 68–9.
70. Harris, *An Ideological Death*, 76.
71. Castel-Bloom, *Halakim enoshiyim* (Human Parts), 42–3.
72. Ibid., 47.
73. Ibid., 248.
74. Bernard, *Rhetorics of Belonging*, 124.
75. Castel-Bloom, *Halakim enoshiyim* (Human Parts), 55.
76. Grossman, *Ha-mavet ke-derekh hayim* (Death as the Way of Life), 119.
77. Quoted in Livne, "Ha-intifada ha-pratit sheli" (My Private Intifada), 29. This contrasts with the analysis of the situation in the novel, in which: "the many terror attacks and the European winter foretold the coming of the Messiah," Castel-Bloom, *Halakim enoshiyim* (Human Parts), 36.
78. Miron, "Mashehu al Orly Castel-Bloom" (Considerations on Orly Castel-Bloom).
79. Gurevitz, *Postmodernism*, 287, 303.
80. Castel-Bloom, "Ha-ma'amar ha-avud" (The Lost Article).
81. Hasak-Lowy, "Postzionism and Its Aftermath," 97.
82. Peleg, *Israeli Culture*, 121.

Chapter 6

1. Levinas, "Reality and Its Shadow," 132.
2. Ibid.
3. Ibid.
4. Levinas, *Totality and Infinity*, 87.
5. Ibid., 42–8.
6. Levinas, "Reality and Its Shadow," 132.
7. Much has been written about Levinas's ambiguous attitude toward literature. See for example, studies by Eaglestone, *Ethical Criticism*; Robbins, *Altered Reading*; Harpham, *Getting It Right*; Gibson, *Postmodernity,*

Ethics and the Novel; Wehrs and Haney (eds.), *Levinas and Nineteenth-Century Literature.*

8. Levinas, *Time and the Other*, 72.
9. Levinas, "The Poet's Vision," 134.
10. Levinas, "Poetry and Resurrection," 7.
11. Ibid., 10.
12. Ibid., 15.
13. Levinas, "The Poet's Vision," 135
14. McDonald, "Aesthetics as First Ethics," 25.
15. Horn, *Himnon la-simha* (Ode to Joy), 1. All quotations from the novel were taken from the English version, translated by the author.
16. Ibid., 2.
17. Ibid., 12–13.
18. Ibid., 16.
19. Ibid., 21.
20. Ibid., 1.
21. Ibid., 56.
22. Critchley, Introduction, 27.
23. Kenaan, *The Ethics of Visuality*, 3.
24. Levinas, "The Trace of the Other," 351.
25. Ibid., 352.
26. Peperzak, *To the Other*, 25, 129.
27. Ibid., 142.
28. Yehoshua, *Shlihuto shel ha-memune* (A Woman in Jerusalem), 4. All quotations from the novel were taken from the English translation by Hillel Halkin.
29. Ibid.
30. Ibid., 4, 9.
31. Levinas, *Totality and Infinity*, 194.
32. Levinas, "The Trace of the Other," 352.
33. Jarvis, *Times of Terror.*
34. Horn, *Himnon la-simha* (Ode to Joy), 45–6.
35. Yehoshua, *Shlihuto shel ha-memune* (A Woman in Jerusalem), 17.
36. Kartun-Blum, "Ha-nahash ve-ha-shablul" (The Snake and the Snail), 23.
37. Horn, *Himnon la-simha* (Ode to Joy), 20.
38. Ibid., 40.
39. Ibid., 32.
40. Ibid., 33.

41. Ibid., 27.
42. Ibid., 90–1.
43. Yehoshua, *Shlihuto shel ha-memune* (A Woman in Jerusalem), 13–14.
44. Shenhav, "Medina mafkira" (Abandoning State), 381.
45. Levinas, *Ethics and Infinity*, 101.
46. Ibid., 98.
47. Levinas, *Totality and Infinity*, 86.
48. Ibid., 199.
49. Kenaan, "Facing Images."
50. Robbins, *Altered Reading.*
51. Horn, *Himnon la-simha* (Ode to Joy), 54.
52. Ibid., 87–8.
53. Yehoshua, *Shlihuto shel ha-memune* (A Woman in Jerusalem), 127.
54. Ibid., 144.
55. Ibid., 166.
56. Ibid., 235.
57. Putnam, "Levinas and Judaism," 38.
58. Levinas, "The Trace of the Other," 359.
59. Ibid.
60. Levinas, *Totality and Infinity*, 79.
61. Yehoshua, *Shlihuto shel ha-memune* (A Woman in Jerusalem), 3–4, 96.
62. In Yehoshua, *Kol ha-sipurim* (The Continuing Silence of a Poet), 141–61.
63. Ibid., 152. Quoted from the English translation by Marsha Pomerantz.
64. Yehoshua, *Shlihuto shel ha-memune* (A Woman in Jerusalem), 31.
65. Lipsker, "Girsaot lohashot" (Whispering Versions), 349; Kartun-Blum, "Ha-nahash ve-ha-shablul" (The Snake and the Snail); Itzhaki, "Shlihuto shel ha-memune" (A Woman in Jerusalem).

    According to Shenhav, the text uses theologization to transform the aggressive exploitative relations between employers and low-ranked employees into relations that demand responsibility and leadership; Shenhav, "Medina mafkira" (Abandoning State).
66. Ben-Dov, "Ve-ha-ir einena kala" (And the City Endures).
67. Yehoshua in Shavit, "Ha-pasion shel Yehoshua" (Yehoshua's Passion).
68. Yehoshua, *Shlihuto shel ha-memune* (A Woman in Jerusalem), 35.
69. Levinas, *God, Death, and Time*, 117.
70. Ibid.
71. Ibid.
72. Peperzak, *To the Other*, 29.

73. Levinas, *Otherwise Than Being*, 151.
74. Eaglestone, *Ethical Criticism*, 147.
75. Peperzak, *To the Other*, 29.
76. Critchley, *Very Little*, 97.
77. Friebach-Heifetz, *Hesed hiloni* (Secular Grace), 195.
78. Derrida, "Adieu," 6.
79. Levinas, "Poetry and Resurrection," 16.
80. Horn, *Himnon la-simha* (Ode to Joy), 94.
81. Levinas, *Alterity and Transcendence*, 162.
82. Horn, *Himnon la-simha* (Ode to Joy), 94.
83. Ibid., 119.
84. Ibid., 186.
85. Levinas, "Reality and Its Shadow," 132.
86. For an in-depth study of "empathy" in the context of literature, see: Keen, *Empathy and the Novel*; Amiel-Houser and Mendelson-Maoz, "Against Empathy."
87. Yehoshua, *Shlihuto shel ha-memune* (A Woman in Jerusalem), 35.
88. Levinas, *Alterity and Transcendence*, 167.
89. Yehoshua, *Shlihuto shel ha-memune* (A Woman in Jerusalem), 89.
90. Ibid., 106; italics in the original.
91. Ibid., 123.
92. Ibid., 133.
93. Ibid., 134.
94. Ibid., 150.
95. Ibid., 166.
96. Ibid., 172.
97. Ibid., 217.
98. Mishani, "Ha-mizrahi ha-samui min ha-ayin" (The Hidden Mizrahi), 387.
99. Yehoshua, *Shlihuto shel ha-memune* (A Woman in Jerusalem), 228.
100. Ibid., 230.
101. Ibid., 137.
102. Shenhav, "Medina mafkira" (Abandoning State), 375.
103. Derrida, "Adieu," 9.
104. Ibid.
105. Kasher, *Sefer katan* (A Little Book), 114–16.
106. Kenaan, "Facing Images," 154.
107. Levinas, "Poetry and Resurrection," 15.

108. Oren, *Ha-siporet ha-israelit* (Israeli Prose).
109. Yehoshua, *Shlihuto shel ha-memune* (A Woman in Jerusalem), 96.
110. Ibid., 122.
111. Ibid., 108–9.
112. Ibid., 7.
113. Ibid., 217.
114. Jaggi, "Power and Pity."
115. Melamed, "Metsi'ut aheret" (Different Reality).
116. Levinas, *Totality and Infinity*, 21.
117. Ibid., 22.
118. Ibid.
119. Peperzak, *To the Other*, 127.
120. Jaggi, "Power and Pity."

Chapter 7

1. Govrin, "Layers of Changing Space," 387–8.
2. On the writing on war by women authors see: Levi-Hazan, *Nashim kotvot al milhama* (Women's Writing on War).
3. Deleuze and Guattari, *A Thousand Plateaus.*
4. Ibid., 6–7.
5. Azoulay and Ophir, "Anu lo shoalim" (We're Not Asking), 125.
6. Friedman, "'Elef mishorim'" ("A Thousand Plateaus").
7. Shapira, *Maslulei nedudim* (Routes of Wandering), 59.
8. In the Hebrew original, the book has no headings, and each part is set in different fonts. In the English translation, the book is divided into sections: New Jersey, Paris, and Jerusalem, creating a classification of the spaces. Photographs were also included to illustrate the descriptions of landscapes in contrast to the original Hebrew version that had no photographs. Adding these headings and pictures may be helpful when reading the work, but also impact its aesthetic purpose. When the snapshots appear without a reference, they emphasize the smooth transitions between spaces.
9. Foucault, *The Order of Things.*
10. Jacobson, "Intimate Relations."
11. Matalon, *Sarah, Sarah* (Bliss), 33. All quotations from the novel were taken from the English translation by Jessica Cohen.
12. Deleuze and Guattari, *A Thousand Plateaus*, 23.

13. Keren, *Ke-yeri'a be-yad ha-rokemet* (Like a Sheet in the Hand of the Embroideress), 188.
14. Hever, "Tnu lo badranim" (Give Him Entertainers), 204.
15. Matalon, *Sarah, Sarah* (Bliss), 262.
16. In Gluzman, "Lehisaret al yedei ha-homer" (Getting Scratched by the Matter), 229.
17. Hever, "Kol ehad tsarikh lada'at" (Everyone Should Know).
18. Matalon, *Sarah, Sarah* (Bliss), 84.
19. Ibid, 49.
20. Ibid., 170.
21. Ibid., 66.
22. Ibid., 105–6.
23. In Calderon, "Sarah, ma sohef be-Sarah?" (Sarah, What Is Stirring in Sarah?).
24. Matalon, *Sarah, Sarah* (Bliss), 193.
25. Ibid., 213–14.
26. In Gluzman, "Lehisaret al yedei ha-homer" (Getting Scratched by the Matter), 244.
27. See: Deleuze and Guattari, *A Thousand Plateaus*, 55.
28. Rimmon-Kenan, "Place, Space," 222.
29. Certeau, *The Practice of Everyday Life*, 117.
30. Bonita and Protevi, *Deleuze and Geophilosophy*, 154.
31. Deleuze and Guattari, *A Thousand Plateaus*, 488.
32. Ibid., 475, 482.
33. Meltzer, "Ha-bhira ha-mevurekhet be-vadaut" (The Blessed Choice of Certainty).
34. Gurevitz and Aranne, "Al ha-makom" (On the Place).
35. Naveh, *Nos'im ve-nos'ot* (Women and Men Travellers), 46–7.
36. Govrin, *Hevzekim* (Snapshots), 18. All quotations from the novel were taken from the English translation by Barbara Harshav.
37. Ibid., 26–7.
38. Ibid., 45.
39. Ibid., 41.
40. Ibid., 2.
41. Ibid., 48–9.
42. Gesser, "Sukkot ve-shmita" (Sukkot and Shmita), 60.
43. Govrin, *Hevzekim* (Snapshots), 284.
44. Ibid., 70.

45. Ibid., 263.
46. Ibid., 282–3; brackets and italics in the original.
47. Ibid., 292.
48. Ibid., 48
49. See: Alon, "Klalat ha-nedudim" (The Curse of Wandering), and Shemtov, "The Bible in Contemporary Israeli Literature," 380–2.
50. In the opera's plot, Don Giovanni tries to seduce Donna Anna, whose father challenges him to a duel. During the duel, the father is killed, but reappears at the end of the opera in the form of a statue that consigns Don Giovanni to hell. In the novel, the dead father does not come to life, but he never ceases to confront the Palestinian lover and the Jewish husband. See: Levitan, "Me-hodu ve-ad kush" (From India to Cush).
51. Govrin, *Hevzekim* (Snapshots), 291.
52. Ibid., 300.
53. Deleuze and Guattari, *Kafka*, 67.
54. Govrin, *Hevzekim* (Snapshots), 301.
55. Deleuze and Guattari, *A Thousand Plateaus*, 494.
56. Shapira, *Maslulei nedudim* (Routes of Wandering), 67.
57. Matalon, *Sarah, Sarah* (Bliss), 67.
58. Naveh, *Nos'im ve-nos'ot* (Women and Men Travelers), 106.
59. Deleuze and Guattari, *A Thousand Plateaus*, 492–4.
60. Matalon, *Sarah, Sarah* (Bliss), 10.
61. Ibid., 66.
62. Ibid., 68.
63. Ibid., 10.
64. Ibid., 11.
65. Ibid., 10.
66. Ibid., 222.
67. Libes and First, "Framing the Palestinian-Israeli conflict," 62. See also: Goren, *The Home Front*, 47–8.
68. Nathansohn, "Metsalmim kibush" (Photographing Occupation), 130.
69. Ibid., 141.
70. Ibid., 147–8.
71. Matalon, *Sarah, Sarah* (Bliss), 64.
72. Govrin, *Hevzekim* (Snapshots), 40.
73. Grosz, *Chaos, Territory, Art*, 11, 16.
74. Govrin, *Hevzekim* (Snapshots), 72–4.
75. Braidotti, *Nomadic Subjects*, 36.

76. Govrin, "Layers of Changing Space," 385–6.
77. Rimmon-Kenan, "Place, Space," 222.
78. Govrin, *Hevzekim* (Snapshots), 114.
79. Karpel, "Oh My Love."
80. Levitan, "Ma lishmot" (What to Drop), 34.
81. Woolf, *Three Guineas.*
82. Hever, "Tnu lo badranim" (Give Him Entertainers), 205, and also *Ha-sipur ve-ha-leom* (The Story and the Nation), 341.
83. Braidotti, *Nomadic Subjects*, 22.
84. See also: Braidotti, "Affirming the Affirmative."
85. Deleuze and Guattari, *A Thousand Plateaus*, 106.
86. Ibid., 277.
87. Irigaray, *This Sex Which Is Not One*, 140–1. See on this subject: Colebrook, Introduction, 10–12. On the connection between Hélène Cixous and Deleuzian thought on becoming, see Conley, "Becoming Woman Now," 25–6.
88. Braidotti, "Nomadism with Difference"; Grosz, "A Thousand Tiny Sexes," 188.
89. Mansbach, "Meha'a al ha-gvul" (Protest on the Border), 89.
90. Lorraine, "Becoming-Imperceptible," 182.
91. Holzman, "Ha-holi ve-ha-si'uv" (The Illness and the Corruption).
92. Shemtov, "The Bible in Contemporary Israeli Literature," 380–2.
93. Govrin, *Hevzekim* (Snapshots), 233–4.
94. Ibid., 233.
95. See: Sivan, "*Snapshots* (review)."
96. Govrin, *Hevzekim* (Snapshots), 76.
97. Ibid., 136.
98. Oppenheimer identifies this contradiction in the figure of Lana. Oppenheimer, "Ha-hayim ha-kfulim" (The Double Life).
99. Eshel, *Futurity*, 5.

Epilogue

1. In Isaksen, *Literature and War*, 108.
2. Kershner, "Jewish-Arab Love Story." See also: Kashti, "Israel Bans Novel."
3. Ibid.
4. Laor, "The Israeli-Palestinian Romance."

5. Grossman, *Ha-zman ha-tsahov* (The Yellow Wind), 211.
6. Ibid., 212.
7. Ibid., 40.
8. Baram, Nir. *Ha-arets she-me'ever la-harim* (A Land without Borders), the quotation is from the introduction to the book, which was translated by Jessica Cohen.
9. Grossman, *Ha-zman ha-tsahov* (The Yellow Wind), 215–16.

Bibliography

Primary Resources

Alterman, Natan. "Magash ha-kesef" (The Silver Platter). *Davar*, Dec. 19, 1947. Republished in *Ha-tur ha-shve'e* (The Seventh Column), 1–3. Tel Aviv: Ha-kibbutz ha-meuhad, 1973.

Amichai, Yehuda. *Me'ahorei kol ze mistater osher gadol* (Behind All This a Great Happiness Is Hiding). Jerusalem: Schocken, 1974.

Amichai, Yehuda. *Patu'ah sagur patu'ah* (Open Closed Open). Jerusalem: Schocken, 1998.

Amichai, Yehuda. *Sh'at ha-hesed* (The Hour of Grace). Jerusalem: Schocken, 1982.

Ben-Ner, Yitzhak. *Ta'atuon* (Delusion). Jerusalem: Am Oved, 1989.

Bernstein, Ilana. "Ma'atsar" (Imprisonment). In *Iyim shel sheket* (Islands of Calm), 174–80. Tel Aviv: Ha-kibbutz ha-meuhad, 1999.

Bernstein, Ilana. *Ha-ir ha-mizrahit* (The East City). Tel Aviv: Yediot, 2013.

Castel-Bloom, Orly. *Dolly City*. Tel Aviv: Zmora-Bitan, 1992. Translated by Dalya Bilu. London: Loki Books, 1997.

Castel-Bloom, Orly. *Halakim enoshiyim* (Human Parts). Tel Aviv: Kinneret, 2002. Translated by Dalya Bilu. Boston: David Godine, 2003.

Evron, Gilad. *Mar'eh makom* (Reference). Tel Aviv: Am Oved, 2003.

Gavron, Assaf. *Tanin pigu'a* (Croc Attack). Or Yehuda: Zmora Bitan, 2006. Translated by Assaf Gavron and James Lever. London: Fourth Estate, 2010.

Gavron, Assaf. *Ha-giv'a* (The Hilltop). Tel Aviv: Yediot, 2013. Translated by Steven Cohen. New York: Scribner, 2014.

Gilboa, Amir. *Shirim ba-boker ba-boker* (Poems in the Morning Morning). Tel Aviv: Ha-kibbutz ha-meuhad, 1953.

Gouri, Haim. *Mishpahat ha-palmah—yalkut alilot ve-zemer* (The *Palmah* Family—Anthology of Stories and Songs), edited by Haim Gouri and Haim Hefer. Jerusalem: The *Palmah* Organization Press, 1977.

Gouri, Haim. *Pirhei ha-esh* (Flowers of Fire). Merchavia: Sifriat Poalim, 1949.

Gouri, Haim. *Shoshanat ruhot* (Compass Rose). Tel Aviv: Ha-kibbutz ha-meuhad, 1960.

Govrin, Michal. *Hevzekim* (Snapshots). Tel Aviv: Am Oved, 2002. Translated by Barbara Harshav. New York: Riverhead Books, 2007.

Green, Dror. *Agadot ha-intifada* (The Intifada Tales). Tsfat: Sfarim, 1989.

Grossman, David. *Hiyukh ha-gdi* (The Smile of the Lamb). Tel Aviv: Ha-kibbutz ha-meuhad, 1983. Translated by Betsy Rosenberg. London: Cape, 1991.

Grossman, David. *Isha borahat mi-bsora* (To the End of the Land). Tel Aviv: Ha-kibbutz ha-meuhad, 2008. Translated by Jessica Cohen, Knopf, 2010.

Horn, Shifra. *Himnon la-simha* (Ode to Joy). Tel Aviv: Am Oved, 2004. Translated by the author. Cornwall: MPG books, 2005.

Iczkovits, Yaniv. *Dofek* (Pulse). Tel Aviv: Ha-kibbutz ha-meuhad, 2007.

Kaniuk, Yoram [Yosef Sharara]. *Aravi tov* (Confessions of a Good Arab). Tel Aviv: Kinneret, 1984. Translated by Dalya Bilu. London: P. Halban, 1987.

Keret, Etgar. *Ga'aguay le-kissinger* (Missing Kissinger). Tel Aviv: Zmora-Bitan, 1994. Translated by Miriam Shlesinger and Sondra Silverston. London: Chatto & Windus, 2007.

Kravitz, Asher. *Ani Mustafa Rabinovitch* (I, Mustafa Rabinovitch). Bnei Brak: Sifriat poalim and Ha-kibbutz ha-meuhad, 2004 (second edition, 2008).

Lahav, Shai. *Lekh le-aza* (Go to Gaza). Tel Aviv: Ma'ariv, 2005.

Laor, Yitzhak. *Laila be-malon zar* (Night in a Foreign Hotel). Tel Aviv: Ha-kibbutz ha-meuhad, 1992.

Laor, Yitzhak. *Rak ha-guf zokher* (Only the Body Remembers). Tel Aviv: Adam, 1985.

Laor, Yitzhak. *Shirim 1974–1992* (Poems 1974–1992). Tel Aviv: Ha-kibbutz ha-meuhad, 2002.

Levin, Hanoch. *Ma ikhpat la-tsipor* (What Does the Bird Care?). Tel Aviv: Ha-kibbutz ha-meuhad, 1987.

Levy, Itamar. *Otiyot ha-shemesh, otiyot ha-yare'ah* (Letters of the Sun, Letters of the Moon). Jerusalem: Keter, 1991.

Levy, Yossi. "Avak shel bustanim" (Dust of Orchards). *Ha-aretz*, Apr. 25, 1989.

Matalon, Ronit. *Sarah, Sarah* (Bliss). Tel Aviv: Am Oved, 2000. Translated by Jessica Cohen. New York: Metropolitan Books, 2003.

Michael, Sami. *Yonim be-trafalgar* (Pigeons in Trafalgar Square). Tel Aviv: Am oved, 2005.

Mosenzon, Yigal. *Be-arvot ha-negev* (In the Negev Desert). Tel Aviv: Trabeski, 1949.

Neumann, Boaz. *Hayal tov* (Good Soldier). Lod: Zmora-Bitan, 2001.

Nevo, Eshkol. *Mish'ala ahat yemina* (World Cup Wishes). Or Yehudah: Zmora-Bitan, 2007. Translated by Sondra Silverston. London: Chatto & Windus, 2010.

Oz, Amos. *Artsot ha-tan: sipurim* (Where the Jackals Howl: And Other Stories). Tel Aviv: Masada, 1965. Translated by Nicholas de Lange and Philip Simpson. London: Chatto & Windus; New York: Harcourt Brace Jovanovich, 1981.

Oz, Amos. *Michael sheli* (My Michael). Tel Aviv: Am Oved, 1968. Translated by Nicolas de Lange in collaboration with the author. New York: Lancer Books, 1970.

Oz, Amos. *Sipur al ahava ve-hoshekh* (A Tale of Love and Darkness). Jerusalem: Keter, 2002. Translated by Nicholas de Lange. London: Vintage Books, 2005.

Polity, Roy. *Arnavonei gagot* (Roof Rabbits). Tel Aviv: Am Oved, 2001.

Rabinyan, Dorit. *Gader haya* (All the Rivers). Tel Aviv: Am Oved, 2014. Translated by Jessica Cohen. New York: Penguin Random House, 2017.

Ron Furer, Liran. *Tismonet ha-mahsom* (Checkpoint Syndrome). Tel Aviv: Gvanim, 2003.

Rowner, Ilai. *Arik* (Deserter). Tel Aviv: Yediot, 2015.

Shalev, Zeruya. *Ke'ev* (Pain). Jerusalem: Keter, 2015.

Shamir, Moshe. *Bemo yadav* (In His Own Hands). Merhavia: Sifriyat poalim, 1951.

Shamir, Moshe. *Hu halakh ba-sadot* (He Walked through the Fields). Merhavyah: Sifriyat poalim, 1947.

Shamir-Tulipman, Ayelet. "Ha'im ata ro'e et ma she-ani shome'a" (Can You See What I Hear). In *Bizman milhama* (In Time of War), 117–70. Jerusalem: Kinneret, 2002.

Shammas, Anton. *Arabeskot* (Arabesques). Tel Aviv: Am Oved, 1986. Translated by Vivan Eden. New York: Harper, 1988.

Shats, Avner. "Te'enim" (Figs). *Ha-aretz*, Apr. 19, 1989.

Shimony, Yuval. "Omanut ha-milhama" (The Art of War). *Siman Kri'a* 20 (1990): 71–83.

Shlonsky, Avraham. *Shirim* (Poems). Merhavyah: Sifriyat poalim, 1954.

Valentain, Avi. *Shahid.* Tel Aviv: Am Oved, 1989.

Yehoshua, Abraham B. *Be-t'hilat kayits—1970* (Early in the Summer of 1970). Jerusalem: Schocken, 1972. Translated by Miriam Arad. New York: Doubleday, 1977.

Yehoshua, Abraham B. *Esh yedidutit* (Friendly Fire). Tel Aviv: Ha-kibbutz ha-meuhad, 2007. Translated by Stuart Schoffman. Florida: Harcourt, 2008.

Yehoshua, Abraham B. *Ha-kala ha-meshahreret* (The Liberated Bride). Tel Aviv: Ha-kibbutz ha-meuhad, 2001. Translated by Hillel Halkin. Orlando: Harcort, 2003.

Yehoshua, Abraham B. *Ha-me'ahev* (The Lover). Jerusalem and Tel Aviv: Schocken, 1977. Translated by Philip Simpson. Florida: Harcourt, 1985.

Yehoshua, Abraham B. *Kol ha-sipurim* (The Continuing Silence of a Poet: The Collected Stories of A. B. Yehoshua). Tel Aviv: Ha-kibbutz ha-meuhad, 1993. Translated by Miriam Arad, Pauline Shrier, and Marsha Pomerantz. London: Halban, 1988.

Yehoshua, Abraham B. *Mar Mani* (Mr. Mani). Tel Aviv: Ha-kibbutz ha-meuhad, 1990. Translated by Hillel Halkin. Florida: Harcourt, 1992.

Yehoshua, Abraham B. *Shlihuto shel ha-memune al mash'abei enosh* (A Woman in Jerusalem). Tel Aviv: Ha-kibbutz ha-meuhad, 2004. Translated by Hillel Halkin. London: Halban, 2006.

Yizhar, S. "Hirbet Hiz'a" (Khirbet Khizeh). In *Arba'a sipurim* (Four Stories), 35–88. Ha-kibbutz ha-meuhad, 1989. Translated by Nicholas de Lange and Yaacob Dweck. Jerusalem: Ibis Editions, 2008. First publication in *The Story of Hirbet Hiz'a.* Merhavyah: Sifriyat poalim, 1949.

Yizhar, S. *Yemei tsiklag* (Days of Tsiklag). Tel Aviv: Am oved, 1958.

Yonatan, Natan. *Shvilei afar* (Dust Roads). Merhavyah: Sifriyat poalim, 1951.

Filmography

Zvi-Riklis, Dina, dir. *Nekudat tatspit* (Lookout). Israel, 1990.

Secondary Resources

Abramson, Glenda. "Oh, My Land, My Birthplace: Lebanon War and Intifada in Israeli Fiction and Poetry." In *Narratives of Dissent: War in Contemporary*

Israeli Arts and Culture, edited by Rachel S. Harris and Ranen Omer-Sherman, 221–40. Detroit: Wayne State University Press, 2013.

Abramson, Glenda. "The Reinterpretation of the Akeda in Modern Hebrew Poetry." *Journal of Jewish Studies* 41, no. 2 (1990): 101–14.

Abujidi, Nurham. "The Palestinian State of Exception and Agamben." *Contemporary Arab Affairs* 2, no. 2 (2009): 272–91. https://doi.org/10.1080/17550910902857034

Agamben, Giorgio. *Means without End.* Translated by Vicenzo Binetti and Cesare Casarino. Minneapolis and London: University of Minnesota Press, 2000.

Agamben. Giorgio. *State of Exception.* Translated by Kevin Attell. Chicago: University of Chicago Press, 2005.

Aginsky, Lea. "Le-Ali ha-katan hayta a'yin mi-zkhukhit" (Little Ali had a Glass Eye). *Hadashot*, May 3, 1989.

Alcoff, Linda. "The Problem of Speaking for Others." *Cultural Critique* 20 (Winter 1991–1992): 5–32.

Algazi, Gadi. "Me'ahorei ha-homa" (Behind the Wall). In *Zman emet* (Time for Truth), edited by Adi Ophir, 241–2. Jerusalem: Keter, 2001.

Almog, Oz. *The Sabra: The Creation of the New Jew.* Translated by Haim Watzman. Berkeley: University of California Press, 2000.

Alon, Ketzia. "Klalat ha-nedudim" (The Curse of Wandering). *Yediot Ahronot Weekend Supplement, Culture, Literature and Art*, Aug. 16, 2002.

Amiel-Houser, Tammy, and Adia Mendelson-Maoz. "Against Empathy: Levinas and Ethical Criticism in the 21st Century." *JLT—Journal of Literary Theory* 8, no. 1 (2014): 199–218.

Amireh, Amal. "Between Complicity and Subversion: Body Politics in Palestinian National Narrative." *South Atlantic Quarterly* 102, no. 4 (2003): 747–72.

Anderson, Benedict. *Imagined Communities.* London and New York: Verso, 1991.

Andre, Judith. "Nagel, Williams, and Moral Luck." *Analysis* 43 (1983): 202–7. https://doi.org/10.2307/3327571

Arendt, Hannah. *Eichmann in Jerusalem: A Report on the Banality of Evil.* New York: Viking Press, 1963.

Arens, Moshe. "Shovrim shtika she-eina kayemet" (Breaking the Silence That Does Not Exist). *Ha-aretz*, Jan. 19, 2016. http://www.haaretz.co.il/opinions/.premium-1.2824670

Avisar, Adar. "Mefaked galey tsahal hish'a et Yoav Kutner" (The Commander of IDF Radio station suspended Yoav Kutner). *Ma'ariv*, Mar. 30, 1988.

Axinn, Sidney. *A Moral Military.* Philadelphia: Temple University Press, 1989.

Azoulay, Ariella, and Adi Ophir. "Anu lo shoalim 'ma ze omer', ela 'eikh ze poel': hakdama l'elef mishorim" (We're Not Asking "What It Means," But "How It Works": An Introduction to "A Thousand Plateaus"). *Teoria u-vikoret* 17 (2000): 123–31.

Bachur, Yona. "Olam shel hitroknut" (A World of Emptying Out). *Yediot Ahronot*, Dec. 12, 1987.

Bakhtin, Mikhail. *Rabelais and His World.* Translated by Helene Iswolsky. Bloomington: Indiana University Press, 1984.

Balaban, Avraham. *Gal aher ba-shiporet ha-ivrit* (A Different Wave in Israeli Fiction). Jerusalem: Keter, 1995.

Ball, Howard. *Prosecuting War Crimes and Genocide.* Lawrence: University Press of Kansas, 1999.

Baram, Nir. *Ha-arets she-me'ever la-harim* (A Land without Borders: My Journey Around East Jerusalem and the West Bank). Tel Aviv: Am Oved, 2016. Translated by Jessica Cohen. Australia and United Kingdom: Text Publishing, 2017.

Barnea, Nahum. *Yorim u-vokhim* (Shooting and Crying). Tel Aviv: Zmora-Bitan, 1981.

Baudrillard, Jean. "The Map Precedes the Territory." In *The Fontana Postmodernism Reader*, edited by Walter T. Anderson, 75–7. London: Fontana Press, 1996.

Ben Ari, Eyal. "Hayalim be-masekhot: tsahal ve-ha-intifada" (Soldiers in Masks: The IDF and the Intifada). In *Ha-milhama ha-shvi'it: hashpaot ha-intifada al ha-hevra be-Israel* (The Seventh War: The Impact of the Intifada on Israeli Society), edited by Reuven Gal, 106–21. Tel Aviv: Ha-kibbutz ha-meuhad, 1990.

Ben-Dov, Nitza. "Ve-ha-ir einena kala" (And the City Endures). *Ha-aretz Culture and Literature*, Apr. 23, 2004. 1.12.2013. https://www.haaretz.co.il/literature/1.960933

Ben-Dov, Nitza. *Ve-Hi Tehilatekha* (Studies in the Works of S. Y. Agnon, A. B. Yehoshua, and Amos Oz). Tel Aviv: Schocken, 2006.

Ben-Eliezer, Uri. *Old Conflict, New War: Israel's Politics toward the Palestinians.* New York: Palgrave Macmillan, 2012.

Ben-Eliezer, Uri, and Yuval Feinstein. "'The Battle over Our Homes': Reconstructing/Deconstructing Sovereign Practices Around Israel's Separation Barrier on the West Bank." *Israel Studies* 12, no. 1 (Spring 2007): 171–92. http://www.jstor.org/stable/30245812

Ben Ezer, Ehud, ed. *Be-moledet ha-ga'aguim ha-menugadim—ha-aravi ba-sifrut ha-ivrit* (Sleepwalkers and Other Stories: The Arab in Hebrew Fiction). Tel Aviv: Zmora-Bitan, 1992. Boulder: Lynne Rienner, 1999.

Ben-Gurion, Arie, ed. *Al tishlah yadkha el ha-na'ar—shirim vedivrei hagut al ha-akeda* (Do Not Lay Your Hand on the Boy—Poems and Essays on the Binding). Jerusalem: Keter, 2002.

Ben-Yosef Ginur, Tzvia. "Ha-distopia ha-tsiyonit al pi Orly Castel-Bloom" (The Zionist Dystopia According to Orly Castel-Bloom). In *Literature and Society in Culture—Papers Presented to Gershon Shaked,* edited by Yehudith Bar-el, Yigal Schwartz and Tamar Hess, 350–463. Tel Aviv and Jerusalem: Ha-kibbutz ha-meuhad and Keter, 2000.

Benziman, Galia. "Disket gibui la-hayim" (Backup for Life). *Ha-aretz Culture and Literature*, May 9, 2008. http://www.haaretz.co.il/literature/1.1323318

Berg, Nancy E. "The Politics of Paternity and Patrimony." *Shofar* 24, no. 3 (2006): 100–14. https://doi.org/10.1353/sho.2006.0044

Bernard, Anna. *Rhetorics of Belonging: Nation, Narration, and Israel/Palestine*. Liverpool: Liverpool University Press, 2013.

Bhabha, Homi K. "Arrivals and Departures." Preface to *Home, Exile, Homeland,* edited by Hamid Naficy, vii–xi. New York: Routledge, 1999.

Bhabha, Homi K. *Location of Culture*. London: Routledge, 1994.

Bhabha, Homi K. *Nation and Narration.* London: Routledge, 1990.

Bhabha, Homi K. "The Other Question: Difference, Discrimination and the Discourse of Colonialism." In *Out There: Marginalization and Contemporary Cultures,* edited by Russell Ferguson et al., 71–88. New York and Boston: New Museum of Contemporary Art and MIT Press, 1990.

Binyaminov, Yisrael. "Ha-akeda ha-leumit" (The National Binding). *Kivunim hadashim* 20 (2009): 268–72.

Blich, Baruch. "Dolly City Me'or ha-dor" (Dolly City, the Generation's Light). *Te'amim* 1 (Dec. 1993): 25–8.

Bonita, Mark, and John Protevi. *Deleuze and Geophilosophy.* Edinburgh: Edinburgh University Press, 2004.

Braidotti, Rosi. "Affirming the Affirmative: On Nomadic Affectivity." *Rhizomes* 11–12 (Fall 2005/Spring 2006). http://www.rhizomes.net/issue11/braidotti.html

Braidotti, Rosi. *Nomadic Subjects: Embodiment and Sexual Difference in Contemporary Feminist Theory.* New York: Columbia University Press, 1994.

Braidotti, Rosi. "Nomadism with Difference: Deleuze's Legacy in a Feminist Perspective." *Man and World* 29 (1996): 305–9.

Breines, Ingeborg, Robert Connell and Ingrid Eide, eds. *Male Roles, Masculinities and Violence: A Culture of Peace Perspective*. Paris: UNESCO Publishing, 2000. http://unesdoc.unesco.org/images/0012/001206/120683e.pdf

Brenner, Rachel Feldhay. *Inextricably Bonded—Israeli Arab and Jewish Writers Re-Visiting Culture*. Wisconsin: University of Wisconsin Press, 2003.

Browne, Brynmor. "A Solution to the Problem of Moral Luck." *Philosophical Quarterly* 42, no. 168 (1992): 345–56.

Burman, Erica. "Innocents Abroad: Western Fantasies of Childhood and the Iconography of Emergencies." *Disasters* 18, no. 3 (1994): 236–53.

Calderon, Nissim. "Sarah, ma sohef be-Sarah?" (Sarah, What Is Stirring in Sarah?). *Ma'ariv Weekend Supplement, Books and Literature*, Feb. 11, 2000.

Cargas, Harry James. "Zionist as a Writer: A. B. Yehoshua Talks with Harry James Cargas." *Shofar* 1 (Fall 1994): 138–43. https://doi.org/10.1353/sho.1994.0075

Carroll, Noël. "The Wheel of Virtue: Art, Literature, and Moral Knowledge." *Journal of Aesthetics and Art Criticism* 60, no. 1 (2002): 3–26.

Castel-Bloom, Orly. "Ha-ma'amar ha-avud" (The Lost Article). *Yediot Ahronot Friday Magazine*, June 11, 1993.

Certeau, Michel de. *The Practice of Everyday Life*. Berkeley, CA: University of California Press, 1984.

Cohen Shabot, Sara. "Towards a Grotesque Phenomenology of Ethical Eroticism." *Women: A Cultural Review* 24, no. 1 (2013): 62–70. DOI: 10.1080/09574042.2012.750922

Colebrook, Claire. Introduction to *Deleuze and Feminist Theory*, edited by Ian Buchanan and Claire Colebrook, 1–17. Edinburgh: Edinburgh University Press, 2001.

Conley, Verena Andermatt. "Becoming Woman Now." In *Deleuze and Feminist Theory*, edited by Ian Buchanan and Claire Colebrook, 18–37. Edinburgh: Edinburgh University Press, 2001.

Critchley, Simon. Introduction to *The Cambridge Companion to Levinas*, 1–32. Cambridge: Cambridge University Press, 2002.

Critchley, Simon. *Very Little . . . Almost Nothing—Death, Philosophy, Literature*. London and New York: Routledge, 1997.

Deleuze, Gilles, and Félix Guattari. *A Thousand Plateaus*. Translated by Brian Massumi. Minnesota: Continuum, 1987.

Deleuze, Gilles, and Félix Guattari. *Kafka: Toward a Minor Literature*. Translated by Dana Polan. Minneapolis and Oxford: University of Minnesota Press, 1986.

Denton, Edgar. *Limits of Loyalty*. Waterloo, Ontario, Canada: Wilfrid Laurier University Press, 1979.

Derrida, Jacques. "Adieu." In *Adieu to Emmanuel Levinas*. Translated by Pascale-Anne Brault and Micheal Naas, 1–13. Stanford: Stanford University Press, 1999.

Domb, Risa. *The Arab in Hebrew Prose*. London: Vallentine, Mitchell, 1982.

Douglas, Mary. *Purity and Danger*. London: Ark Paperback, 1966.

Eaglestone, Robert. *Ethical Criticism: Reading after Levinas*. Edinburgh: Edinburgh University Press, 1997.

Elias, Norbert. *The Civilizing Process*. Translated by Edmund Jepcott. New York: Urizen Books, 1978 [1939].

Enoch, David, and Andrei Marmor. "The Case against Moral Luck." *Law and Philosophy* 26 (2007): 405–36. https://doi.org/10.1007/s10982-006-9001-3

Eshel, Amir. *Futurity: Contemporary Literature and the Quest for the Past*. Chicago and London: University of Chicago Press, 2013.

Fanon, Frantz. *Black Skin, White Masks*. Translated by Charles Lam Markmann. New York: Grove Press, 1967.

Feige, Michael. *Shtei mapot la-gada* (One Space, Two Places). Jerusalem: Magnes, 2002.

Feldman, Yael. *Glory and Agony*. Stanford, CA: Stanford University Press, 2010.

Feldman, Yael. "Shel mi ha-korban haze, la'azazel? aliyato ve-nefilato shel avraham ha-oked bi-shnot ha-hamishim" (Whose Sacrifice Is It? The Rise and Fall of Abraham the Binder in the 50's). *Mikan* 9 (May 2008): 125–57.

Feldman, Yael. "The Other Within in Contemporary Israeli Fiction." *Middle East Review* (Fall 1989): 53–60.

Feldman, Yael. "Yits'hak o Oedipus—migdar ve-psychopolitika be-gilgulei ha-akeda" (Isaac or Oedipus—Gender and Psychoanalysis in the Metamorphosis of the Binding). *Alpayim* 22 (2001): 53–77.

Foucault, Michel. *Discipline and Punish: The Birth of the Prison*. Translated by Alan Sheridan. New York: Vintage Books, 1979.

Foucault, Michel. *Power/Knowledge*. Translated by Colin Gordon. Brighton: Harvester Press, 1980.

Foucault, Michel. Preface to *Anti-Oedipus: Capitalism and Schizophrenia*. Translated by Robert Hurley, Mark Seem, and Helen R. Lane, xiii–xvi. London: Continuum, 2004 [1977].

Foucault, Michel. *The Order of Things*. London: Tavistock, 1970.

Friebach-Heifetz, Dana. *Hesed hiloni* (Secular Grace). Tel Aviv: Resling, 2009.

Friedman, Liat. "'Elef mishorim': mahalakh anti-nietszche'ani" ("A Thousand Plateaus": An Anti-Nietzschean Move). *Teoria u-vikoret* 19 (2001): 234–8.

Frykman, Jonas, and Orvar Lofgren. *Culture Builders: A Historical Anthropology of Middle Class Life*. Translated by Alan Crozier. New Brunswick: Rutgers University Press, 1987.

Gantz, Haim. "Ha-herut lelaket zradim" (The Freedom to Collect Twigs). *Siman Kria* 5 (1976): 291–4.

Gertz, Nurit. "Imprisoning the National Identity: The West Bank in *The Smile of the Lamb* (the Book and the Film) and *Yellow Wind*." *Contemporary Theatre Review* 3, no. 2 (1995): 193–205. https://doi.org/10.1080/10486809508568349

Gesser, Nechama. "Sukkot ve-shmita—hevzek? mabat psycho'analiti" (Sukkot and Shmita—A Snapshot? A Psychoanalytical Gaze). *Et Lacan* 2 (2006): 59–63.

Gibson, Andrew. *Postmodernity, Ethics and the Novel*. London and New York: Routledge, 1999.

Gilad, Elon. "Matai hit'halnu lehishtamesh ba-mila hitkarnefut" (When Have We Started to Use the Word Rhinoceros). *Ha-aretz*, Jan. 18, 2013. http://www.haaretz.co.il/magazine/the-edge/mehasafa/1.1909611

Glassner, Arik. "Isha borahat mi-bsora" (To the End of the Land). *Ma'ariv*, Apr. 19, 2008.

Gluzman, Michael. *Ha-guf ha-zioni—leumiyut, migdar ve-miniyut ba-sifrut ha-ivrit ha-hadasha* (The Zionist Body—Nationality, Gender and Sexuality in Modern Hebrew Literature). Tel Aviv: Ha-kibbutz ha-meuhad, 2007.

Gluzman, Michael. "Im lo tihi'ye Yerushalaim" (If There Would Be No Jerusalem). *Ha-aretz*, May 5, 2008. http://www.haaretz.co.il/literature/1.1322595

Gluzman, Michael. "'Lehisaret al yedei ha-homer, lo lehitrapek alav': re'ayon im Ronit Matalon" ("Getting Scratched by the Matter, Not Clinging to It": An Interview with Ronit Matalon). *Mikan* 2 (2001): 228–48.

Gluzman, Michael. "The Politics of Intertextuality in Anton Shammas's Arabesques." *Modern Jewish Studies* 3, no. 3 (2004): 319–35. doi/pdf/10.1080/1472588042000292385

Golan, Avirama. "Ha'im ha-sipur shelo hu ha-sipur shelanu" (Is His Story Our Story?). *Ha-aretz Literary Supplement* 653, Aug. 31, 2005. http://www.haaretz.co.il/literature/1.1040323

Gold, Nili. *Haifa—City of Steps*. Waltham, MA: Brandeis University Press, 2017.

Goldshmid, Tali. "Ha-gvul shel ha-sifrut—al musag ha-gvul be-sifrut ha-sikhsukh" (The Border of Literature—On the Concept of Border in the Literature of the Conflict). *Alpayim* 21 (2008): 60–82.

Goren, Shiri. *The Home Front: Literary Engagement with Political Crises in Israel, 1993–2006*, PhD dissertation, Department of Hebrew and Judaic Studies, New York University, 2011.

Govrin, Michal. "Layers of Changing Space in Jerusalem: View from a Hilltop." *Hebrew Studies* 47 (2006): 385–8. http://www.jstor.org/stable/27913808

Grassiani, Erella. "The Phenomenon of 'Breaking the Silence' in Israel." In *The Moral Dimension of Asymmetrical Warefare: Counter-Terrorism, Democratic Values and Military Ethics*, edited by Th. A. van Baarda and D. E. M. Verweij, 247–59. Leiden and Boston: Martinus Nijhoff, 2009.

Greenbaum, Charles, and Yoel Elitzur. "Ha-hashlakhot ha-psychologiot ve-ha-musariot shel kibush ha-shtahim ha-falastiniyim al ha-hevra ha-israelit" (The Psychological and Moral Implications of the Occupation of the Palestinian Territories on Israeli Society). In *Hashpa'at ha-kibush al ha-hevra ha-israelit* (The Influence of the Occupation on Israeli Society), edited by Daniel Bar-Tal and Itzhak Shanel, 310–34. Tel Aviv and Jerusalem: The Tami Steinmetz Center for Peace Research, Tel Aviv University and Bialik Institute, 2013.

Grossman, Dave. *On Killing*, Toronto, Canada: Little, Brown, 1995.

Grossman, David. *Ha-mavet ke-derekh hayim* (Death as the Way of Life). Tel Aviv: ha-kibbutz ha-meuhad, 2003. Translated by Haim Watzman, edited by Efrat Lev. New York: Farrar, Straus and Giroux, 2003.

Grossman, David. *Nokhehim nifkadim* (Present Absentees). Bnei-Brak: Ha'kibbutz ha'meuhad, 1992. Translated by Haim Watzman as *Sleeping on a Wire: Conversations with Palestinians in Israel.* New York: Farrar, Straus and Giroux, 1993.

Grossman, David. *Ha-zman ha-tsahov* (The Yellow Wind). Tel Aviv: Ha-kibbutz ha-meuhad, 1987. Translated by Haim Watzman. New York: Farrar, Straus, and Giroux, 1988.

Grossman, David. *Writing in the Dark.* Translated by Jessica Cohen. New York: Farrar, 2008.

Grosz, Elizabeth. "A Thousand Tiny Sexes: Feminism and Rhizomatics." In *Gilles Deleuze and the Theater of Philosophy*, edited by Dorothea Olkowski and Costantin V. Boundas, 187–210. New York: Routledge, 1994.

Grosz, Elizabeth. *Chaos, Territory, Art.* New York: Columbia University Press, 2008.

Grosz, Elizabeth. *Volatile Bodies.* Bloomington and Indianapolis: Indiana University Press, 1994.

Grover, Yerach. *Zionism: The Limits of Moral Discourse in Israeli Hebrew Fiction.* Minneapolis: University of Minnesota Press, 1994.

Grumberg, Karen. "Female Grotesque: Orly Castel-Bloom and the Israeli Woman's Body." *Nashim* 23, no. 3 (2012): 145–68. https://doi.org/10.2979/nashim.23.145

Grumberg, Karen. *Place and Ideology in Contemporary Hebrew Literature*. Syracuse: Syracuse University Press, 2011.

Gurevitz, David. *Postmodernism*. Tel Aviv: Zmora-Bitan, 1997.

Gurevitz, Zeli, and Gideon Aranne. "Al ha-makom" (On the Place). *Alpayim* 4 (1993): 9–44.

Hall, Stuart. "Cultural Identity and Diaspora." In *Identity: Community, Culture, Difference*, edited by John Rutherford, 222–37. London: Lawrence and Wishart, 1990.

Hall, Stuart. "Ethnicity: Identity and Difference." In *Becoming National*, edited by Geoff Eley and Ronald Grigor, 339–48. Oxford: Oxford University Press, 1996.

Hannah, Robert. "Morality 'De Re': Reflections on the Trolley Problem." In *Ethics: Problems and Principles*, edited by John Martin Fischer and Mark Ravizza, 318–36. Fort Worth, TX: Harcourt Brace Jovanovich College, 1992.

Harpham, Geoffrey Galt. *Getting It Right*. Chicago: University of Chicago Press, 1992.

Harpham, Geoffrey Galt. *On the Grotesque: Strategies of Contradiction in Art and Literature*. Princeton, NJ: Princeton University Press, 1982.

Harris, S. Rachel. *An Ideological Death—Suicide in Israeli Literature*. Evanston: Northwestern University Press, 2014.

Harsonsky, Yossi. "Ovrim le-reshet gimel" (Moving to Gimel Radio Station). *Ma'ariv*, Apr. 3, 1988.

Hasak-Lowy, Todd. "Postzionism and Its Aftermath in Hebrew Literature: The Case of Orly Castel-Bloom." *Jewish Social Studies* 14, no. 2 (2008): 86–112. muse.jhu.edu/article/242640

Hazaz, Haim. "Ha-sifrut ha-ivrit ba-zman ha-ze" (Hebrew Literature in This Era). *Daf* 11 (July 1956): 3–5.

Hersh, Seymour M. "Torture at Abu Ghraib." *The New Yorker*, May 10, 2004. http://www.newyorker.com/magazine/2004/05/10/torture-at-abu-ghraib

Herzog, Omri. "Journey to the Hills in the Land of Settlers." *Ha-aretz*, Feb. 5, 2013. https://www.haaretz.co.il/literature/prose/1.1921790

Hever, Hannan. *Ha-sipur ve-ha-leom* (The Story and the Nation). Tel Aviv: Resling, 2007.

Hever, Hannan. "Kol ehad tsarikh lada'at et ha-makom shelo" (Everyone Should Know His Place). *Ha-aretz Literary Supplement* 362, Feb. 2, 2000.

Hever, Hannan. "Mapa shel hol—mi-sifrut ivrit le-sifrut israelit" (Map of Sand—From Hebrew Literature to Israeli Literature). *Teoria u-vikoret* 20 (2002): 165–90.

Hever, Hannan. *Producing Modern Hebrew Canon: Nation Building and Minority Discourse*. New-York: New York University Press, 2001.

Hever, Hannan. *Sifrut she-nikhtevet mi-kan* (Literature Written from Here). Tel Aviv: Yediot Ahronot, 1999.

Hever, Hannan. "Tnu lo badranim—ve-yanua'h be-shalom: canoni ve-populari be-idan shel kibush" (Give Him Entertainers, and He Will Rest in Peace). In *Canoni ve-populari* (Canonic and Popular), 193–208. Tel Aviv: Resling, 2007.

Hever, Hannan. "'We Have Not Arrived from the Sea': A Mizrahi Literary Geography," *Social Identities*, 10, no. 1 (2004): 31–51.

Hochberg, Gil Z. *Visual Occupations: Violence and Visibility in a Conflict Zone*. London: Duke University Press, 2015.

Holmes, Richard. *Acts of War—The Behavior of Men in Battle*. New York: The Free Press, 1985.

Holzman, Avner. "Ha-holi ve-ha-si'uv" (The Illness and the Corruption). *Yediot Ahronot Weekend Supplement*, Jan. 21, 2000.

Horn, Bernard. *Facing the Fires: Conversations with A. B. Yehoahua*. New York: Syracuse Univesity Press, 1997.

Humphreys, Stephen. "Legalizing Lawlessness: On Giorgio Agamben's State of Exception." *European Journal of International Law* 17, no. 3 (2006): 677–87. https://doi.org/10.1093/ejil/chl020

Irigaray, Luce. *This Sex Which Is Not One*. Translated by Catherine Porter with Carolyn Burke. Ithaca, NY: Cornell University Press, 1985.

Isaksen, Runo. *Literature and War—Conversation with Israeli and Palestinian Writers*. Translated by Kari Dickson. Massachusetts: Olive Branch Press, 2009.

Itzhaki, Yedidya. "'Shlihuto shel ha-memune al mash'abei enosh' ke-dialog yehudi-notsri" ("A Woman in Jerusalem" as a Judeo-Christian Dialogue). In *Mabatim mitstalvim—iyunim be-yetsirat A. B. Yehoshua* (Intersecting Perspectives: Essays on A. B. Yehoshua's Oeuvre), edited by Amir Banbaji, Nitza Ben-Dov, and Ziva Shamir, 356-61. Tel Aviv: Ha-kibbutz ha-meuhad, 2010.

Izikovitch, Gili. "Si'ah lohamim—me'ahorei ha-nitsahon ha-gadol shel '67 histatra shura shel pish'ei milhama" (Fighters' Discourse—Behind the Great Victory of '67, War Crimes Were Hidden). *Ha-aretz*, June 6, 2015. http://www.haaretz.co.il/gallery/cinema/.premium-1.2651353#hero__bottom

Jacobson, David C. "Intimate Relations between Israelis and Palestinians in Fiction by Israeli Women Authors." *Shofar* 25, no. 3 (Spring 2007): 32–46. https://doi.org/10.1353/sho.2007.0074

Jaggi, Maya. "Power and Pity." *The Guardian*, June 23, 2006. http://www.theguardian.com/books/2006/jun/24/featuresreviews.guardianreview11

Jarvis, Lee. *Times of Terror: Discourse, Temporality and the War on Terror.* Basingstoke, England, and New York: Palgrave Macmillan, 2009.

Jensen, Henning. "Morality and Luck." *Philosophy* 59 (1984): 323–30.

Karpel, Dalia. "Oh My Love, Comely as Jerusalem." *Ha-aretz* English Edition, Apr. 18, 2002. http://www.haaretz.com/oh-my-love-comely-as-jerusalem-1.47474

Kartun-Blum, Ruth. "Ha-nahash ve-ha-shablul" (The Snake and the Snail). *Keshet ha-hadasha* 12 (2005): 22–31.

Kartun-Blum, Ruth. "Me'ayin ha-etsim ha-ele be-yadi: ha-akeda ke-mikre bohan ba-shira ha-ivrit ha-hadasha" (Where Do These Trees Come From—The Binding of Isaac as a Test Case in Modern Hebrew Poetry). *Moznayim*, 62, no. 9–10 (1988): 9–14.

Kasher, Asa. *Sefer katan al mashmaut ha-hayim* (A Little Book on the Meaning of Life). Tel Aviv: Ha-kibbutz ha-meuhad and Amutat Yehoraz, 2002.

Kashti, Or. "Israel Bans Novel on Arab-Jewish Romance from Schools for 'Threatening Jewish Identity.'" *Ha-aretz* English Edition, Dec. 31, 2015. https://www.haaretz.com/israel-news/.premium-israel-bans-novel-depicting-arab-jewish-romance-from-schools-1.5383970

Kashua, Sayed. "Welcome to the Israeli Arab Ghetto." *Ha-aretz* English Edition, Jan. 15, 2016. https://www.haaretz.com/opinion/.premium-welcome-to-the-israeli-arab-ghetto-1.5390893

Kayser, Wolfgang. *The Grotesque in Art and Literature*. Translated by Ulrich Weisstein. Toronto and New York: McGraw-Hill, 1966.

Keen, Suzanne. *Empathy and the Novel.* Oxford: Oxford University Press, 2007.

Kemp, Adriana. "Ha-gvul ki-fnei Janus—merhav ve-toda'a leumit be-Israel" (The Border as Janus's Face—Space and National Identity in Israel). *Teoria u-vikoret* 16 (2000): 13–43.

Kenaan, Hagi. "Facing Images: After Levinas." *Angelaki*: *Journal of the Theoretical Humanities* 16, no. 1 (2011): 143–59. https://doi.org/10.1080/0969725X.2011.564370

Kenaan, Hagi. *The Ethics of Visuality: Levinas and the Contemporary Gaze.* London: I. B. Tauris, 2013.

Keren, Nitza. *Ke-yeri'a be-yad ha-rokemet—nashim kotvot ve-ha-tekst ha-hegemoni* (Like a Sheet in the Hand of the Embroideress—Women Authors and the Hegemonic Text). Ramat Gan: Bar-Ilan University, 2010.

Kershner, Isable. "Jewish-Arab Love Story Excluded from Israeli Classrooms." *New York Times*, Dec. 31, 2015. https://www.nytimes.com/2016/01/01/world/middleeast/borderlife-dorit-rabinyan-israel-ministry-education.html

Kidron, Peretz, ed. *Ad kan—eduyot shel sarvanim* (Refusenik! Israel's Soldiers of Conscience). Tel Aviv: Hargol, 2004. London: Zed Books, 2004.

Kimmerling, Baruch. *The Israeli State and Society: Boundaries and Frontiers*. New York: State University of New York Press, 1989.

Kishon, Ephraim, and Gardosh (Dosh) Kariel. *Sliha she-nitsahnu* (We Apologize for Our Victory). Tel Aviv: Ma'ariv, 1967.

Klein, Uta. "'Our Best Boys': The Making of Masculinity in Israeli Society." In *Male Roles, Masculinities and Violence: A Culture of Peace Perspective*, edited by Ingeborg Breines, Robert Connell and Ingrid Eide, 163–80. Paris: UNESCO Publishing, 2000. http://unesdoc.unesco.org/images/0012/001206/120683e.pdf

Kochavi, Avner. "Degel shahor e'had gadol" (One Large Black Flag). In *Ad kan—eduyot shel sarvanim* (Refusenik! Israel's Soldiers of Conscience), edited by Peretz Kidron, 144. Tel Aviv: Hargol, 2004.

Kristeva, Julia. *Power of Horror: An Essay on Abjection*. Translated by Leon S. Roudiez. New York: Colombia University Press, 1982.

Laor, Yitzhak. "A. B. Yehoshua ve-ha-sin'a ha-mizrahit la-aravim" (A. B. Yehoshua and the Mizrahis' Hatred of the Arabs). *Mita'am* 2 (2005): 43–60. http://mitaam.co.il/mit2laor.htm

Laor, Yitzhak. "Ha-roman shel shuliyat ha-kosem" (The Novel of the Sorcerer's Apprentice). *Ha-aretz Culture and Literature*, Oct. 26, 2001. http://www.haaretz.co.il/misc/1.742706

Laor, Yitzhak. "Mahshavot al tsenzura ve-'si'ah lohamim: ha-slilim ha-gnuzim'" (Thoughts on Censorship and "Fighters' Discourse: Censured Voices"). *Ha-aretz*, Nov. 20, 2015. http://www.haaretz.co.il/literature/study/.premium-1.2781062

Laor, Yitzhak. "Motar ha-mizrahan al ha-mizrahi" (The Orientalist Is Preferable to the Oriental). *Ha-aretz Culture and Literature*, Nov. 2, 2001. http://www.haaretz.co.il/misc/1.745148

Laor, Yitzhak. "The Israeli-Palestinian Romance That Doesn't Dare." *Ha-aretz* English Edition, Sep. 23, 2014.

Levi-Hazan, Yael. *Nashim kotvot al milhama ba-sifrut ha-ivrit* (Women's Writing on War in Hebrew Literature), PhD dissertation, Department of Hebrew Literature, Ben-Gurion University of the Negev, 2015.

Levinas, Emmanuel. *Alterity and Transcendence*. Translated by Michael B. Smith. London: Athlone Press, 1999.

Levinas, Emmanuel. *Ethics and Infinity—Conversation with Philip Nemo*. Translated by Richard A. Coher. Pittsburgh, PA: Duquesne University Press, 1985.

Levinas, Emmanuel. *God, Death, and Time*. Translated by Bettina Bergo. Stanford, CA: Stanford University Press, 1993.

Levinas, Emmanuel. *Otherwise Than Being, or Beyond Essence*. Translated by Alphonso Lingis. Pittsburgh, PA: Duquesne University Press, 1998 [1974].

Levinas, Emmanuel. "Poetry and Resurrection: Notes on Agnon." In *Proper Names*. Translated by Michael B. Smith, edited by Werner Hamacher and David E. Wellbery, 7–16. Stanford, CA: Stanford University Press, 1996.

Levinas, Emmanuel. "Reality and Its Shadow." In *The Levinas Reader*. Translated by Alphonso Lingis, edited by Sean Hand, 129–43. Oxford and Cambridge: Blackwell, 1989 [1948].

Levinas, Emmanuel. "The Poet's Vision." In *Proper Names*. Translated by Michael B. Smith, edited by Werner Hamacher and David E. Wellbery, 127–39. Stanford, CA: Stanford University Press, 1996.

Levinas, Emmanuel. "The Trace of the Other." In *Deconstruction in Context*. Translated by A. Lingis, edited by Taylor C. Mark, 345–59. Chicago, IL: University of Chicago Press, 1986.

Levinas, Emmanuel. *Time and the Other and Additional Essays*. Translated by Richard A. Cohen. Pittsburgh, PA: Duquesne University Press, 1987.

Levinas, Emmanuel. *Totality and Infinity: An Essay on Exteriority*. Translated by Alphonso Lingis. Pittsburgh, PA: Duquesne University Press, 1991 [1961].

Levitan, Amos. "Ma lishmot, ma le'ehoz?" (What to Drop, What to Keep?). *Iton 77* 269 (2002): 33–5.

Levitan, Amos. "Me-hodu ve-ad kush" (From India to Cush). *Iton 77* 320–1 (May–June 2007): 34–6.

Levy-Barzilai, Vered. "Yefei ha-nefesh, nim'astem" (Sensitive Souls, Enough). *Ha-aretz*, Aug. 8, 2002. http://www.haaretz.co.il/misc/1.1558851

Levy, Gideon. "I Punched an Arab in the Face." *Ha-aretz* English edition, Nov. 20, 2003. https://www.haaretz.com/1.4766243

Levy, Lital. "Nation, Village, Cave: A Spatial Reading of 1948 in Three Novels of Anton Shammas, Emile Habiby, and Elias Khoury." *Jewish Social*

Studies: History, Culture, Society 18, no. 3 (Spring/Summer 2012): 10–26. https://doi.org/10.2979/jewisocistud.18.3.10

Levy, Shimon. "Shvuim be-bid'yon—ha-aravim ba-sifrut ha-ivrit ha-hadasha" (Prisoners of Imagination: The Arabs in New Hebrew Literature). *Moznaim* 5–6 (October–November 1983): 70–3.

Levy, Yagil. *Mi sholeṭ al ha-tsava? bein pikuah al ha-tsava le-shelita bi-tsva'iyut* (Who Governs the Military? From Control over the Military to Control of Militarism). Jerusalem: Magnes Press, 2010.

Libes, Tamar, and Anat First. "Framing the Palestinian-Israeli conflict." In *Framing Terrorism: The News Media, the Government and the Public*, edited by Pippa Norris, Montague Kern, and Marion Just, 59–64. New York and London: Routledge, 2003.

Libes, Tamar, and Shoshana Blum-Kulka. "Yorim u-vokhim? al hitmodedut im dilemot musariyot ba-sherut ha-tsva'i ba-shtahim" (Shooting and Crying? On Coping with Moral Dilemmas in the Military Service in the Occupied Territories). In *Ha-milhama ha-shvi'it: hashpaot ha-intifada al ha-hevra be-Israel* (The Seventh War: The Impact of the Intifada on Israeli Society), edited by Reuven Gal, 85–105. Tel Aviv: Ha-kibbutz ha-meuhad, 1990.

Lieblich, Amia. *Transition to Adulthood during Military Service*. Albany: State University of New York Press, 1989.

Lieblich, Amia, and Meir Perlow. "Transition to Adulthood during Military Service." *Jerusalem Quarterly* 47 (1988): 40–76.

Linn, Ruth. "Soldiers with Conscience Never Die—They Are Just Ignored by Their Society: Moral Disobedience in the Israel Defense Force." *Journal of Military Ethics* 1, no. 2 (2002): 57–76. https://doi.org/10.1080/150275702320231280

Lior, Ilan. "Breaking the Silence: Why Take the Message Abroad?" *Ha-aretz* English Edition, Dec. 18, 2015. https://www.haaretz.com/israel-news/.premium-why-take-the-message-abroad-1.5378846

Lipsker, Avidov. "Girsaot lohashot be-'shlihuto shel ha-memune al mash'abei enosh'" (Whispering Versions in "A Woman in Jerusalem"). In *Mabatim mitstalvim—iyunim be-yetsirat A. B. Yehoshua* (Intersecting Perspectives: Essays on A. B. Yehoshua's Oeuvre), edited by Amir Banbaji, Nitza Ben-Dov, and Ziva Shamir, 345–55. Tel Aviv: Ha-kibbutz ha-meuhad, 2010.

Livne, Neri. "Ha-intifada ha-pratit sheli" (My Private Intifada). *Ha-aretz Friday Supplement*, Apr. 5, 2002. http://www.haaretz.co.il/misc/1.784160

Lockard, Joe. "Somewhere between Arab and Jew: Ethnic Re-Identification in Modern Hebrew Literature." *Middle Eastern Literatures* 5, no. 1 (2002): 49–62. https://doi.org/10.1080/14751790220103774

Lorraine, Tamsin. "Becoming-Imperceptible as a Mode of Self-Presentation." In *Resistance, Flight, Creation: Feminist Enactments of French Philosophy*, edited by Dorothea Olkowski, 179–94. Ithaca, NY: Cornell University Press, 2000.

Lubin, Orly. *Isha koret isha* (A Woman Reads Woman). Or Yehudah: Haifa University Press and Zmora-Bitan, 2006.

Lustick, Ian. *Unsettled States, Disputed Lands*. Ithaca New York: Cornell University Press, 1993.

Mackie, J. L. *Ethics, Inventing Right and Wrong*. London: Penguin Books, 1977.

Majumdar, Gaurav. *Migrant Form*. New York: Peter Lang, 2010.

Malach-Pines, Ayala. "Et mi shoheket ha-intifada?" (Who Suffers Burnout from the Intifada?). In *Ha-milhama ha-shvieit: hashpaot ha-intifada al ha-hevra be-Israel* (The Seventh War: The Impact of the Intifada on Israeli Society), edited by Reuven Gal, 55–64. Tel Aviv: Ha-kibbutz ha-meuhad, 1990.

Mann, Barbara. *A Place in History: Modernism, Tel Aviv, and the Creation of Jewish Urban Space*. Stanford, CA: Stanford University Press, 2006.

Mann, Barbara. *Space and Place in Jewish Studies*. New Brunswick, NJ: Rutgers University Press, 2012.

Mansbach, Daniela. "Meha'a al ha-gvul: koha shel ha-dualiyut be-praktikot ha-meha'a shel tnuat mahsom-watch" (Protest on the Border: The Power of Duality in the Protest Actions of MachsomWatch). *Teoria u-vikoret* 31 (2007): 77–99.

Maoz, Azaryahu. *Pulhanei medina—hagigot ha-atsmaut ve-hantsahat ha-noflim 1948–1956* (Rituals of State—The Celebrations of Independence and the Commemoration of the Fallen 1948–1956). Sde Boker: Ben-Gurion University, 1995.

Maoz, Rivka. "D'yokano shel Na'im ke-mitbolel tsair" (A Portrait of Na'im as a Young Assimilator). In *Rega shel huledet—mehkarim ba-sifrit ha-ivrit u-ve-sifrut ha-idish likhvod Dan Miron* (A Moment of Birth—Studies in Hebrew and Yiddish Literature in Honor of Dan Miron), edited by Hannan Hever, 519–38. Jerusalem: Bialik Institute, 2007.

Margalit, Ruth. "Assaf Gavron's 'The Hilltop' Excels at Unmasking Israel's Contradictions." *Ha-aretz* English edition, Nov. 3, 2014. https://www.haaretz.com/life/books/.premium-a-view-from-on-high-1.5322265

Masalha, Salman. "Hutspa israelit" (Israeli "Hutspa"). *Hadashot*, May 3, 1989.

Mayer, Tamar. *Gender Ironies of Nationalism: Sexing and Nation*. London: Routledge, 2000.

McDonald, Henry. "Aesthetics as First Ethics: Levinas and the Alterity of Literary Discourse." *Diacritics* 38, no. 4 (2008): 15–41.

Meisels, Ofra. "Likrat giyus" (Before Recruitment). In *Mitbagrim be-Israel—hebetim ishiyim, mishpahtiyim ve-hevratiyim* (Adolescents in Israel—Individual, Familial and Social Characteristics), edited by H. Plum, 177–200. Even Yehuda: Rekhes, 1995.

Melamed, Ariana. "Ha-epos ha-eimtani shel ha-imahut" (The Formidable Epos of Motherhood). *Hadashot*, Apr. 10, 1992.

Melamed, Ariana. "Mehir ha-shtika" (The Price of Silence). *Ynet*, Apr. 3, 2008. http://www.ynet.co.il/articles/0,7340,L-3527203,00.html

Melamed, Ariana. "Metsi'ut aheret" (Different Reality). *Ynet*, Mar. 20, 2004. http://www.ynet.co.il/articles/0,7340,L-2892059,00.html

Meltzer, Yoram. "Ha-bhira ha-mevorekhet be-vadaut" (The Blessed Choice of Certainty). *Ma'ariv Weekend Supplement, Literature and Books*, June 14, 2002.

Meltzer, Yoram. "Ha-metsi'ut hi uvda ba-shetah" (Reality Is a Fact on the Ground). *Ma'ariv Books*, May 16, 2002.

Meltzer, Yoram. "Sfarim lema'an ha-rega she-lifnei ovdan ha-vadaut" (Books for the Instant before the Loss of Meaning). *Ma'ariv Books*, May 10, 2002.

Mendelson-Maoz, Adia. "Amos Oz's 'A Tale of Love and Darkness' in a Framework of Immigration Narratives in Modern Hebrew Literature." *Journal of Modern Jewish Studies* 9, no. 1 (March 2010): 71–87. https://doi.org/10.1080/14725880903263101

Mendelson-Maoz, Adia. "Borders, Territory, and Sovereignty in the Works of Contemporary Israeli Women Writers." *Women's Studies* 4, no. 6 (2014): 788–822. https://doi.org/10.1080/00497878.2014.921511

Mendelson-Maoz, Adia. "Checkpoint Syndrome—Violence, Madness, and Ethics in the Hebrew Literature of the Intifada." In *Textual Ethos Studies, or: Locating Ethics*, edited by Anna Fahraeus and AnnKatrin Jonsson, 209–27. Amsterdam and New Jersey: Rodopi, 2005.

Mendelson-Maoz, Adia. "Ethics and Literature: Introduction." *Philosophia* 35, no. 2 (2007): 111–16. https://doi.org/10.1007/s11406-007-9068-6

Mendelson-Maoz, Adia. "Hurled into the Heart of Darkness—Moral Luck and the Hebrew Literature of the Intifada." *Hebrew Studies* 52 (2011): 315–39. https://doi.org/10.1353/hbr.2011.0019

Mendelson-Maoz, Adia. "On 'Human Parts'—Orly Castel-Bloom and the Israeli Contemporary Extreme." In *Novels of the Contemporary Extreme*, edited by Naomi Mandel and Alain-Philippe-Durand, 163–73. London and New York: Continuum, 2006.

Mendelson-Maoz, Adia. "Situatsiot kitsoniyot—zva'atiyut ve-groteskiyut be-yetsiratam shel Castel-Bloom ve-Keret" (Extreme Situations—The Horrendous and the Grotesque in the Works of Castel-Bloom and Keret). *Dapim—Research in Literature* 11 (1998): 162–77.

Mendelson-Maoz, Adia. "The Bereaved Father and His Dead son in the Works of A. B. Yehoshua." *Social Jewish Studies* 17, no. 1 (Fall 2010): 116–40. http://www.jstor.org/stable/10.2979/jewisocistud.17.1.116

Menuchin, Ishai. "Ha-hayal ha-tov" (The Good Soldier). In *Kibush ve-siruv* (Occupation and Refusal), edited by Ishai Menuchin, 22–32. Jerusalem: Sifrei November, 2006.

Metres, Philip. "Vexing Resistance, Complicating Occupation: A Contrapuntal Reading of Sahar Khalifeh's 'Wild Thorns' and David Grossman's 'The Smile of the Lamb.'" In *Narratives of Dissent: War in Contemporary Israeli Arts and Culture*, edited by Rachel S. Harris and Ranen Omer-Sherman, 81–109. Detroit: Wayne State University Press, 2013.

Miron, Dan. "Mashehu al Orly Castel-Bloom" (Considerations on Orly Castel-Bloom). *Al Hamishmar*, June 16, 1989.

Miron, Dan. *Mul ha-ah ha-shotek: al shirat ha-atsmaut* (In Front of the Silent Brother—On the Poetry of the War of Independence). Jerusalem: Open University and Keter Press, 1992.

Mishani, Dror. "Ha-mizrahi ha-samui min ha-ayin" (The Hidden Mizrahi). In *Mabatim mitstalvim—iyunim be-yetsirat A. B. Yehoshua* (Intersecting Perspectives: Essays on A. B. Yehoshua's Oeuvre), edited by Amir Banbaji, Nitza Ben-Dov and Ziva Shamir, 384–91. Tel Aviv: Ha-kibbutz ha-meuhad, 2010.

Morahg, Gilead. "New Images of Arabs in Israeli Fiction." *Prooftexts* 6 (1986): 147–62. http://www.jstor.org/stable/20689149

Morahg, Gilead. "Simanim mukdamin—ha-tahazit ha-koderet shel 'ha-kala ha-meshahreret'" (Early Indications—the Gloomy Forecast of "The Liberated Bride"). *Mikan* 9 (2008): 5–18.

Morgenstern, Avi. "Yorim u-vokhim—bli tsenzura" (Shooting and Crying—No Censorship). *Ma'ariv*, Apr. 6, 1998.

Munk, Yael. *Golim be-gvulam—ha-kolnoa ha-israeli be-mifne ha-elef* (Exiled in Their Borders: Israeli Cinema at the Turn of the Century). Ra'anana: Open University Press, 2012.

Murdoch, Iris. "Against Dryness: A Plemic Sketch." *Encounter*, January [1961]: 16–20.

Nagel, Thomas. *Mortal Questions*. UK: Cambridge University Press, 1979. Translated into Hebrew by Ronen, Z. Tzadka as *She'elot almavet*. Jerusalem: Magnes Press, 2010.

Nagel, Thomas. *The View from Nowhere*. New York and London: Oxford University Press, 1986.

Nassar, Hala Khamis. "Stories from under Occupation: Performing the Palestinian Experience." *Theatre Journal* 58, no. 1 (March 2006): 15–37. https://doi.org/10.1353/tj.2006.0083

Nathansohn, Regev. "Metsalmim kibush: sotsiologya shel yitsug hazuti" (Photographing Occupation: Sociology of Visual Representation). *Teoria u-vikoret* 31 (Winter 2007): 127–54.

Naveh, Hannah. *Nos'im ve-nos'ot: sipurei masa ba-sifrut ha-ivrit ha-hadasha* (Women and Men Travellers: The Travel Narative in Hebrew Literature). Tel Aviv: Ministry of Defense, 2002.

Ne'eman, Oded. "Aliyatam ve-nefilatam shel yefei ha-nefesh—kri'a be-'si'ah lohmim' u-ve-eduyot 'shovrim shtika'" (The Rise and Fall of the Sensitive Souls—Reading "Fighters' Discourse" and the Testimonies of "Breaking the Silence"). *Teoria u-vikoret* 33 (2008): 225–38.

Niv, Kobi. "Yorim u'bokhim" (Shooting and Crying). *Ha-olam ha-ze,* Dec. 15, 1976. *http://www.tarabut.info/he/articles/article/shooting-and-crying/*

Norvin, Richards. "Luck and Desert." *Mind* 95, no. 378 (1986): 198–209. https://doi.org/10.1093/mind/XCV.378.198

Nussbaum, Marta C. *The Fragility of Goodness: Luck and Ethics in Greek Tragedy and Philosophy*. Cambridge: Cambridge University Press, 1986.

Ofrat, Gidon, ed. *Akedat Yits'hak ba-omanut ha-israelit* (Isaac's Binding in Israeli Art). Ramat Gan: Museum of Israeli Art, 1980.

Omer-Sherman, Ranen. "Guests and Hosts in A. B. Yehoshua's 'The Liberated Bride.'" *Shofar* 31, no. 3 (2013): 25–63. https://doi.org/10.1353/sho.2013.0056

Omer-Sherman, Ranen, "On the Verge of a Long-Craved Intimacy: Distance and Proximity between Jewish and Arab Identities in A. B. Yehoshua's 'The Liberated Bride.'" *Journal of Jewish Identities* 2, no. 1 (January 2009): 55–84. https://doi.org/10.1353/jji.0.0005

Ophir, Adi. "Al ktiva postmodernit ve-efsharut hatsdakata ha-musarit" (On Post-Modern Writing and the Possibility of Its Moral Justification). *Mikan* A (May 2000): 115–33.

Ophir, Adi, ed. *Zman emet* (Time for Truth). Jerusalem: Keter, 2001.

Ophir, Adi, and Ariella Azoulay. *Mishtar ze she-eino ehad* (This Regime Which Is Not One). Tel Aviv: Resling, 2008.

Oppenheimer, Yochai. "Aliyato u-nefilato shel ha-si'ah ha-musari" (The Rise and Fall of Moral Discourse). In *Leumiyut u-musar* (Nationalism and Morality), edited by Efraim Lavie, 281–304. Jerusalem: Carmel, 2014.

Oppenheimer, Yochai. "Ha-hayim ha-kfulim shel ha-utopia" (The Double Life of Utopia). *Ha-aretz Books*, June 5, 2002. http://www.haaretz.co.il/misc/1.799629

Oppenheimer, Yochai. *Me'ever la-gader: itsug ha-aravim ba-siporet ha-ivrit ve-ha-israelit 1906–2005* (Barriers: The Representation of the Arab in Hebrew and Israeli Fiction, 1906–2005). Tel Aviv: Am oved and Sapir, 2008.

Oppenheimer, Yochai. "The Arab in the Mirror: The Image of the Arab in Israeli Fiction." *Prooftexts* 19, no. 3 (September 1999): 205–34. muse.jhu.edu/article/408176

Oren, Yosef, "Ha-sifrut ha-israelit—sti'ya miderekh ha-yashar" (Hebrew Literature—Deviation from the Path of Righteousness). *Nativ* 122, no. 3 (2008): 55–67.

Oren, Yosef. *Ha-siporet ha-israelit bi-shnot ha-intifada* (Israeli Prose in the Years of the Intifada). Rishon le-tsion: Yehad, 2005.

Oren, Yosef. "Pitputon mishpahti ve-manifest kna'ani" (Family Chatters and a Canaanite Manifest). *Nativ* 116, no. 3 (2007): 63–70.

Parr, Adrian (ed.). *The Deleuze Dictionary*. Edinburgh: Edinburgh University Press, 2005.

Parush, Adi. "Bikoret mivhan 'ha-degel ha-shahor'" (A Critique of the "Black Flag" Test). In *Kafr Qasim—eiru'im u-mitos* (Kafr Qasim—Events and Myths), edited by Ruvik Rosenthal, 131–77. Tel Aviv: Ha-kibbutz ha-meuchad, 2000.

Patton, Paul. *Deleuzian Concepts: Philosophy, Colonization, Politics*. Stanford, CA: Stanford University Press, 2010.

Patton, Paul. "Deterritorialization and Politics." In *The Deleuze Dictionary*, edited by Adrian Perr, 72–4. Edinburgh: Edinburgh University Press, 2010.

Peled, Shimrit. *Ha-ribon ha-israeli- ha-sia'h ve-ha-roman 1967–1973* (The Israeli Sovereign: Discourse and Novel 1967–1973), Jerusalem: Magnes Press, 2014

Peleg, Yaron. *Israeli Culture between the Two Intifadas: A Brief Romance*. Austin: University of Texas Press, 2008.

Peperzak, Adriaan. *To the Other—An Introduction to the Philosophy of Emmanuel Levinas*. Indiana: Purdue University Press, 1993.

Perry, Menakhem. "The Israeli-Palestinian Conflict as a Metaphor in Recent Israeli Fiction." *Poetics Today* 7, no. 4 (1986): 603–21.

Putnam, Hilary. "Levinas and Judaism." In *The Cambridge Companion to Levinas*, edited by Simon Critchley and Robert Bernasconi, 33–62. Cambridge: Cambridge University Press, 2002.

Ramras-Rauch, Gila. *The Arab in Israeli Literature*. Bloomington and Indianapolis: Indiana University Press, 1989.

Rawls, John. *Theory of Justice*. Cambridge, Massachusetts: Harvard University Press, 1971.

Raz-Krakotzkin, Amnon. "Be-hipus ahar ha-anima" (In Search of the Anima). *Ha-aretz*, Jul. 29, 1989.

Rescher, Nicholas. "Luck." *Proceedings of the American Philosophical Association* 64, no. 3 (1990): 5–20.

Rimmon-Kenan, Shlomit. "Place, Space, and Michal Govrin's *Snapshots*." *Narrative* 17, no. 2 (May 2009): 220–34. https://doi.org/10.1353/nar.0.0019

Robbins, Jill. *Altered Reading: Levinas and Literature*. Chicago, IL: University of Chicago Press, 1999.

Rondel, David. "Equality, Luck and Pragmatism." *Journal of Speculative Philosophy* 21, no. 2 (2007): 115–23. https://doi.org/10.1353/jsp.2007.0029

Rosebury, Brian. "Moral Responsibility and 'Moral Luck.'" *Philosophical Review* 104, no. 4 (1995): 499–524. https://doi.org/10.2307/2185815

Rozen, Roli, and Ilana Hammerman. *Meshorerim lo ikhtevu shirim: be-madim be-erets Ishmael, sipurim ve-teudot* (Poets Will Not Write Poetry: In Uniform in Israel, Stories and Documents). Tel Aviv: Am Oved, 1990.

Sagi, Avi. "The Meaning of the *Akeda* in Israeli Culture and Jewish Tradition." *Israel Studies* 3, no. 1 (1998): 45–60. http://www.jstor.org/stable/30246795

Said, Edward W. *Orientalism*. New York: Vintage Books, 1979.

Said, Edward W. "Permission to Narrate." In *The Edward Said Reader*, edited by Mustafa Baoji and Andrew Rubin, 243–66. New York: Vintage Books, 2000.

Sansom, Ian. "The Hilltop by Assaf Gavron Review—'An Extraordinary View of Contemporary Israeli Society.'" *The Guardian*, Dec. 19, 2014. https://www.theguardian.com/books/2014/dec/19/the-hilltop-assaf-gavron-review-novel

Schafer, Arthur. "The Buck Stops Here—Reflections on Moral Responsibility." In *Democratic Accountability and Military Values*. Canada: Commission of Inquiry into the Deployment of Canadian Forces to Somalia, 1997.

Schiff, Ilan. "Bizkhut mivhan 'ha-degel ha-shahor'" (In Support of the "Black Flag" Test). In *Kafr Qasim—eiru'im u-mitos* (Kafr Qasim—Events and Myth), edited by Ruvik Rosenthal, 117–30. Tel Aviv: Ha-kibbutz ha-meuhad, 2000.

Schwartz, Yigal. "'Human Engineering' and Shaping Space in the New Hebrew Culture." *Jewish Social Studies* 11, no. 3 (2005): 92–114. https://doi.org/10.1353/jss.2005.0026

Schwartz, Yigal. "Mi-'makom aher' le-'Dolly City'" (From "Different Place" to "Dolly City." *Ha-aretz*, June 16, 1995.

Schwartz, Yigal. *Ma she-ro'im mi-kan: Sugiot ba-historyographia shel ha-sifrut ha-ivrit* (What We See from Here: Issues in Hebrew Literature's Historiography). Tel Aviv: Dvir Publishing House, 2005.

Schwartz, Yigal. *Ha-yadata et ha-arets sham ha-limon pore'ah? Handasat ha-adam u-mahshevet ha-merhav ba-sifrut ha-ivrit ha-hadasha* (Did You Know the Land Where the Lemon Tree Blooms? Space Engineering in Modern Hebrew Literature). Tel Aviv: Dvir Publishing House, 2007.

Shaked, Gershon. *Gal hadash ba-siporet ha-ivrit* (A New Wave in Hebrew Prose). Merhavya and Tel Aviv: Poalim and Ha-kibbutz ha-meuhad, 1972.

Shaked, Gershon. "The Arab in Israeli Fiction." *Modem Hebrew Literature* 3 (Fall 1989): 17–21.

Shalev, Mordechai. "Hotam ha-akeda be-'shlosha yamim ve-yeled', 'be-t'hilat kayits 1970' u-ve-'mar Mani'" (The Signs of the Binding in "Three Days and a Child," "Early in the Summer of 1970" and "Mr. Mani"). In *Ba-kivun ha-negdi—kovets mehkarim al 'mar Mani' shel A. B. Yehoshua* (In the Opposite Direction—Essays on Yehoshua's "Mr. Mani"), edited by Nitza Ben-Dov, 399–448. Tel Aviv: Ha-kibbutz ha-meuhad, 1995.

Shamir, Ziva, "Bein sof levein saf—A. B. Yehoshua, 'esh yedidutit'" (Between an End and a Threshold—A. B. Yehoshua's "Friendly Fire"). *E-mago*, Feb. 23, 2007. http://www.e-mago.co.il/Editor/literature-1531.htm

Shapira, Anita. "'Ha-siper ha-zioni' shel Amos Oz" (Amos Oz's "Zionist Narrative"). *Israel* 7 (Spring 2005): 163–71.

Shapira, Anita. "Hirbet Hizah: Between Remembrance and Forgetting." *Jewish Social Studies* 7, no. 1 (2000): 1–62. https://doi.org/10.1353/jss.2000.0022

Shapira, Anita. *Yehudim hadashim, yehudim yeshanim* (New Jews, Old Jews). Tel Aviv: Am Oved, 1996.

Shapira, Avraham, ed. *Si'ah lohamim* (Fighters' Discourse). Tel Aviv: Friends of the Kibbutzim Movement, 1968.

Shapira, Sarit. *Maslulei nedudim* (Routes of Wandering). Jerusalem: Israel Museum, 1991.

Shavit, Ari. "Ha-pasion shel Yehoshua—re'ayon im A. B. Yehoshua" (Yehoshua's Passion—An Interview with A. B. Yehoshua). *Ha-aretz Supplement*, Mar. 15, 2004. http://www.haaretz.co.il/misc/1.953188

Shavit, Ari. "Ha-yehudi ha-sored—re'ayon im Amos Oz" (The Surviving Jew—An Interview with Amos Oz). *Ha-aretz Supplement*, Mar. 1, 2002. http://www.haaretz.co.il/misc/1.775818

Shemtov, Vered. "The Bible in Contemporary Israeli Literature: Text and Place in Zeruya Shalev's 'Husband and Wife' and Michal Govrin's 'Snapshots.'" *Hebrew Studies* 47 (2006): 363–84. http://www.jstor.org/stable/27913807

Shenhav, Yehuda. "Halalei ribonut, he-harig u-matsav ha-herum—le'an ne'elma ha-historia ha-imperialit" (Casualties of Sovereignty, the Exceptional and the State of Emergency—Where Has the Imperial History Gone). *Teoria u-vikoret* 29 (2006): 205–18.

Shenhav, Yehuda. "Medina mafkira, ahrayut shel ta'agid ve-ha-optsia ha-post-hilonit: kri'a be-'shlihuto shel ha-memune al mash'abei enosh'" (Abandoning State, Corporate Responsibility and the Post-Secular Alternative: Readings in "A Woman in Jerusalem"). In *Mabatim mitstalvim—iyunim be-yetsirat A. B. Yehoshua* (Intersecting Perspectives: Essays on A. B. Yehoshua's Oeuvre), edited by Amir Banbaji, Nitza Ben-Dov, and Ziva Shamir, 362–83. Tel Aviv: Ha-kibbutz ha-meuhad, 2010.

Shiffman, Smadar. "Motherhood under Zionism." *Hebrew Studies* 44 (2003): 139–56. http://www.jstor.org/stable/27913657

Shiffman, Smadar. "Orly Castel-Bloom and Yoel Hoffmann: On Israeli Postmodern Prose Fiction." *Hebrew Studies* 50 (2009): 215–27. http://www.jstor.org/stable/27913934

Shiffman, Smadar. "Re'alizm mugaz" (Carbonated Realism). *Ha-aretz Books*, Apr. 24, 2002. http://www.haaretz.co.il/misc/1.788799

Silberstein, Laurence J. *The Postzionism Debate: Knowledge and Power in Israeli Culture.* New York: Routledge, 1999.

Sinai, Ruti. "Ke-shlish me-ha-israelim nehsefu le-pigu'ei terror" (A Third of all Israelis Were Personally Exposed to Terror Attacks). *Ha-aretz*, Dec. 3, 2004.

Sion, Liora. *Dimuyei gavriyut etsel lohamim: ha-sherut be-hativot heil raglim ke-tekes ma'avar mi-na'arut le-bagrut* (Images of Masculinity among Combat Soldiers: Military Service in the Israeli Infantry as a Rite of Passage from Youth to Adulthood). Jerusalem: Dayan Center for Social Science Research, Hebrew University, 1997.

Sivan, Miriam. "*Snapshots* (review)." *Shofar* 27, no. 4 (2009): 203–5. https://doi.org/10.1353/sho.0.0382

Spivak, Gayatri Chakravorty. "Can the Subaltern Speak?" In *Marxism and the Interpretation of Culture*, edited by Cary Nelson and Lawrence Grasberg, 271–313. Urbana: University of Illinois Press, 1988.

Stanovsky, Derek. "Stealing Guilt: Freud, Twain, Augustine and the Question of Moral Luck." *American Imago* 63, no. 4 (2007): 445–61. https://doi.org/10.1353/aim.2007.0009

Statman, Daniel, ed. Introduction to *Moral Luck*, 1–33. Albany: State University of New York Press, 1993.

Sverdlik, Steven. "Crime and Moral Luck." *American Philosophical Quarterly* 25 (1988): 79–86. http://www.jstor.org/stable/20014225

Svirsky, Marcelo. *Arab-Jewish Activism in Israel-Palestine*. Farnham, UK: Ashgate, 2012.

Tamar, David. "Hazon Yeshayahu" (Yeshayahu's Prophecy). *Ma'ariv*, Feb. 12, 1988.

Taub, Gadi. "Mehapsim safa aheret" (Looking for Another Language). *Ha-ir*, Dec. 11, 1998.

Thomson, Philip. *The Grotesque*. London: Methuen, 1972.

Tsur, Reuven. "Tsafnat pa'ane'ah ve-ha-nehiya ahar ha-vada'ut" (Solving Riddles and the Quest for Certitude). *Ha-sifrut* 2, no. 34 (1985): 142–60.

Urian, Dan. "Cinema and Stage—Representations of War in Israeli Drama and Theater." In *Narratives of Dissent: War in Contemporary Israeli Arts and Culture*, edited by Rachel S. Harris and Ranen Omer-Sherman, 181–299. Detroit, MI: Wayne State University Press, 2013.

Usher, Graham. "Children of Palestine." *Race and Class* 321, no. 4 (1991): 1–18.

Walker, Margaret U. "Moral Luck and the Virtues of Impure Agency." In *Moral Luck*, edited by Daniel Statman, 235–50. Albany, New York: State University of New York Press, 1993.

Wehrs, Donald R., and David P. Haney, eds. *Levinas and Nineteenth-Century Literature: Ethics and Otherness from Romanticism through Realism*. Newark, DE: University of Delaware Press, 2010.

Weiss, Hillel. "He'arot livhinat akedat Yits'hak ba-siporet ha-ivrit bat zmanenu" (Comments on Isaac's Binding in Contemporary Hebrew Literature). In *Ha-akeda ve-ha-tokheha* (The Binding and Its Punishment), edited by Zvi Levi, 25–31. Jerusalem: Magnes, 1991.

Weitz, Gidi, and Dror Mishani. "Esh yedidutit—re'ayon im A. B. Yehoshua" (Friendly Fire—An Interview with A. B. Yehoshua). *Ha-aretz*, Feb. 15, 2008. http://www.haaretz.co.il/misc/1.1304726

Weizman, Eyal. *Hollow Land—Israel's Architecture of Occupation*. London and New York: Verso, 2007.

Williams, Bernard. *Moral Luck*. Cambridge: Cambridge University Press, 1982.

Williams, Bernard. "Postscript." In *Moral Luck*, edited by Daniel Statman, 251–8. Albany: State University of New York Press, 1993.

Woolf, Virginia. *Three Guineas*. London: Penguin, 1978 [1938].

Yaar-Edelbaum, Iris. "Normali ze hakhi, Bulli" (Normal Is the Best, Bulli). *Time Out Tel Aviv* 229, Mar. 29, 2007.

Yehoshua, A. B. "Hatima: levatel et ha-akeda al yedei mimusha" (Sealing: To Annul the Binding by Actualizing It). In *Ba-kivun ha-negdi—kovets mehkarim al 'mar Mani' shel A. B. Yehoshua* (In the Opposite Direction—Essays on Yehoshu's "Mr. Mani"), edited by Nitza Ben-Dov, 296–397. Tel Aviv: Ha-kibbutz ha-meuhad, 1995.

Yehoshua, A. B. *Ahizat moledet* (Homeland Grasp). Tel Aviv: Ha-kibbutz ha-meuhad, 2008.

Yosef, Raz. *The Politics of Loss and Trauma in Contemporary Israeli Cinema*. New York: Routledge, 2011.

Young, Robert J. C. *Colonial Desire*. London: Routledge, 1995.

Zartal, Moshe. "Al si'ah lohamim" (On Fighters' Discourse) *Al ha-mishmar,* Feb. 9, 1968, 5–6.

Zimmerman, Michael J., "Luck and Moral Responsibility." *Ethics* 97, no. 2 (1987): 374–86. http://www.jstor.org/stable/2381355

Zimmerman, Michael J., "Taking Luck Seriously." *Journal of Philosophy* 99, no. 11 (2002): 533–76. https://doi.org/10.2307/365575

Žižek, Slavoj. "A Soft Focus on War." *In These Times* 35, no. 5 (May 2010): 30–2.

Index

Y

Z